To the memory
of my father John
and of my brother John

Contents

Acknowledgments

An earlier version of chapter 3 has appeared in *Understanding Origins*, ed. Jean-Pierre Dupuy and Francisco Varela (Dordrecht, Netherlands: Kluwer, 1991).

An earlier version of chapter 4 first appeared in *Postmodernism and Continental Philosophy: Selected Studies in Phenomenology and Existential Philosophy 13*, ed. Hugh Silverman and Donn Welton (Albany, N.Y.: SUNY Press, 1988). The Appendix is reprinted here with slight changes from my essay in *Helios* 17:1 (1990). My thanks to the editors for their permission to include this work here. My thanks also to Loyola University of Chicago for its consistent support of my research efforts, including an academic leave of absence that enabled me to bring them to a conclusion. Translations, where not cited from published editions, are my own.

Abbreviations

DBB   *"To Double Business Bound": Essays on Literature, Myth,
       Mimesis and Anthropology* (Girard)
DDN   *Deceit, Desire and the Novel: Self and Other in Literary
       Studies* (Girard)
OG   *Of Grammatology* (Derrida)
PP   "Plato's Pharmacy" (Derrida)
THFW *Things Hidden since the Foundation of the World* (Girard)
VO   *Violent Origins: Walter Burket, René Girard and Jonathan
       Z. Smith on Ritual Killing and Cultural Formation*
       (Hamerton-Kelly, ed.)
VS   *Violence and the Sacred* (Girard)
WD   *Writing and Difference* (Derrida)

1

Introduction:
Philosophy in Spite of Itself

Aristotle defines man as the political and rational animal, but the readings in this book are guided by his observation that "man differs from other animals in his greater aptitude for imitation." Aristotle points to this aptitude amidst his meditations on tragedy in his *Poetics* (book 4.2), but it is a scene from a Molière comedy that best demonstrates its preeminence. This scene very cogently and deliberately dramatizes humankind's political, rational, and mimetic "natures," somewhat in that order of ascendancy. It furthermore dramatizes the conflict of these properties while recalling the philosopher's foundational concern for the difference between humans and animals:

Enter the PHILOSOPHER

MONSIEUR JOURDAIN.	Ah, Mr. Philosopher. You've arrived in the nick of time with your philosophy. Come and make peace between these fellows.
PHILOSOPHER.	What is it? What is going on, gentlemen?
MONSIEUR JOURDAIN.	They've got so angry about which of their professions is the most important that they started insulting each other and very nearly came to blows.
PHILOSOPHER.	Come, come, gentlemen! Why let yourselves be carried away like this? Have you not read Seneca *On Anger*? Believe me there is nothing so base and contemptible as a passion which

	reduces men to the level of wild animals! Surely, surely, reason should be mistress of all our actions!
DANCING MASTER.	But, my good sir, he's just been insulting the pair of us and sneering at music, which is this gentleman's profession, and dancing which is mine.
PHILOSOPHER.	A wise man is superior to any insults which can be put upon him, and the proper response to unseemly behavior is patience and moderation.
FENCING MASTER.	They had the audacity to compare their professions with mine.
PHILOSOPHER.	Well, my friend, why should that move you? We should never compete in vainglory or precedence. What really distinguishes men from one another is wisdom and virtue.
DANCING MASTER.	I maintain that dancing is a form of skill, a science, to which sufficient honor can never be paid.
MUSIC MASTER.	And I that music has been held in foremost esteem all down the ages.
FENCING MASTER.	And I still stick to my point against the pair of them that skill in arms is the finest and most necessary of all the sciences.
PHILOSOPHER.	And what then is the place of philosophy? I consider you all three presumptuous to speak with such arrogance before me and impudently give the title of science to a set of mere accomplishments which don't even deserve the name of arts and can only be adequately described under their wretched trades of gladiator, minstrel, and mountebank.
FENCING MASTER.	Oh get out! You dog of a philosopher!
MUSIC MASTER.	Get out! You miserable pendant!
DANCING MASTER.	Get out! You beggarly usher!
PHILOSOPHER.	What! Rascals like you dare to— (*He hurls himself upon them and all three unite to beat him.*) (*Le Bourgeois gentilhomme* act 2, scene 3)

In scarcely more than a page Molière sets out virtually all the themes of this book and more than somewhat insinuates its conclusions.

Here is humankind's political nature in the form a community of individuated members with rival claims to ascendancy. Here is our rational nature in the person of the Philosopher, whose role is to adjudicate these claims according to reason, which he, like Aristotle, asserts to be what distinguishes humans from animals. And here is humankind's mimetic nature, to which even reason, even philosophy, falls prey in an undifferentiated bid for ascendancy. Humanity's rational nature, its stipulated claims to science, is at war with its political nature, the claims of community, and the name for this war is mimesis. The result is the loss of difference not only between philosophy and what it pretends to adjudicate but also between humans and wild animals. This irrational result issues from a pattern, or a structure; it springs from a rigorous logic that reason (or philosophy) cannot claim as its own.

The serially cadenced claims of the Dancing, the Music, and the Fencing Master about the honor and necessity of their sciences are an irresistible lure; they serve as a model, projecting a desideratum for which the Philosopher abandons all restraint in denouncing their presumptions. Another cadenced series, this time of insults, provides the model and the impetus for physical violence on the part of his rivals. All differences dissolve in a violent mêleé in which humanity's highest faculty gets the worst of it. Reason is overturned, or turned inside out, not in spite of it claims but just because of them. Philosophy is neither the arbiter of transcendence nor the guardian of the transcendental signified, wisdom, but a signifier of vainglory. What pretends to prevail as the origin and locus of value betrays instead the militant etymon of value as mere valor, or violence itself.

Anyone who has been reading René Girard will welcome this scene as a spectacular representation of his theory of mimetic desire as it leads to violent indifferentiation resulting in the arbitrary selection of a scapegoat (in this case, the Philosopher). Girard has in fact commented on this scene in support of his sacrificial hypothesis about human culture (in *"To Double Business Bound,"* chap. 6, henceforth *DBB*), and I will return to details of his originary scenario in this and subsequent chapters.

As with any great literary text however, the ramifications of Molière's play are manifold, and anyone who has been reading the texts of Jacques Derrida could just as well applaud this scene in the name of what he calls the deconstruction of philosophy. Because Derrida's texts are so notoriously difficult and resistant to paraphrase, I will award them the lion's share of commentary.

Although the word *deconstruction* has been put to a wide, not to say wild, variety of uses in past decades, it is meant here in the sense that Derrida uses it when he states that "Peirce goes very far in the direction that I have called the de-construction of the transcendental signified, which, at one time or another, would place a reassuring end to the reference from sign to sign. I have identified logocentrism and the metaphysics of presence as the exigent, powerful, systematic and irrepressible desire for such a signified" (*Of Grammatology* 49, henceforth *OG*). Molière's Philosophy Master incarnates just this desire, which Derrida identifies with that of philosophy as such: the hierarchical, value-laden ordering of signs and their referents, be they abstract or concrete, in terms of such binary oppositions as precedence and sequence, essence and accident, reality and appearance, origin and copy, and so on. This order corresponds to the difference between true signifieds, or truth itself, whose mastery is the role of philosophy, and extraneous, superficial signifiers, which have the same inferior status as vainglory and precedence when opposed to wisdom and virtue. This order derives from the postulate (or rather imposture) of original presence or being, of which language is but a copy. Such a view is at times designated as theologocentrism to designate a superhuman vantage point that presides over what is human and what is not, just as it presides over the physical and the metaphysical, the concrete and the abstract. Philosophy's traditional task has been variously to discover, invent, construct, or perfect the language that best represents what (truly) is, a task resulting in the classical notion of science as "une langue bien faite." Deconstruction upsets this entire order when it focuses on language in its most concrete physical manifestation, that is, as writing.

Molière's Philosopher is called on to put a reassuring end to the conflict of signs and of sciences. He views himself as the proprietor of what is proper to humans. His violent impropriety flatly contradicts that view, however; what is metaphysical about his desire is mimetic, mediated by the model of his rivals' desire. This is Girard's view of things, but it is inextricably bound up with the questions Derrida poses to philosophy in terms of what is proper and improper to language, what is literal or figurative in representation. All the Philosopher does is repeat, imitate, or re-present his rivals' desires, which *figure* as science or transcendence, but whose literal sense is violence.

Philosophy's comic fall from grace corresponds very closely to what Derrida describes as a "necessary overturning" within a " 'general economy,' a kind of *general strategy of deconstruction*": "To do justice to this necessity is to recognize that in a classical philosophical opposition we are not dealing with a peaceful coexistence of a *vis-a-vis*, but rather with a violent hierarchy. One of the two terms governs the other (axiologically, logically, etc.), or has the upper hand. To deconstruct the opposition, first of all, is to overturn the hierarchy at a given moment. To overlook this phase of overturning is to forget the conflictual and subordinating structure of opposition" (*Positions* 41). The Philosopher's recourse to violence fairly parodies the violence of hierarchy described here. To say that Molière deconstructs philosophy is to observe about this scene what Derrida observes about the workings of a certain kind of general textuality:

> This is why this work cannot be purely "theoretical" or "conceptual" or "discursive." I mean it cannot be the work of a discourse entirely regulated by essence, meaning, truth, consciousness, ideality, etc. What I call *text* is also that which "practically" inscribes and overflows the limits of such a discourse. *There is* such a general text everywhere that (that is everywhere) this discourse and its order (essence, sense, truth, meaning, consciousness, ideality, etc.) are *overflowed*, that is everywhere that their authority is put back into the position of a *mark* in a chain, though the structural illusion of this authority is to wish and believe it commands the chain. (*Positions* 59–60, trans. modified)

This structural illusion is shared by both the philosopher and his employer, and its deconstruction is the work of Molière's text, its comically leveling effect. "Laughter is proper to man"—and, it seems, to deconstruction too, where the joke is on philosophy. Philosophy presumes to speak from outside a difference within which it is compromised; it is but a mark within what it claims to demarcate; the claims of consciousness and order are prey to the unconscious, destructuring violence of mimesis. According to the paralogic of differance, which will be examined in these pages, philosophy differs less from what it marks as other than human than from itself. Here the unconscious is structured not, as Jacques Lacan avers, like a language, with its differentiating functions, but rather, as Philippe Sollers quips in *To Honor René Girard*, like a lynching (192).

Numerous passages from Derrida are available to support this claim, namely, that Molière's text challenges metaphysical hierarchies, that it *performs* in every sense of the word a critique of difference between signifier and signified as between the inside and outside of philosophy. Molière's play is cannily and archly concerned with difference as a theme, beginning with the one between bourgeois and gentleman inscribed in and as its title. No difference, social or semiological, is immune to its comic subversions, its overflowings or overturnings, including the notorious and richly problematic difference between verse and prose. Our very notion of what constitutes language, of what discourse *is*, takes an unconscious blow from the Philosopher—"everything that is not prose is verse; and everything that is not verse is prose"—and this problematic descends all the way down to the elements of signification, to the difference between writing and speech that, beginning with Derrida's reading of signs in Husserl, gives rise to deconstruction.

Monsieur Jourdain knows how to read and write: "Oui, je sais lire et écrire," he says to his Philosophy Master, who asks him whether he has any principles, any beginnings of knowledge. But he wants to know how to spell. "Que voulez-vous donc que je vous apprenne?" "Apprenez-moi l'orthographe." From there he wants to learn the almanac, "so as to know when there is a moon and when there is not." He could look outside, but such material evidence does not exemplify knowledge. What is inside and outside representation, or representation and its other, is the theme of this writing lesson.

The pupil's contradiction, in the form of his ignorance of a big word like *orthographe* as it refers to what he already knows, makes plain the structure of his ignorance, or rather, his ignorance as a structure. It consists in not knowing what he knows and what he does not. The role of philosophy is to occupy this difference, to inhabit it, to secure and propagate it in a highly ambiguous way. It teaches this difference, and in so doing it maintains it, authorizing it and itself at once. Philosophy is not founded on knowledge but on another's ignorance, that is, on a difference between knowledge and ignorance that it institutes and that in turn constitutes it as knowledge. Philosophy is founded on itself, which is no foundation at all. Philosophy itself has designated this gesture as a category error, an error of set-theoretic typing whereby philosophy governs a class of which it is a member. The result is a tangled hierarchy that structures philosophy in a double bind as it obeys the contradictory imperatives of reason and order. It is the very same contradiction that previously ensnared philosophy in the violence it sought to quell. Derrida has made much of this "stricture" of the double bind, though without ever tracing it to the contradictions of mimetic desire. That, in part, will be the task of this book.

The arbitrary, not to say bogus, authority invested in this difference has been astutely analyzed with reference to Aristotle and Molière by the philosopher Vincent Descombes in *L'Inconscient malgré lui*. More germane to the arguments of this book is the speech lesson administered by the Philosopher in Molière's play: it resembles for all the world an incipient, albeit unconscious, grammatology, a science of the letter that questions the very possibility of scientific foundations, of rigorous and coherent representation:

PHILOSOPHER.   Very well. Now, to follow your idea and at the same time to treat the matter philosophically one must begin, according to the proper order of things, by an exact understanding of the nature of letters and of the different manner of pronouncing them. And in this connection I must explain that the letters are divided into vowels, so called because they express vocal sounds; and consonants, so named because they sound "con" or with the vowels and only mark the various articulations of the voiced sounds. There are five vowels or voiced sounds: A, E, I, O, U. (2.4)

As the philosopher proceeds to teach Monsieur Jourdain what he already knows, the scene quickly deteriorates to nonsense: "A, E, I, I, I, I. It's true. Long live science!" It is no ordinary nonsense, though, but nonsense that contaminates meaning in the same astructural way that letters contaminate speech with their mute inanity.

PHILOSOPHER.   The vowel O is formed by reopening the mouth and bringing the opposing corners of the lips closer together: O.
MONSIEUR JOURDAIN.   O. O. Nothing could be more true. A, E, I, O, I, O. It's wonderful! I, O, I, O. (2.4)

Here is a true philosopher in the maieutic sense: he has taught his pupil what he already knows. He is a false philosopher, nonetheless, for having taught his pupil nothing, only noise. His knowledge consists in a knowledge of representation that by its representation becomes nonrepresentation, for the letters mean nothing and are farther removed from meaning with their witless repetition.

This is an archly superficial critique, and it is as such that it commands attention, for it brings to the surface the inanity of the signifying system, or at least the inanity of its foundational elements, namely, letters. Representation is not representable, at least not meaningfully so. The difference between something and nothing here hinges on nothing but the letter (writing), which is nothing but a mark of a difference. But it is not altogether nothing, for there it is, the insignificant mark of a difference between something and nothing. Because Molière's play is concerned with difference at every level, including the differentiating function of levels, it is not surprising that the concern extends to the arch difference with which deconstruction originates and on which it develops its critique of origins and foundations. If the originality of Derridean deconstruction is attention to letters, to the gramm, as the archetypal difference, then it finds in Molière a droll precursor.

PHILOSOPHER.   The opening of the mouth makes just a little circle which represents an O. [L'ouverture de la bouche fait justement comme un petit rond qui représente un O.]

MONSIEUR JOURDAIN.   O, O, O. You are right. O. Ah! it's such a fine thing to know something! [O, O, O. Vous avez raison. O. Ah! la belle chose que de savoir quelque chose!] (2.4)

The buccal *O* physically representing the letter parodies the idea of language as a direct representation of reality. That it is no such thing, and that writing is the proof of this, is exemplified in and by the unintentional wordplay of the pupil's response: *raison* is compromised by the word *chose*, which means both something one knows and just some thing, "un petit rond." *O* is indeed a *chose*, though closer to nothing, to zero in fact, than to anything like *savoir*, so that its nothingness contaminates "savoir quelque chose," or *savoir* itself. *Savoir* emerges as the representation of no thing but representation, letters, or writing, which is barely anything. And it is not at all clear by this stage whether letters represent sounds or are represented in turn by them—which would make writing the origin of language. Perhaps letters alone arrest the noise that is as undifferentiated as the violence that engulfed philosophy a scene earlier.

In short, letters are things of whose nature there is no exact knowledge, no adequate or intelligible representation, and whose representation as knowledge overflows into utter nonsense. The elements of representation represent nothing. This is not a novel philosophical observation; Plato's *Cratylus* discusses this gap between meaning and its elements, between signifiers and signifieds. But Derrida is the first to mark that gap with the letters philosophy hastens to forget. Traced back to the undecidable origin of letters in sounds or sounds in letters, the foundations of meaning and knowledge are overturned, ceaselessly overturning; pinned down to the elements of language, sense oscillates hopelessly and helplessly between sense and nonsense. In no time at all, the "linguistic turn" in philosophy turns on itself. Deconstruction installs itself in and as that oscillation and must maintain an ongoing flirtation with nonsense. Even Rudolf Kuenzli's insightful correlation between deconstruction and the derealizing impulses of Dadaism (see his "Derridada") resonates in Molière's text: "Da, Da. Oui, Ah! les belles choses! les belles choses!"

Molière is indeed a philosopher in spite of himself if, with Derrida, we identify deconstruction as the historical destiny of philosophy marking the closure of metaphysics. It accomplishes this not from above, not from any theoretical horizon, which is ever a metaphysical gesture, but from below—or rather, from within the text of philosophy, by this disclosure of writing, or the gramm, which philosophy represses. What Derrida holds for a "new 'concept' " of writing against the *ancien régime* of philosophy holds for Molière's text: "And this holds first of all for a new concept of writing, that *simultaneously* provokes the overturning of the hierarchy speech/writing, and the entire system attached to it, *and* releases the dissonance of a writing within speech, thereby disorganizing the entire inherited order and invading the entire field" (*Positions* 42). Molière's play very successfully exploits this dissonance, and the inherited order he disorganizes extends up through the hierarchical differences between bourgeois and gentleman.

Given enough time, we might be able to read all French literature through Molière's play, as well as the cultural order variously reflected and challenged in that literature. In fact, Derrida's statement about a general textuality ends with a pro-gram for literary history as a letterly history of a widely, not to say totally, interdisciplinary kind: "This general text is not limited, of course, as will (or would be) quickly understood, to writing on the page. The writing of this text, moreover, has the exterior limit only of a certain *re-mark*. Writing on the page, and then 'literature,' are determined types of this re-mark. They must be investigated in their specificity, and in a new way, if you will, in the specificity of their 'history,' and in their articulation with the other 'historical' fields of the text in general" (*Positions* 60). Such a comprehensive field for deconstruction is not surprising in view of the ubiquity with which the question of difference can be posed. The notion is indispensable to examining all meaning systems, all social institutions, all historical specificities. Mimetic desire, especially as it erodes difference, has the same ubiquity for Girard, it being the defining trait of the human. Reading Derrida and Girard together holds out prospects of relating social institutions and meaning systems in a new way. Elsewhere I have attempted integrative readings of Girard and Derrida with a view to correlating rhetorical and social structures (see my "Flaubert's Freudian Thing," "*Tartuffe*," and "Double Talk: Two Baudelairean Revolutions"). Perhaps the greatness of a literary work can be measured by its capacity to reveal rather than merely reflect just such correlations, by its ability to link the operations of signs to the machinations of the socius. Rather than reduce a text to the dimensions and dynamics of a tropological system, far more work needs to be done toward showing the text's own intelligence of such connections. But that is not the aim of this book, which issues instead from theoretical considerations provoked by such readings.

On the other hand, such integrative readings are perilous in view of the way Girard's and Derrida's theories diverge—or rather, the way Derrida demurs from the possibilities of theory:

> The necessary decentering cannot be a philosophic or scientific act as such, since it is a question of disclosing, through access to another system linking speech and writing, the founding categories of language and the grammar of the *epistemè*. The natural tendency of *theory*—of what unites philosophy and science in the *epistemè*—will push rather toward filling in the breach than forcing the closure. It was normal that the breakthrough was more secure and more penetrating on the side of literature and poetic writing: normal also that it, like Nietzsche, at first destroyed and caused to vacillate the transcendental authority and dominant category of the *epistemè:* being. (*OG* 91–92)

Being is henceforth to be written "under erasure," for the term denotes illusory presence that language presumes to re-present. It is an illusion dispelled by literature and poetic writing, owing to their dedication to signifiers as they solicit other signifiers rather than refer to something outside the text. The apparent privilege accorded to literature results from its resistance to systematizing, to theory as such, desire for which in this view abets a desire for a transcendental signified, or logocentrism. Theory necessarily tends to overlook or repress just what literature, and especially poetry, values: the irrepressible agency of signifiers as incarnate in writing. Theory reflects unifying and totalizing ambitions that are fulfilled only at the expense of writing or what writing represents, namely, whatever resists illusions of full presence, immediacy, parousia.

This pro-grammed resistance to theory explains why Derrida's texts are so self-involved, why they so regularly turn in on themselves, why the difference between theory (or philosophy) and its other (namely, literature) is among the first to go the way of deconstruction. As Derrida writes of his own texts, which he denies the unifying designation of *books*, "under these titles it is solely a question of a unique and differentiated textual 'operation,' if you will, whose unfinished movement assigns itself no absolute beginning, and which, although it is entirely consumed by the reading of other texts, in a certain fashion refers only to its writing" (*Positions* 3). This is such a telling description of so much literature—from Villon, Rabelais, Montaigne, and Cervantes down through Flaubert, Joyce, Proust, and the postmoderns—that it is easy to understand the success of deconstructive criticism in literature departments. It serves to blur the boundaries of literature and theory and to warrant the oft-repeated claims of certain critics as to the literary status of their own criticism. Quotation marks serving to designate an "original" text variously superabound and disappear in a general meltdown instigated by the precipitating agency of the grapheme. As a consequence, the human sciences are forlorn of an object, being fatally wed to autobiography, however unconscious. The fate is structural, or rather poststructural, for it issues from the deconstruction of the difference between literature and theory.

I will return to this issue at various times, especially in my conclusion—though it is a foregone conclusion for some Derrideans, a theory of literature in either the subjective or objective sense of the genitive being doomed from the start as a contradiction in terms. What is at least clear at this stage is that between Derrida, who holds out for a boundless textuality, and Girard, who holds out for a unified theory in the human sciences, we have a debate of the first magnitude. It is a debate between literature and theory and within them as well, a debate that at times opposes them and at times divides them within themselves.

Although it is tempting to do so, I will not take these differences out on Molière, who has served as but a pretext to engage the texts of

Derrida and Girard, to interrelate their curiously rival and complementary readings. In their symmetrical emphasis on texts and an institutions, they conform to a relation of rival brothers, of "frères
ennemis," the very relation that in fact determines all mimetic, oppositional structures for Girard. This is the same for Derrida as the
relations of signifier to signified, of gramm to logos, as I show when I
consult his reading of the *Phaedrus* in the next chapter (2), where I
read Derrida's essays on Plato and Descartes across Girard's sacrificial
scenario. I test Girard's theory of linguistic and cultural origins against
the Derridean critique of origins in chapter 3. The focus there is on
the antifoundationalist critique in *Of Grammatology* and on the deconstructive motifs imbedded in Girard's theory of human origins as the
latter relates to Derrida's reading of Rousseau and Claude Lévi-Strauss.
This yields historical and institutional implications that are prolonged
into the history of our century in the next two chapters, which deal
with postmodernism (chap. 4) and the state's relation to violence ar-
chetypally exemplified by the Greenpeace scandal in France (chap.
5). These two chapters also engage reflection on holocaust as it refers
inextricably to both the prospect of global violence and the indubitable reality of genocide, requiring a focus on the thematics of survival
and victimage. In the concluding chapter I confront the choices
implied by these readings as they concern the epistemological stand-
ing of the victim, testing this epistemology in a discussion of Richard
Rorty's "postphilosophical" views and of the controversy surrounding
the wartime journalism of Paul de Man. In the appendix I essay
Girard's victimary hypothesis across some readings in Hebrew and
Christian Scripture.

    In sum, the deconstructive critique of metaphysics, logocentrism,
ontotheology, essentialism, and the like, corresponds in its structure
and dynamics to Girard's critique of sacrificial practices. The occlu-
sions and exclusions to which writing, the grapheme, are subjected
correspond to the destiny of the sacrificial victim. It is as if Derrida
describes as happening to the linguistic signifier something that Girard describes as happening at the foundation of cultural institutions.
There is an opportunity here to relate what appears to many to be but
a formalist critique, concerned only with texts, to real institutional
practices and, accordingly, to substantive issues. There are possibilities for real knowledge in deconstruction, which has to be redeemed
from some of its formalist or nihilist temptations.

I make a propaedeutic effort throughout to explicate Derrida and Girard via each other and to explicate both with reference to issues in the public realm. This explains in part the preeminence accorded to Girard in this book, its aim being to render deconstruction intelligible, to translate and secularize it in the sense both of laicizing its vocabulary and of historicizing it—and therefore, via Girard, of anthropologizing it. In the human sciences, a theory is worth only the historical or institutional understanding it offers or the ethical insights its guarantees. Confronting Girard's and Derrida's work one with the other yields more in these respects than either one does on its own terms.

The necessity of choosing engages methodological considerations that will take up the rest of this introductory chapter.

Doubtless Molière's play, its play of differences, makes sense on its own terms, without recourse to advanced literary theory. The nonsense it makes of overweening claims to sense and difference is effectively demonstrated by the laughter it provokes at the collapse of difference. But the equally demonstrable fact that it is translatable in both Girardian and Derridean terms—as mimesis or differance—suggests important theoretical possibilities that I explore in this book.

Of course, other critical approaches apply as well, particularly that of Jacques Lacan, whose "sujet supposé savoir," ever the dupe of his own desire, finds its near perfect figure in Molière's Philosopher. As a result, Molière's text, like that of many another, could be explored as an advertisement for a critical pluralism. Such an enterprise would be sanctioned, in ascending order of rigor, by such prevailing ideas as (1) the liberal humanist truism that measures the greatness of a literary work by the sheer variety of interpretations to which it lends itself; (2) an argument about the futility of seeking "final vocabularies" to interpret anything (Rorty 1988); and (3) evidence against the possibility of any fully adequate translation, particularly as it draws fresh rigor from the deconstructive critique of representation.

I do not proceed this way for a number of reasons: (1) although it would serve a useful pedagogical aim, it would frustrate the unifying aims of scientific theory, which not even deconstruction can oppose without unifying everything around autobiography, the grapheme, "la cendre," or some such notion; (2) Baudelaire's objections to eclecticism in art apply to criticism as well: "Qui embrasse trop mal étreint" (the more you embrace, the less you grasp), a sound methodological

principle if method means a way to go (meta-hodos), which is finally
nowhere if, as Baudelaire states, an eclectic is a boat wishing to sail by
all four winds at once (*Oeuvres complètes* 251); and (3) the issues here
concern possibilities for literary and cultural criticism, which ultimately requires choice to be properly critical. Accordingly, Marvin
Harris's objection to eclecticism serves to warrant the correlation attempted here: "fragmentation and inconsistency do not reflect the
nature of socioculture phenomena but rather the absence of principles
capable of producing a research effort consistently along lines that
could conceivably produce a coherent corpus of interpenetrating theories" (*Cultural Materialism* 291–92). Girardian monism and Derridean
dissemination are alike critiques of dualism, and "in a certain fashion"
they function alike. Neither is hospitable to theoretical indifferent-
ism; where the choice is between polemism and pluralism, their place
is with the former. The question is whether, or to what degree, they
are hospitable to each other. That is the matter of this book: can we,
following one orientation, deconstruct the difference Girard/Derrida?
Or, following the other orientation, can we reduce deconstruction to
anthropological terms? Let us grant to the imperium of autobiography
that we are all telling our own story. We may still go on to ask whether
it is not, in some structural sense, the same story.

I will briefly take up the second question as a means of at least le-
gitimizing the aim proposed by the first. This involves sketching Girard's originary hypothesis with a view to showing its intersection with
Derrida. The original motivation for this study springs from the observation that there are moments, movements, and formulations in
Derrida's critique of presence, of difference and of origin itself, that
conform so rigorously to the paradoxes of the sacred on which Girard's
theory is founded that they support rather than oppose its logic and
promote rather than contest its theoretical import.

According to Girard's hypothesis, the human species originates in
the aleatory selection of a victim whose elimination puts an end to a
mêlée of appropriative violence. The violence of all against all, in the
midst of which no community can form itself, still less survive, becomes the violence of all against one when some one member is arbitrarily singled out for destruction. Girard draws on ethological studies
of animal behavior that record dominance patterns and instinctual
brakes to violence that, as history shows, are utterly lacking among

humans. Appropriative or acquisitive violence divides members of a group, but as it intensifies, it passes beyond the object of appropriation to become conflictual mimesis, which, as it intensifies, is destined to unite them against a single victim:

> Acquisitive mimesis is contagious, and if the number of individuals polarized around a single object increases, other members of the community, as yet not implicated, will tend to follow the example of those who are; conflictual mimesis necessarily follows the same course because the same force is involved. Once the object has disappeared and the mimetic frenzy has reached a high degree of intensity, one can expect conflictual mimesis to take over and snowball in its effect. Since the power of mimetic attraction multiplies with the number of those polarized, it is inevitable that at one moment the entire community will find itself unified against a single individual. Conflictual mimesis therefore creates a *de facto* allegiance against a common enemy, such that the conclusion of the crisis is nothing other than the reconciliation of the community. (*Things Hidden since the Foundation of the World* 26, henceforth *THFW*)

(It is noteworthy that the passage here from acquisitive to conflictual mimesis as leading to a unique victim is legible in Molière's scene, where the Philosopher unites all against him once the rivalry for precedence among the sciences cedes to violence itself.) The victim of this conflict is retrospectively perceived as the origin of reconciliation, the founder of the newborn community, and accordingly as sacred, as unaccountably, incommensurably powerful. "The victim is held responsible for the renewed calm in the community and for the disorder that preceded this return. It is even believed to have brought about its own death" (*THFW* 26). The victim represents the violence of the community and its subsequent peace as coming from outside itself, as other than its own. In sacralizing the victim, the community turns its violence inside out, and it is just this inversion from effect to cause that (1) affords the possibility of experiencing an inside and an outside, (2) generates for the first time its temporal coordinates of a before and an after, and (3) generates the very notions of cause and effect, of consequentiality itself. The victim is sacralized for representing the origin of both the community and the unanimous violence that ends with the destruction of the victim. The sacred is just this quid pro quo, which takes the effect of violence for its cause; the sacred is this misconstruction of its origin by the community.

From a structural point of view, which is that of the community, the community originates in a sacred both exterior and prior to it. According to this hypothesis, the sacred is not the origin itself but the origin that the community postulates for itself. Indeed, it is an imposture, for the community postulates an origin it itself has produced in the sacralization of the victim. The community has produced itself not by parthenogenesis but by retrogenesis, by attributing an origin it has produced.

According to this deconstruction of events the sacred is nothing but the illusion that the community sustains about its (own) origin and that in turn sustains the community in ritual sacrifice. As long as it sacrifices to its divinity, its own violence will remain a *mysterium tremendum* to it; as long as it repeats this scenario it will achieve the unity necessary to its conservation. It places the origin of its violence before its existence in time and outside its existence in space, whence notions of time and space as before and after and inside and outside accrue to experience. Otherwise stated, the sacred is a deluded *ex post facto* construct that accounts for the *de facto* peace and/in unanimity. This view may in every sense be labeled poststructural.

It is here, at the structural level, that the victimary hypotheses intersects with the deconstruction of speech as original presence of mind, which for Derrida is an origin that never takes place prior to its representation, prior, that is, to the violent and mystified exclusion of writing. We are regularly asked, *à propos* Saussure, Husserl, Rousseau, and Plato, to conceive of writing as the "origin" (under erasure) of speech, of logos, of original presence of mind, whose originarity is misconceived, misconstrued *ex post facto* by the exclusion of writing. The victim occupies the place—within and without the community— in Girard's view of cultural origins that writing occupies in Derrida's critique of origins or of original presence, of which language is but the representation and writing the secondary representation, the forlorn and occluded trace. The victim, like writing, is a supplement of a supplement (speech), a stand-in, an arbitrary substitute for any and all members of a community that does not exist prior to the victim's expulsion. In several essays Derrida shows writing as the origin of the language it represents, which is a contradictory notion designating writing as the mark and model of the instituted trace without which language is inconceivable: "The supplement comes in the place of a lapse, a nonsignified or a nonrepresented, a nonpresence. There is no present before, it is not preceded by anything but itself, that is to say by another supplement. The supplement is always the supplement of a supplement. One wishes to go back *from the supplement to the source:* one must recognize that there is a *supplement at the source"* (*OG* 303–4).

The inherent and literal *absurdity* of the sacred, its mute irrationality, comparable to that of writing, also inheres in the Derridean supplement:

> Il s'agit donc d'un supplément originaire, si cette expression absurde peut être risquée, tout irrecevable qu'elle est dans une logique classique. Supplément d'origine plutôt: qui supplée l'origine défaillante et qui pourtant n'est pas dérivé; ce supplément est, comme on dit d'une_ pièce, d'origine. (*De la grammatologie* 442)
> [The question is of an originary supplement, if this absurd expression may be risked, totally unacceptable as it is within classical logic. Rather the supplement of origin: which supplements the failing origin and which is yet not derived; this supplement is, as one says of a spare part [*une pièce*] of the original make [*d'origine*] (or a document establishing the origin). (*OG* 313)]

A passage like this takes the reader back to the epicentral translation problem, for it includes the problem of translating Derrida. It is one that engages questions of style and *substance* literally, the question of what *underlies* language, which for Girard is the surrogate victim, the origin of all cultural substitutions, and which for Derrida is the letter, the gramm, which on the contrary renders any quest for origins self-contradictory. It is because Girard hypothesizes human origins in and and as the contradictions surrounding the victim that I may proceed with my inquiry.

It is accordingly the premise of this study that Derridean poststructuralism, or deconstruction, is translatable, that what Derrida is saying can be made clear. It has something to say that does not depend on the peculiar, idiosyncratic arrangement of his signifiers; deconstruction is not an idiolect, nor is it *simply* irrational. Its irrationality is complex and structural, issuing from a critique of difference that can yield positive results.

The "strange essence of the supplement" ("not to have essentiality") conforms rigorously to the ambiguity of the sacred as the community's inside turned outside, as an otherness consisting in a mystified sameness. Derrida insists that no ontology, as it confides in the categories of being/nothing, before/after, presence/absence, and so on, can think its operation. It is indeed the wager of this book that only a fundamental anthropology, rooted in the violent origin of the sacred, can think through the paradoxes evoked everywhere by Derrida when he challenges our conceptions of origins.

To deconstruct the sacred is to show this reversal of cause and effect, this coimplication or complication of inside and outside, to show the origin of the structure in the victimary supplement. This is not an easy task because of the differential, diacritical character of language, which depends for sense on oppositions like before and after, inside and outside, and cause and effect. The anarchitectonics of Derridean deconstruction or poststructuralism as a challenge to inveterate differences and theologocentric delusions of transcendental origin can be enlisted in this task—though with a critical eye to the self-defeating limits it sets for its explanation of human affairs.

A basic paradox of deconstructive discourse is its simultaneously radical and reticent character: it ably subverts widely held tenets of rationality only to issue in a textual labyrinth from which positive results, or positionality of any kind, are formally excluded. I contend to the contrary that this discourse offers an explanatory potential for human affairs once it is yoked to an anthropological hypothesis. The labyrinth, let us recall, originally houses a corpse—or a god. The victimary hypothesis, as it explains the generation of the sacred, helps show this to be the same thing, for the immortality of the sacred, its transcendental, generative agency, masks the structural illusion of its violent origin; the before- and afterlife of the sacred constitute an obscure allusion, a misconstruction of the victim's foundational and enduring role. For Derrida, the labyrinth of language, its contortions and tropes, serves a homologous delusion whose epicenter is the grapheme, the dead letter, the cryptogram, whose properly sacrificial destiny appears throughout Derrida's reading of philosophy. There is no common measure in the fate of signifiers and of victims, but there is a common structure, or rather poststructure, such that the form of Derridean readings is deemed worth salvaging from the apparent wreckage it instigates in our mental, or structural, habits.

In the forthcoming chapters, then, I review the originary scenario with reference to different texts, themes, issues, and institutions, shuttling back and forth between Girard's and Derrida's contributions to its intelligibility and between its explanatory power for the operation of signs and for the machinations of the socius.

The chapters accordingly move back and forth between the public realm of social and historical reference, on the one hand, and textual analysis, on the other. This is itself an exercise in translation requiring massive textual citation and commentary to show the correspondence between texts and issues, the way the texts respond to each other's concerns and analyses, though very often at different levels. This difference of levels is of no slight consequence, however, for it involves what remains only—and in my view regrettably—implicit in Derrida's texts but is developed explicitly and thematically in Girard's. The very motif of what remains, of traces and marginalia, is essential to Derridean discourse; its real historical and institutional valence emerges only by recourse to Girard's theory. Consequently, the reader will regularly encounter a decided preference for Girardian themes, however much they gain their fuller articulation and application by recourse to Derridean analyses. The logic of that preference, its real cognitive advantage, is the burden of the chapters to follow, where I show how deconstruction very ably discovers exclusionary and occlusionary mechanisms while shying away from the anthropological implications of its own discovery. This shyness is congenital to deconstruction's linguistic hypersensitivity, whereby its textual involvement yields to a kind of involution that obstructs its best insights and the intellectual project they solicit. I have already alluded to deconstruction's reticence, its irresolution or resolute nonpositionality, whereby, as I argue in the conclusion, it makes impossible demands on representation. It is one thing to hold out for the importance of margins and traces in discourse; it is another to allow them to cannibalize the referential potential of discourse.

Thus, to evoke the fullest possible significance from their correlation, it is tempting to defer questions of a critical choice between Derrida and Girard until the conclusion. This in a sense would already be a *deferral* to Derrida, however (in but one of the Derridean senses of that word), for it would maintain a strategy of suspense, or suspense as a strategy. This is how Derrida styles his own writing activity, as "a strategy without any finality, . . . the aleatory strategy of someone who admits that he does not know where he is going" ("The Time of a Thesis" 50). Yet it is just this inconclusiveness and self-propelling obliquity that is being taken to task in deconstruction. Among its essential theses, argued with great skill, is that symbolic indirection and misrepresentation are structural and systemic, and that a certain violence transpires in the determination of concepts and differences. Nonetheless, there is no reason to suppose that the detection and scrutiny of such phenomena cannot lead to positive conclusions.

Moreover, any respectable suspense story supplies clues to its dénouement. The fact that I chose Molière to begin this book expresses a theoretical privilege accorded to the literary text of a kind that does not, *pace* Derrida, oppose theory and literature but rather conjoins them.

> A basic contention of this essay [*Deceit, Desire and the Novel*] is that the great writers apprehend intuitively and concretely, through the medium of their art, if not formally, the system in which they were first imprisoned together with their contemporaries. Literary interpretation must be systematic because it is the continuation of literature. It should formalize implicit or already half-explicit systems. To maintain that criticism will never be systematic is to maintain that it will never be real knowledge. The value of a critical thought depends not on how clearly it manages to disguise its own systematic nature or on how many fundamental issues it manages to shirk or to dissolve but on how much literary substance it really embraces, comprehends, and makes articulate. (Girard, *Deceit, Desire and the Novel* 3, hereafter *DDN*)

The theory is a kind of critical realism, designating literature as best capable of revealing our relations to signs and to each other, though not all literature as such, which is appraised critically according to whether it reveals or reflects the "romantic lie" of desire's originality and autonomy. "Instead of interpreting the great masterpieces in the light of modern theories, we must criticize modern theories in the light of these masterpieces, once their theoretical voice has become explicit" (*DBB* x). But the logic of my choice will be justified only by evidence advanced in the forthcoming chapters.

Girard concludes the lengthy passage just quoted with a remark resounding with finality about his systematic ambitions for criticism: "The goal may be too ambitious but it is not outside the scope of literary criticism. It is the very essence of literary criticism. Failure to reach it should be condemned but not the attempt. Everything else has already been done" (*DDN* 3). Such a note of closure risks putting off readers, yet it merits consideration, for a lot has been done since this remark was appended to this 1965 translation of *Mensonge roman-tique et vérité romanesque*. Above all, there is structuralism and post-structuralism, the book's affinity with which is signaled by the subtitle to the translation: *Self and Other in Literary Structure*. It is with just these theoretical advances that my book is concerned; I aim to show their correlation with, rather than opposition to, the mimetic hypoth-esis, which after all is a critique of difference, a poststructural critique of just those differences in which structuralism confides.

In the last quarter-century theory has become a text that we huddle around, explicating and advertising it with a diligence formerly ac-corded only to literary texts. This book arises from the conviction that this development is irreversible, that the investment in theory is not a passing craze that will be superseded by some sort of return to more genteel and leisurely discussion, be it impressionistic gloss or histor-icist positivism. Theory today has become autoprobatory. Once it is a theme of our reflection, we cannot anathematize it without bringing it further into relief. We cannot repress it without its being there to re-press, and the more deliberately we attempt to repress it, the more it becomes manifest, not to say intellectually contagious. Antisystematic "resistance to theory," as it is sometimes called, no doubt will persist and continue to produce important insights, ones inaccessible to the blinders that theory adopts in pursuit of its unifying aims. But a the-oretical or structural resignation to blindness in the name of a self-immolating rigor cannot be an aim for criticism if the latter, as argued here, is to contribute to real knowledge. What all forms of resolute inconsequence, however otiose or methodological and programmatic, have in common is not so much skepticism, which may be formally irrefutable, but dandyism, which substantially refutes itself, for as Baudelaire remarks of that "étrange spiritualisme," its only sacrament is suicide (*OC* 560). Anyway, a text like Molière's, for instance, does not ultimately discourage systematic reflection.

Literary works for the most part do end, and when one ends like *Le Bourgeois gentilhomme* we are justified in thinking that it consists in and coheres as a sustained meditation on mimesis, that it consti-tutes a veritable philosophy of mimetic behavior—indeed, one of the best we have. When Cléonte publicly demonstrates his essential, in-trinsic nobility in a lengthy disquisition about "l'imposture" behind "le mot," "le nom" in favor of "les sentiments," and "l'honneur," when he renounces false claims to nobility as "indigne d'un honnête

homme," he is abruptly dismissed as a suitor for Monsieur Jourdain's
daughter (3.12). "That settles it then, my daughter is not for you" is
all he gets in response to his miniseminar on appearance versus reality,
on the outward sign versus the thing itself. He succeeds only when he
apes Monsieur Jourdain's mimetic strategy and hyperbolizes it by im-
personating an emissary of the Grand Turk and dubbing Jourdain
Mammamouchi—a pure signifier whose phonemes imitate one another
rather than accumulate to any reference in the world of social reality.
Needless to say, the success of this stratagem effectively deconstructs
the difference that Molière's society attempts to stabilize between
the "gentilhomme," who originates in a name, and the "honnête
homme," who originates in a substantial self. Molière is at the apex,
or provides the nexus, of seventeenth-century France's sociology, and
his semiology, not to say his grammatology, is a party to it.

The text, then, voices a theory, even a theory of voice versus letters. The better the text, the more coherent the theory, even if it is a
theory of incoherence—though not as aleatory nonsense but as internal contradiction, as skewed, mystified ontology, and as it issues not
from metaphysics but from metaphysical—that is, mimetic—desire.
Sooner or later it is necessary to test these theories against each other,
to read them across each other, to decide what theory accounts for the
best in literature as well as, concomitantly, what literature accounts
best for what makes us human and for what goes on among us, including what makes us behave in ways we regard as inhuman. According to the mimetic hypothesis, real knowledge of human affairs is
massively accessible once we understand the unreality of desire.

In a sense, this book is only a prologue to such an account, inter-
relating two of the most prominent contemporary theorists—and not
just any two, but precisely those two whose differences beckon correlation by their very symmetry. Where they differ is on the question
of difference and its consequences for knowledge. Accordingly, they
serve to polarize the question of theory in a way that is new and, I
think, ultimately productive (I would even say constructive): not in
terms of literature versus philosophy, for deconstruction very ably conflates the two when it reads the latter as a text like any other, but in
terms of divergent views of literature. Of course, deconstruction is opposed to polarization in fact and in principle; breaking down the binary oppositions that nourish what it calls logocentrism, metaphysics,
or simply philosophy is what is does best. It does not for all that aspire

to a higher synthesis or to a third way beyond the differences it deconstructs; rather, it demonstrates the withinness of difference, the mutual contamination of differences resulting in the impossibility of anything beyond literature. That is how I translate Derrida's archly ambiguous phrase in a note on Mallarmé, "L'au-delà de la littérature—ou rien" ("Hors Livre" in *La Dissémination* 62), meaning that there is nothing beyond literature but also that what literature demonstrates as its content is that there is no beyond ("l'au-delà"): no hidden essences, no transcendence. Because Derrida emphatically denies that this is nihilism or skepticism, it is worthwhile confronting it with theoretical aspirations for the human sciences that also claim their roots in literature. Derrida and Girard must each mean something very different by *literature—rien* for Derrida, real knowledge for Girard. Of course, by *rien* Derrida means nothing but the gramm or the grapheme, which I will show to be subject to a sacrificial process in whose apprehension Girard locates real knowledge.

I have stated the case for this correlation using Molière as a pretext; I then restated it by eliciting the astructural homology between the supplement and the surrogate victim. The case can be stated further on its own terms, that is, by considering the symmetry of the difference between Girard and Derrida. The very facility with which they can be opposed suggests that a deconstruction is in order.

Girard's work originates as theory of mimetic, mediated desire as revealed in the novels of Cervantes, Dostoyevsky, Stendhal, Flaubert, and Proust. It culminates with *Things Hidden since the Foundation of the World* in a theory of human origins of a decidedly paradoxical, not to say contradictory, stamp: the theory lays claim to being a scientific hypothesis while asserting its source in the scriptural rehabilitation of the victim in Judeo-Christian tradition. This tradition desacralizes the world, turning to Scripture for its scientific rather than soteriological resources.

According to Derrida's autobiographical thesis defense in 1980, his work originates as a theory of literature that, by questioning the very fact of writing, contests the possibility of coherent theory. "The project [on "the ideality of the literary object"] went astray with the first questions it posed: 'What is literature?' And first of all what is it 'to write'? How is it that the fact of writing can disturb the very question 'what is?' and even 'what does it mean?' " ("The Time of a Thesis" 37). For Girard, the imperium of mimesis is grounds for universal scientific inquiry, leading back to a hypothesis of human origins and cultural foundations, to a fundamental anthropology. For Derrida, to the contrary, the critique of difference instigated by the gramm, the critique of logocentrism in the (non)name of differance, the internal difference inhabiting and destabilizing any identity, cuts the ground from beneath the systematic ambitions of the human sciences.

In a sense, Derrida does something alarmingly simple. He reads philosophy as it is written, as a text, so that he ends up questioning the difference between literature and philosophy in a way corresponding to the richly problematic difference between signifier and signified. This leveling process extends to all sorts of nonfiction discourse, revealing its unconscious poetry—and its unconscious violence. Whereas Girard advances a theory of violence, Derrida is concerned with the violence of theory.

Girard offers a genetic hypothesis anchored in the victim; Derrida presents a critique of origins focused on writing and its analogues, "its nonsynonymous equivalents," which by their very nature—or rather, lack of nature or essence—cannot be anchored to anything. For Girard the victim is a means of grounding his theory in historical and cultural fact, whereas for Derrida, just as inevitably, the signifier in its paradoxical inanity and playfulness defies the possibility of anchoring any discourse.

Consequently, Girard appears concerned primarily with institutions, with signifieds and their referents, whereas Derrida is drawn to the play of signifiers, to which he devotes scrupulous and nonetheless ludic attention. As a result, referents posited outside language are regularly folded back within it, issuing in counterintuitive statements like "the things itself is a sign" and "there is nothing outside the text" (or, more literally, "There is no outwork" ["Il n'y a pas de hors texte"]). I say "appears" because it is precisely the structural continuity between these levels that this book seeks to uncover—notwithstanding deconstruction's inveterate quarrel with the hierarchical violence implied by the very notion of levels.

These differences easily lend themselves to caricature. The two discourses are as unlike as the titles of their books imply, Girard being concerned with things hidden since the foundation of the world and Derrida with propagating groundless dissemination; or again, the two are as different as a book grounding the human sciences in the Bible (*The Scapegoat*) is from a book-length meditation on a postcard (*La Carte Postale*) that perversely represents Plato dictating to Socrates.

It is beginning to look as if I can oppose Girard and Derrida, or translate their difference, in terms of the difference between prose and poetry (As does Molière's Philosopher? Derrida comments that "philosophy is the invention of prose. Philosophy speaks prose." [*OG* 287]), between seminar and salon, or the serious and playful, indeed, between the tragic and the comic. Surely the appeal of Derrida's readings is due in no small measure to the comic effects achieved by his wordplay, whereby a semantic loss of difference is realized in the way words imitate words. But Girard does not simply emerge as the *trouble fête* here. He has no more confidence in philosophy than does Derrida, and no one has matched his claims for the explanatory potential of comic genius, whereby the likes of Flaubert, Cervantes, Dostoyevsky, Proust, and Shakespeare testify to a loss of difference, to the breakdown of ontological delusions, in a way that outstrips the insights of the social sciences. The problem of levels resurfaces insistently, with Girard focusing on the agency of desire and Derrida on the agency of the signifier that logocentric desire occludes.

I could multiply, ramify, and complicate such differences indefinitely. Indeed, an entire book could perhaps be written on why this book should not be extended in such a manner. In a sense, many such books already exist; to see that one need only consider both the countless studies devoted to Derrida, deconstruction, and poststructuralism that contain no reference to Girard and those, fewer in number, devoted to Girard that contain no reference to Derrida, or only derogatory dismissal. (Some prominent exceptions are treated within.) Such massive bibliographical evidence might serve as material proof of this book's improbability—if not, as argued here, for its necessity. It is the necessity of a cross-referencing that is warranted as much by the symmetry of their differences as by the questions of theory they pose to each other. It is the necessity, in other words, of attending to the symmetrical allergy to the sacred and to signifiers that besets so many critics today, for the differences between them correspond to virtually all the differences which deconstruction puts into question. Reason enough, then, to follow the impetus Derrida himself gives to our interpretive faculties and thereby to attempt the desconstruction of the difference between Derrida and Girard.

If literature is to have the last word in such matters, it is not yet
clear what that term means. What is clear is that literature does not
betray the previously mentioned allergy in its exploration of meaning
and order. Monsieur Jourdain's elevation to the rank of Mammamouchi is accomplished to the rhythmic beat of a cadenced pummeling,
accompanied by a Moslemized, mongrelized French: "Dara, dara,/
Bastonnara, bastonnara." "The Turks repeat the same verses, beating
him to music" (*Le Bourgeois gentilhomme* 4.5). This comic violence
points to the loss of meaning, or of difference, that Monsieur Jourdain's pretensions instigate. The scene parodies an initiatory rite.
The bourgeois's imaginary metamorphosis into gentleman recalls the
sacrificial origins of kingship, of sovereign Difference, of which Monsieur Jourdain is the befuddled possessor, the comic exemplar, the
be(k)nighted victim.

The play concludes with the "Ballet des Nations." Sung in several
languages to music composed by Lulli, it appears to symbolize the reconciliation of differences.

2

Philosophy and Sacrifice in Plato and Descartes

"Plato's Pharmacy"

When René Girard interrogates mythological texts he uncovers a scapegoat mechanism that he argues lies at the foundation of human culture. When Jacques Derrida interrogates philosophical texts he uncovers a systematic exclusion of writing, of the gramm or the signifier, and he argues that this exclusion is necessary to the generation and stabilization of concepts. Notwithstanding the substantial difference between a discourse concerned with signifiers and one concerned with victims, there is a *formal* or *structural* resemblance in the processes of expulsion and mystification analyzed by these two writers. I think that this can be shown in the case of Derrida's reading of Plato and of Descartes and furthermore, that a case can be made on the basis of these same readings for Girard's claim about the distinctly revelatory power of Scripture in human affairs.

When Derrida explores the origins of Western philosophy in "Plato's Pharmacy" (in *Dissemination;* "Plato's Pharmacy" is henceforth referred to as PP), what he uncovers is a mechanism of exclusion and mystification, a logic of sacrifice as articulated by Girard. In the *Phaedrus* Plato recalls the myth of Theuth, in which writing is portrayed as a dangerous drug offered to Ra, the father-god, as an aid to memory. The gift is rejected for impeding memory, for usurping its active functioning. "If men learn this," the king says, "it will implant forgetfulness in their souls; they will cease to exercise memory because they rely on that which is written, calling things to remembrance no longer

from within themselves, but by means of external marks" (*Phaedrus* §
275). Writing is invented as a supplement to speech, to presence of
mind, to the origin as logos and logos as origin, and it is expelled for
threatening to supplant it altogether. Accordingly, Plato labels it a
pharmakon, a remedy-poison, and the subsequent translations of this
word as either remedy or poison reflect the rejection by philosophic
tradition of a radical ambiguity or originary bivalence to whose expulsion the Platonic text is arduously dedicated.

The Derrida shows thereafter that the two terms share more than just
their lexical ties, that writing as *pharmakon* has structural and functional affinities with the *pharmakos* in Greek culture: the scapegoat,
the sacrificial victim whose violent expulsion purifies the community.
This role is extended to that of Socrates himself, who figures at times
in the dialogues as enchanter, sorcerer, beguiler, or *pharmakeus*.
Socrates, moreover, regards his own poisoning as a remedy releasing
his soul to immortality, and he is recorded as having been born on the
day of purification, Thargelies, a sacrificial day. Derrida marks Plato's
silence about these affinities, but as another reader of Plato has
pointed out (Bandera, in "Literature and Desire"), he is silent in turn
about the properly sacrificial dimension of philosophical discourse, a
dimension in which his own silence is implicated.

The sacrificial origins of philosophy are in fact manifold. They are
formal and substantial, textual as well as institutional or historical, for
as even Derrida reminds us, it is Platonism that installs Western metaphysics in its conceptuality (PP 76): the very opposition of mythos to
logos, though it antedates the dialogues (see Burkert, *Greek Religion*
312), draws its subsequent authority from Plato (PP 168), and Plato,
we are reminded, writes "from out of the death of Socrates" (PP 148,
153). Girard himself comments concisely on the pertinence of Derrida's reading of Plato for his own hypothesis in *Violence and the Sacred*.
Indeed, he states that "the Platonic *pharmakon* functions like the human pharmakos and leads to similar results" (*Violence and the Sacred*
296, hereafter *VS*). The fate of the signifier in Derrida's reading is the
same as that of the victim in Girard's analysis, but it is worthwhile to
demonstrate the rigorous homology between Derrida's reading of the
philosophical text and Girard's reading of culture.

Derrida shows that it is not simply as representation, as sensible
marking, that writing poses a threat; what makes it noxious is not its
difference from the origin, from the selfsame presence of the idea

(*eidos*), but its indifference to origins, whence its paradoxical likeness to the origin it supplants:

> Why is the surrogate or supplement dangerous? It is not, so to speak, dangerous in itself, in that aspect of it that can present itself as a thing, as a being present. In that case it would be reassuring. But the supplement *is* not, is not a being (*on*). It is nevertheless not a simple nonbeing (*me on*) either. Its slidings slip it out of the simple alternative presence/absence. *That* is the danger. And that is what enables the types always to pass for the original. As soon as the supplementary outside is opened, its structure implies that the supplement itself can be "typed," replaced by its double, and that a supplement to the supplement, a surrogate for the surrogate, is possible and necessary. Necessary because this movement is not a sensible, "empirical" accident: it is linked to the ideality of the eidos as the possibility of the repetition of the same. (PP 109)

To repeat: if truth were not repeatable, it would not be true. Because it is repeatable, its relation to another, bad repetition—writing—is problematic; worse, it is undecidable, for the formal difference between memory and recollection, between *mnesis* and *hypomnesis*, between presence of mind and representation, is "hardly perceptible" (PP 111).

Plato's suspicion of writing conforms to Pascal's suspicion of imagination, down to the letterly figures by which Pascal marks its unreliability: "It is that deceitful part in man, that mistress of error and falsity, the more deceptive that she is not always so; for she would be an infallible rule of truth, if she were an infallible rule of falsehood. But being most generally false, she gives no sign [*marque*] of her nature, impressing [*marquant*] the same character on the true and the false" (*Pensées*, Brunschvicg ed. § 82, 95).

Because of this radical ambiguity, Derrida figures Plato as perplexed and fascinated by the scandalous alternation of a good and bad repetition: "As a substitute capable of doubling for the king, the father, the sun, and the word, distinguished from these only by dint of representing, repeating, and masquerading, Theuth was naturally also capable of totally supplanting them and appropriating all their attributes. He is added as the essential attribute of what he is added to, and from which almost nothing distinguishes him. He differs from speech or divine light only as the revealer from the revealed. Barely" (PP 90). Writing is not itself a harmful substance; it is harmful because it is not a substance, because it is not itself. Existing only as repetition, its identity is its nonidentity (93), its difference is its in-difference to difference, on which depends any notion, any formal or institutional possibility, of meaning, order, and structure.

What is wrong with writing is that there is nothing wrong with it. It is not a thing that can be right or wrong. It merely represents the formal possibilities of representation, or mimesis—and that is what is wrong with it: "that the supplement itself can be 'typed,' replaced by its double," means that there is no limit to the contagion of mimesis, to the proliferation of doubles, which, as I shall show, has substantial consequences in the life of the polis. The reason for its expulsion from Plato's philosophy is homologous to the fate of twins in sacrificial ritual, as evoked by Girard: "In the case of twins, symmetry and identity are represented in extraordinarily explicit terms; nondifference is present in concrete, literal form, but this form is itself so exceptional as to constitute a new difference. Thus the *representation* of nondiffer-ence ultimately becomes the very exemplar of difference, a classic monstrosity that plays a vital role in sacred ritual" (*VS* 64). What twins represent, fairly incarnate, is the opposition of like to like; they are the very *figure* of violent indifferentiation, of mimetic conflict, which sacrifice seeks to allay. Twins resemble the parricide, the usurper, the incestuous son, as slayers of distinction (*VS* 74). They symbolize the dissolution of normative differences, or desymbolization itself: "Ulti-mately, the insufficient difference in family relationships serves to symbolize the dissolution of family distinctions; in other words, it *desymbolizes*" (*VS* 62).

Sacrifice restores order by restoring difference: between the sacra-lized victim, arbitrarily chosen, and the rest of the community, which is unanimous in its expulsion of violence. As all are violent, any one can substitute for all the others, all the enemy brothers that each member strives to banish from the community. For the suspicion of each against each to become the conviction of all against one, "noth-ing, or almost nothing is necessary. The slightest hint, the most groundless accusation, can circulate with vertiginous speed and is transformed into irrefutable proof" (*VS* 79, trans. modified). The se-lection of the victim is aleatory; all that is necessary is an insignificant mark, the least significant mark, "l'indice le plus dérisoire,"—the ar-bitrary mark as such, like the gramm or the grapheme in Derrida's reading of Plato.

Homologously, philosophy installs order by marking the difference between a good and bad repetition, the bad repetition being that of the mark itself, that of writing. In Derrida's commentary on Plato it bears all the monstrous traits assigned to the sacrificial victim: it is a "living dead," a "reprieved corpse," an "outlaw," a "pervert," a "bad seed" (PP 143), above all a "parricide" (146). Because of its ambiguous being, Derrida identifies writing as a *"fantôme,"* a ghost (103), whereby it connects with the *hallucinatory* character of the double as depicted by Girard: "The 'Dionysiac' state of mind can and, . . . often does erase all manner of differences: familial, cultural, biological, and natural. The entire everyday world is caught up in the whirl, producing a hallucinatory state that is not a synthesis of elements, but a formless and grotesque mixture of things that are normally separate" (*VS* 160). The otherness, the structural alterity of monstrosity, as of parricide and incest as well, is indifference to difference, for instance, between human and beast, father and son, or mother and child: Oedipus slays his father and marries his mother; Pentheus dresses as a woman and is slain by his mother. Writing also foments "the destruction of differences," which is the expression Girard uses to characterize a sacrificial crisis (*VS* 74).

In the *Republic* this indifferentiation appears as a political allegory of democracy, where the bid for equality represents the crisis of difference as a crisis of desire: "This errant democrat, wandering like a desire or like a signifier freed from *logos*, this individual who is not even perverse in a regular way, who is ready to do anything, to lend himself to anyone, who gives himself equally to all pleasures, to all activities— eventually even to politics or philosophy . . . —this adventurer, like the one in the *Phaedrus*, simulates everything at random and is really nothing. Swept off by every stream, he belongs to the masses; he has no essence, no truth, no patronym, no constitution of his own" (PP 145). Writing's capacity to represent anything derives from the fact that it represents nothing in particular. What Plato contemns in writing is mimesis precisely as it represents the dynamics of the crowd, the revolutionary mob, whose violence is quelled only by the arbitrary expulsion of one of its members. Writing is thus expelled as a supplanter of origins in Plato's text for the same reason that the scapegoat, such as Oedipus, is expelled from the city: he represents its mimetic fury. He is its inside turned out.

There is profound irony in this structural contortion, for writing emerges as the origin of the opposition (including that of father and son or original and copy) that subsequently functions to exclude it:

> It is not enough to say that writing is conceived out of this or that series of oppositions. Plato thinks of writing and tries to comprehend it, to dominate it on the basis of *opposition* as such. In order for these contrary values (good/evil, true/false, essence/appearance, inside/outside, etc.) to be in opposition, each of the terms must be simply external to the other, which means that one of these oppositions (the opposition between inside and outside) must already be accredited as the matrix of all possible opposition. And one of the elements of the system (or of the series) must also stand as the very possibility of systematicity or seriality in general. (PP 103)

Seriality or systematicity is the obscure synonym of the stereotype it excludes. The *pharmakon* is the origin, the foundation of oppositions that come into "being" by its expulsion. Far from being dominated by any oppositions, writing is the condition of the very possibility of opposition; it cannot be contained by any oppositions, but remains ever in excess of them. Writing is insubordinate in principle and, more importantly, of principle as such. The emergence of the logos as the condition of truth, of the presence of the idea to itself, it thus traced to the expulsion of an otherness in which it originates.

Derrida's argument is that writing does not fit into preconceived categories as something bad. Rather, for such a category to exist, writing or "something like the *pharmakon*" (103), the double or mimesis, must be expelled. This obstacle to truth, the rival to truth, is likewise its originary model. This opposition of same to same, where rival, model, and obstacle are one, displays the dynamics of violent mimesis of the victimary hypothesis. It argues that the violence of all against all in the mêlée of appropriative rivalry yields at a certain point to the violence of all against one, against the victim, whose vulnerability marks it out for destruction. The death of the victim restores calm to the group and instaurates for the first time an order of before/after (the violence) and inside/outside (the group), the victim being the outside on and against which the group as an inside, a community, is founded. In sum, it is the order of space and time. All subsequent cultural differentiations (what Derrida calls seriality or systematicity) derive from this inaugural expulsion, whose mistake, whose misprision, is essential to their maintenance and credibility (*THFW* 103–4).

The victim is the matrix of difference for Girard (*THFW* 162) for the same reason that writing is the matrix of difference for Derrida: both succumb to a mystified expulsion to which order and difference owe their origin, their institution. The victim in Girard's scenario plays the same structuring role as writing in Derrida's reading of Plato, that of the "*supplément d'origine,*" "the supplement of (at) the origin" (*OG* 313).

The homology here is not merely formal or thematic: it is functional, operational, and pragmatic. It works. It produces philosophy along with other cultural institutions whose survival and credibility depend on concealing their violent origins. The efficacy of sacrificial mechanisms, as Girard shows, depends on the occlusion of arbitrary exclusion, which is why such mechanisms work to both good and ill effect. Sacrifice alienates violence from the community; it protects the community from its own violence, which is good. But as it mystifies the origin of violence by assigning it to the victim, it also protects violence from any understanding that would serve to eliminate it definitively. Consequently, the community is ever in search of new victims, in which it blindly seeks what Derrida calls its "réserve d'arrière-fond," its "store of deep background" (PP 128). As Derrida writes, "there is no such thing as a harmless remedy. The *pharmakon* can never be simply beneficial" (99). To translate or interpret this supplement as simply beneficial—or simply the opposite—is to perpetuate the violence that gives rise to all interpretation and all valuations coterminous with it: "All translations into languages that are the heirs and depositories of Western metaphysics thus produce on the *pharmakon* an *effect of analysis* that violently destroys it, reduces it to one of its simple elements by interpreting it, paradoxically enough, in the light of the ulterior developments it itself has made possible. Such an interpretative translation is thus as violent as it is impotent: it destroys the pharmakon but at the same time forbids itself access to it, leaving it untouched in its reserve" (PP 99). This effect in philosophy is the same, structurally and functionally, as the mystifying effect of sacrificial substitution analyzed in *Violence and the Sacred:* "It is the knowledge of violence, along with the violence itself, that the act of expulsion succeeds in shunting outside the realm of consciousness" (*VS* 135). What Derrida calls the "reserve," a supplement that both precedes and exceeds the concept, is just this indifference that violence expels and that is the essential characteristic of violence itself.

The violence of interpretation cited by Derrida does not lead to the nihilistic conclusion that all interpretations are of equal value, still less that all valuation is bad because it is violent. Precisely because some readings of Derrida seem to favor this conclusion, however, Girard's focus on the victim is necessary. If violence is bad, then those interpretations that reveal its agency, however unconscious, are good and true. And violence is always to some degree unconscious to the extent that it is not a function of autonomous will but of mimetic desire. This is the epistemological argument of *The Scapegoat* and *Job: The Victim of His People*, which make explicit what is often only implicit in Derrida's interpretive activity. What Girard does is thematize the moral impulse of deconstruction in its ever more subtle detections of unconscious violence. This is an impulse all too often ignored by both advocates and adversaries of deconstruction, which uncovers violence in texts only to concern itself thereafter with textuality and not with violence. This in itself might be considered an instance of symbolic repression, the more-or-less ritualized oblivion of the violence to which Derrida's reading of the text nonetheless beckons our attention.

There is evidence for this oblivion even in Derrida's own text, for example, when he links the ambiguity of writing to the simulated reversal of values that takes place at festivals: "The entrance of the *pharmakon* on the scene, the evolution of the magic powers, the comparison with painting, the politicofamilial violence and perversion, the allusion to makeup, masks, simulacra—all this couldn't *not* lead us to games and festivals, which can never go without some sort of urgency or outpouring of sperm" (149–50). Derrida then proceeds to graph the oppositive motifs of the game (*paidia*), the holiday (*heortè*), and the serious (*spoudè*): "On the one hand cultivation, agri-culture, knowledge, economy; on the other, art, enjoyment and unreserved spending" (150). Plato's metaphor of knowledge as serious farming serves to condemn writing as a kind of "writing in sand"; no "sensible farmer" would be "using his pen to sow words (*melani speiron dia kalamou meta logon*) that can't either speak in their own support (*boèthein*) or teach the truth adequately" (*Phaedrus* § 276c, as cited in PP 151). This is the occasion for Derrida to link sperm and ink to the liquiform mutability of writing: "Sperm, water, ink, perfumed dye: the *pharmakon* always penetrates like a liquid; it is absorbed, drunk, introduced into the inside, which it first marks with the hardness of the type, soon to invade it and inundate it with its medicine, its brew, its drink, its potion, its poison" (PP 152). So sperm, like ink, flows out, then in. What seems to evade Derrida's attention amid these juicy associations is the notorious fact that if festivals are the occasion for the outpouring of sperm, it is because they are only a somewhat deritualized representation of desire, whence the masks and other simulacra that *perform* mimesis and its concomitant loss of individualized identity (see *VS* 66–68), even sexual identity. The outpouring of sperm is but the prelude to the outpouring of blood, which until the medicine of this century poured only one way: out toward death. This is when the mimetic desires focus on a single victim. This singular omission unfortunately characterizes most of the critical literature that, following the publication of Bakhtin's *Rabelais and his World,* focuses on the festival and the carnivalesque. We are regaled with the thematics of transgression, of overturning traditional values, and so on, without any recollection that the carnival played on the margins of Ash Wednesday, that Mardi Gras was a prelude to the Passion, as Saturnalia was to sacrifice. We can desire to perpetuate the seemingly emancipatory antivalues of the festival against repressive institutions only if we forget that the very free-play of its antistructuring proclivities is a sacrificial institution (see Turner, *The Ritual Process: Structure and Anti-Structure*). It is only in relatively modern times that such free-play is not the foreplay to bloodletting.

It should be clear by now that one could indefinitely multiply passages to this effect in Derrida and Girard, revealing the victim effect in Derrida's reading of philosophy, whereby the victimary hypothesis lends anthropological reference to such Derridean antinotions or foreconcepts as "trace," "mark," "supplement," and "differance" itself. Indeed the violence of the letter is both hidden and revealed in the last term, a heterographic neologism whereby Derrida seeks to uncover "the alterity of allergy or of polemics," in which differentiation—that of *phonè* versus *grammè* for instance—originates: "But the word 'difference' (with an e) could never refer to differing as temporalizing or to difference as *polemos*" (*Margins of Philosophy* 8, trans. modified)—that is, to the present participial sense of active opposition: violence, in a word. The whole of *Violence and the Sacred* can be viewed as a commentary, an explication, of the Heraclitean dictum that Girard cites in chapter 3 and evokes again in the last sentence of his book: "'Strife [*polemos*] is the father and king of all. Some it makes gods, others men; some slaves, and others free'" (*VS* 88). We may cite, as Derrida's explication of this dictum, what he says of the "play of traces or supplements," which, he insists, "no reality, no absolutely external reference, no transcendental signified can come to limit, bound or control": "One would not have understood anything of this 'linguistic' 'immanence' if one saw it as the peaceful milieu of a merely fictional war, an inoffensive word play, in contrast to some raging *polemos* in reality. It is not in any reality foreign to the 'play of words' that Theuth also frequently participates in plots, perfidious intrigues, conspiracies to usurp the throne. He helps the sons do away with the father, the brothers do away with the brother that has become king" (PP 89). For sons to do away with the father, brothers with brothers, or father with sons is all one: *polemos*. It is the same difference that governs the text of philosophy and the text of culture. When Plato translates the struggles of logos with its other (its other self as *pharmakon*) into human terms, it is *polemos*, as Derrida shows, that is "father and king of all."

"Differance," Derrida insists, "is neither a word nor a concept" (*Margins of Philosophy* 3). Still less is it a theme. Rather, it is the structuring principle of difference, or "difference under erasure," as another critic has observed (Siebers, *The Ethics of Criticism* 81). What erases here is the very "thing" that marks it. Otherwise stated, it is the astructural, atheistic *anathememe* (my coinage, conflating theme and anathema) that defies the unity of a concept for marking the fundamental disunity, or dysunity, that gives rise to concepts and that they thereafter function to conceal. Derrida uses the audibly imperceptible *a* of differance, the first letter of the alphabet, to suggest the primacy of writing as that which a text conceals in the deployment of its signifieds, its themes. The very first sentence of "Plato's Pharmacy" reads "A text is not a text unless it hides from the first comer, from the first glance, the law of its composition and the rules of its game. A text remains, moreover, forever imperceptible" (63). Of course, this is presumably no longer the case after Derrida, in whose text a certain concealment is revealed, and with it a certain violence.

Because the letter has no privilege, no primacy, it symbolizes the "cryptogram" that every text buries as its originary trace. The Derridean cryptogram is a play on words, a "pleonastic proposition" suggesting the hiddenness of the letter as tomblike, tending, as he says, "to take shelter in its crypt" (PP 105). It is pleonastic because what is hidden is the tomb and the body it entombs—or entomes, as in a book. The Derridean cryptogram is the victimary status of the letter and the mechanisms of concealment of which the entire philosophical edifice is constructed, in the same way that the body of the victim is what founds the entire cultural edifice for Girard (*THFW* 165).

The effect on human bodies is disproportionate to that on dead letters—indeed, incommensurate—but the structure of the operation is the same. If this is not mere coincidence, a fluke, it is a warrant for the victimary hypothesis as a unified theory of cultural institutions, philosophy among them. It is thus not surprising that "Plato's Pharmacy" reads like an allegory of this theory, a symbolic representation of institutional occurrences. Philosophy is an institution like many another; if the origin of culture and cultural institutions is sacrificial, philosophy will not be immune to sacrificial mechanisms. Rather, philosophy is accomplice to them when it thematizes the *pharmakon* while remaining silent about the *pharmakos*. This silence is in turn the theme of Cesareo Bandera's reflections:

> If Girard is right and the violent ritual of the expulsion of the human *pharmakos* is in itself a *repetition*, a cover up, a replica of an original expulsion, a *real* killing which is disguised in the very act of being meticulously, ritualistically re-produced, the silence of the philosophical text could in turn be read as a textual parallel of the ritual, a *repetition* of the ritual, a cover up of the cover up, so to speak. The text itself would thus appear to be inscribed in the violent ritual, and not *vice-versa*. The original expulsion, the *real* killing would become the unspoken text, the father, the king of the text in precisely Derrida's sense, while all other texts (*l'écriture*) would constitute themselves as text by killing the father, or rather by inevitably disguising and concealing the *real* violence of such a killing. ("Literature and Desire" 36)

Bandera offers this as a "hypothesis," "since," he says, "we cannot go into a detailed analysis." The analyses I present here were undertaken independently of Bandera's intuitions and are being advanced as a confirmation of his hypothesis.

This revealing coincidence suggests the possibility of further homologies—with Scripture, for instance. Jesus' rebuke of the Pharisees for being "whitened sepulchers" (Matt. 23:27) reproaches them for occluding the violence at the foundation of religion (*THFW* 164). It resonates with Derrida's critique of philosophy as a "white mythology," in which properly mythical origins are bleached out as concepts: "White mythology—metaphysics has erased in itself the fabulous scene which produced it, the scene that nevertheless remains active and stirring, inscribed in white ink, an invisible design covered over in the palimpsest" (*Margins of Philosophy* 213). I have shown that this "fabulous scene" conforms to the dynamics of a foundational murder, which is why Derrida finds that the "structural laws" of Plato's tale betray a "contagion of mythemes" among cultures (PP 85). According to Girard's reading of Scripture, which he alleges is Scripture's reading of culture, all religion effaces its violent origins, burying the tomb in which culture originates:

> R.G.: Luke compares the Pharisees not just to tombs but to underground tombs, that is to say, invisible tombs—tombs that are perfect in a double sense, if we can put it like that, since they conceal not only death, but also their own existence as tombs. "Woe to you! for you are like graves which are not seen, and men walk over them without knowing it" (Luke 11:14).
>
> J.-M. O.: This double concealment reproduces the way in which cultural differentiation develops on the basis of the founding murder. This murder tends to efface itself behind the directly sacrificial rituals, but even these rituals risk being too revealing and so tend to be effaced behind post-ritual institutions, such as judicial and political systems or the forms of culture. These derived forms give way nothing of the fact that they are rooted in the original murder. (*THFW* 165)

My reference to Scripture at this stage may seem unwarranted, not to say irreverent, yet Girard claims for Scripture the revelatory key to every sacrificial mechanism, and Derrida, willy-nilly, shows philosophy to be one such mechanism. In his fascination with labyrinths and palimpsests, as with their cryptograms, Derrida snoops around the foundational tombs of culture—though without finally deciding whether to venture into them or to adorn them further. In "White Mythology" Derrida unveils the metaphors underlying the so-called proper senses of words, thereby breaking down philosophy's construct of itself as presiding over this difference (between rhetoric as external and philosophy as internal to thought). It differs from itself as metaphor rather than from literature, which it defines as its other. "This self-destruction still has the form of a generalization, but this time it is no longer a question of extending and confirming a philosopheme, but rather, of unfolding it without limit, and wresting its borders of propriety from it. And consequently to explode the reassuring opposition of the metaphoric and the proper, the opposition in which the one and the other have never done anything but reflect and refer to each other in their radiance" (*Margins of Philosophy* 270). This self-destruction of philosophy again exhibits the *polemos* of rival twins, the pathos of mistaken identity.

Consequently, it is neither accident nor mere formal coincidence that these Derridean paradoxes, paralogisms, and *coincidentia oppositorum* (a figure employed provisionally by both Girard and Derrida to designate a violent paradox rather than a harmonious synthesis) correspond to certain parabolic dicta, such as "the first shall be last and the last shall be first," which we are to understand as fulfilled, as definitively revealed, in such announcements as "I am the Alpha and the Omega, the first and the last, the beginning and the end" (Rev. 22:13). Here again, passages could be multiplied indefinitely, because, as Shakespeare's Richard II would not fail to perceive in the anguish of his dethronement and imminent murder, scriptural texts often "set the word itself against the word" (*Richard II*, act 5, scene 5). This is not accomplished as a merely formal exercise, as some commentary suggests (Crossan, *The Dark Interval*, after Kermode, *The Sense of an Ending*). Still less is it enunciated in service to *polemos*, which to the contrary depends on illusions of selfsame identity and external difference. According to Girardian exegesis, such statements definitively reveal *polemos* by showing the mechanisms that occlude its agency.

It is the altogether startling argument of *Things Hidden since the Foundation of the World* and *The Scapegoat* that Scripture reveals the structuring principle of sacrificial expulsion, its cultural and historical efficacy—that Scripture is the keystone of a "fundamental anthropology." Girard further argues this revelation of the victim as the foundation of human culture to be, in the person of Jesus, a decisive historical event that must subsequently work to deconstruct sacrificial institutions and, concomitantly, to reveal violence as wholly human rather than holy or sacred. Where Derrida is concerned, this principle is perhaps most succinctly formulated in the following dictum: "The stone which the builders have rejected has become the cornerstone" (cf. Ps. 118:22; Luke 20:17). If that is not but a facile paradox, or a cryptogram in a merely hermetic sense, then it deserves to stand as the epigraph—literally, and the epitaph also—to "Plato's Pharmacy," as well as to the many other texts by Derrida in which writing is revealed as a *scandalon* to *logos*, a stumbling block to philosophy.

Derrida's irrepressible play with the signifiers, with letters, with the imperceptible building blocks of discourse, perpetuates this

scandal in the philosophical community. The crisis of difference between father and son, speech and writing, inside and outside, original
and copy, center and margin, as well as true and false, good and bad
(repetition), and so on—that is, virtually all the categories of Western
thought to whose structural laws Plato conforms his narrative—necessarily extends to the difference between philosophy and literature.
This crisis has prompted Richard Rorty to classify philosophy as just
another literary genre, "a kind of writing" that began with Plato and
has pretty much run its course with Derrida (*Consequences of Pragmatism* chap. 6).

Of course, the debate between literature and philosophy is as old as
philosophy itself; after all, it was Plato who expelled literature from
his republic. For his repudiation of writing, Plato incarnates what
Derrida describes as the "*dream*" of philosophy: "truth as distinct
from its sign, being as distinct from types, . . . memory with no sign"
(PP 109). Derrida uncovers the violence of this dream as a white mythology that occludes the exclusion of the sign, showing traces of victimage in the name of a universal Truth. Derrida's critique of
philosophy is in this regard continuous with Girard's critique of mythology, whose purpose, as defined in *The Scapegoat* (chap. 7), is to
erase the traces of violent expulsion and the founding role of the victim. It is therefore to Derrida's credit that I quote the Pauline version
of what I have suggested as a plausible epigraph to "Plato's Pharmacy": "Behold I am laying in Zion, a stone that will make men stum-
ble, a rock that will make them fall; and he who believes in him will
not be put to shame" (Rom. 9:33; cf. Isa. 28:16; 8:14–15). This is not
the place to debate the merits of religious belief or faith, which Girard
affirms and Derrida eschews altogether, but their shared disbelief in
nonviolent origins, their rigorously informed suspicion of an origin distinct from violence, can be established with the utmost clarity. If the
origin of this revelation is located in Scripture, as Girard has argued,
then Derrida's critical activity, strategically located on the margins of
philosophy, can function as a paving stone rather than as a stumbling
block to understanding the revelation.

Plato's *Letters*

Plato's *Letters* contains an interesting sequel, a historical supplement,
to this story of the sacrificial origins of philosophy in the expulsion by

the logos of its other, its brother, its rival father-son. This sequel is all the more interesting for the fact that Derrida does not detect it, though it confirms the tragic dimension of philosophical origins. Instead, Derrida cites the *Letters* only at the end of his essay, as an instance of Plato's distrust of writing: "It is a very great safeguard," Plato writes to Dionysius of Syracuse, "to learn by heart instead of writing," an admonition that ends with the command to "burn this letter after reading it many times" ("Letter 2" § 314b–c).

In the body of the letter, Plato recounts how the unjust death of Socrates caused him to withdraw from public life. The fear of being "nothing but words" ("Letter 7" § 328c) caused him to renew his attempts to reconcile theory and practice, philosophy and government. In letters 3, 4, and 7 Plato narrates his properly tragic experience as counselor to Dionysius, tyrant of Syracuse, and as friend of Dion, whom the former suspects of attempting to usurp his throne. It is another skewed family scene, with Dion, the middle-aged contemporary and friend of Plato, being exiled by Dionysius for allegedly trying to supplant him. And it is Dionysius's groundless though murderous rivalry with Dion that causes Plato to withdraw philosophical inquiry definitively from the scene of public life.

Plato particularly reproaches Dionysius for wishing to be preferred to Dion, for imagining a rivalry between Dion and Dionysius over which Plato would be the arbiter in the latter's favor: "He did indeed grow more and more to like me as time passed and as he learned to know my life and character, but he wanted me to commend him more than Dion, to think him rather than Dion a special friend. In fact his ambition in this respect was surprising. He shunned, however, the best method of attaining his object, if it could be attained at all—that is, of course, by receiving instruction and hearing me discourse on philosophy, to become my intimate friend and disciple. The reports circulated by our enemies made him afraid he might somehow be entangled and so Dion have accomplished his desire" ("Letter 7" § 330a–b). The design, in Dionysius's imagination, is that of getting him so wrapped up in philosophy, getting his intelligence so "yielded to the spell of education, that he should lose interest in government" and allow himself to be supplanted by Dion ("Letter 7" § 333c). The latter, in Plato's construction, figures as a good "father" for both the wisdom of his years and the generosity of his advice ("Letter 3" § 316c; "Letter 7" § 332c).

In view of the disputed authorship of Plato's letters, it is probably not worthwhile attempting to get to the truth of these charges and countercharges. Their structure is nonetheless revealing as viewed on either a horizontal or vertical plane. The former shows the rivalry of (imaginary) doubles; the latter, the pathology of discipleship. Moreover, the dynamics of the second plane repeat those of the first, for Dionysius's resentment of his imagined rival is replicated by Plato's resentment of Dionysius, which develops when Plato discovers in his disciple an obstacle to his role as a model. Whereas the enemy brothers rival for Plato's recognition, Plato rivals with Dionysius for recognition as a philosopher.

This is the familiar scene of rival brothers, in which Dionysius plays the role of Cain against Abel, of Jacob against Esau, for the blessing of the godhead or the father. It is the structural replica, or replay, of the mythical rivalry between Eteocles and Polyneices for the domination of Thebes in Euripides' *Phoenecian Women*. In Euripides' play, the city is saved by the mutual destruction of the rivals. In Sophocles' version of this story, Creon seeks to save the city by instituting an arbitrary difference between them, but this results only in the sacrificial murder of Antigone, who contests that difference. In Plato's version, the philosopher's withdrawal and subsequent institution of the academy are meant to keep the city safe from such a catastrophe as befalls the enemy twins, whose difference is grounded in the pursuit of a mistakenly identical object, a compound case of mistaken identity. The philosopher withdraws from the city to contemplate it, thereby sacrificing himself.

This marginal role continues to haunt philosophy. It accounts in part for the contemporary interest, the (anti)philosophical investment, in the marginal, in margin-alea, in chance, in what is not reducible to system or assimilable to power; such issues are centrally important to philosophers like Derrida, who strategically writes on the margins of philosophy, that is, where philosophy rubs against or overlaps with literature. But the margins of philosophy are many, and its institutional origins implicate the state as well as religion. If it is possible to envisage the origins of philosophy in and as the sacrificial expulsion of the letter, literature, it is necessary also to consider its origins in a resentment of the state. The author of the second letter believes that "it is a natural law that wisdom and great power attract each other" ("Letter 2" § 310e). What is not stated, though it is exhibited in the tale that the letters unfold, is the potential for rivalry in this attraction, that wisdom's desire for power and power's desire for wisdom are mimetic, a fact that places their attraction on a collision course. Perhaps the most decisive contribution to a theory governing that relationship is provided by Molière in the person of his violent Philosopher, especially in the sequel to the previously cited imbroglio. The Philosopher swears to avenge himself on his rivals with a satire "which will tear them to pieces," a design that suggests the interest of Eric Gans's theory of high culture as originating in resentment (see *The End of Culture*, especially part 3). At any rate, such a view finds confirmation in Stanley Cavell's observation that "skepticism's 'doubt' is motivated not by (not even where it is expressed as) a (misguided) intellectual scrupulousness but by a (displaced) denial, by a self-consuming disappointment that seeks world-consuming revenge" (*Disowning Knowledge* 5–6). Whether it concerns system builders or system destroyers, one need only imagine Molière's Alceste with a Ph.D.

Of course, one might object that Molière's Philosopher, like his pedants and "précieux," his doctors, hypochondriacs, and hypocrites, is just a comic mask, a hyperbolic stereotype in a play whose principle interest is the ritual of comic expulsion. But it is precisely the comprehensive import of Girard's theory that no institution is immune to the sacrificial practices on which culture is founded (see chap. 3 of this book, "Tracing Institutions"). On the other hand, some further qualifications about philosophy are in order, lest I appear to sacrifice a whole living discipline to the consequently violent reconciliation of Girard and Derrida. As Girard himself has remarked, we are only too eager to make scapegoats of our institutions. ("The Logic of the Undecidable" 20–21). Their ostensible impersonality opens them to charges of inhumanity.

Derridean deconstruction provides an antifoundationalist critique, though it is not the first to do so. In fact, deconstruction shares antifoundationalism with nearly the entire Anglo-American tradition of analytic philosophy (see Reed Way Dasenbrock, ed., *Redrawing the Lines: Analytic Philosophy, Deconstruction, and Literary Theory*). It is a tradition that, despite solicitation by Richard Rorty, deconstruction has mostly "refused to engage" (*Redrawing* 17). When Derrida evokes philosophy, he is mostly concerned with what is called its Continental or metaphysical tradition: Plato, Aristotle, Cartesian rationalism, and German idealism, including the latter's twentieth-century vestiges in

Husserl and Heidegger. Except for his latter-day exploitation of J. L. Austin's notion of performative utterances, Derrida's almost only brush with the analytic tradition (as in "Limited Inc.") is to show up *its* metaphysical presuppositions. Such presuppositions, I argue, betray sacrificial mythemes and mechanisms, whence the proposed alliance between Derrida and Girard.

But there is a possible irony here at deconstruction's expense, for I suspect at times that something variously called philosophy, metaphysics, or logocentrism and its cognates serves deconstruction itself as a scapegoat for violence both within and without the academic community. To cite one example among many, here is Eric Santner's gloss on poststructuralist discourses: "These discourses propose a kind of perpetual leave-taking from fantasies of plenitude, purity, centrality, totality, unity and mastery. Such fantasies and their various narrative performances, whether cast in the rhetoric of totalization or of liberation, are in turn seen as the primary sources of violence in history, the Third Reich being only the most extreme example in a long historical series" (*Stranded Objects* 7). As I argue in subsequent chapters (especially chaps. 4 and 5), there is something to this, but it has to be balanced by an observation like Hannah Arendt's that "after all it wasn't the German language that went crazy" (in Young-Bruehl, *Hannah Arendt* 3). The expulsion of philosophy with a capital *P,* as master discipline, only serves to replicate and perpetuate rather than rationally resolve misunderstanding.

Moreover, a symmetrical danger inheres in the analytical tradition, with its "minimalist" and "deflationary" accounts of truth as inscribed with a decidedly small *t.* Such accounts regularly take place in the absence of any attention to the mediating role of others and, consequently, to social and historical contexts. There is near unanimity among analytic philosophers about truth being contained in sentences, about it being a matter of propositions (e.g., Rorty, in Dasenbrock, *Redrawing* 207, and Paul Horwich, *Truth* 17). In short, the analytic tradition lacks just that structural, dialectical, interactive, intersubjective dimension to which Girard's work compels our attention. In analytic philosophy, the reliability or soundness of propositions is regularly essayed against logically "true" arguments about imaginary beings, unicorns and centaurs being the most popular. Yet the *real* significance of such monsters lies in an anthropology that ac-

counts for their hallucinatory invention and expulsion amidst the clash
of ubiquitously violent doubles.

Another consistent strain in the analytic tradition is the postulation
of such deliberate, reflective, and epistemically rational individuals as
we are likely to find only in the pages of textbooks, which Girard's
notion of "interdividuality," of subjects divided from their own consciousness by their mimesis of others' desires, very plausibly puts into
question. The existence of such amiably goal-seeking beings as occupy the pages of Richard Foley's *Theory of Epistemic Rationality* or
Robert Nozick's *Philosophical Explanations* is devoutly to be wished,
but their agency in culture or in history is as dubious as the countless unicorns and centaurs, and as the ritually evoked Alpha Centauri
and brains-in-a-vat manipulators (of which we are the imaginings),
that are conjured up to test our best intentions, our noblest and intellectually cleanest designs. Here again, the remorseless and nervy
realism of Hannah Arendt is apposite: "The stubbornness of reality is
relative," she appended to a letter from David Reisman: "Reality
needs us to protect it. If we can blow up the world, it means that God
has created us as guardians of it; just so, we are the guardians of
Truth" (in Young-Bruehl, *Hannah Arendt* 255). A similar concern resonates in Bernard Williams's rhetorical question: "What will the professor's justification do, when they break down the door, smash his
spectacles, take him away?" (*Ethics and the Limits of Philosophy* 23).
Truth, to be sure, has known a bewildering variety of applications and
implications, at least since the seventeenth-century secularization of
philosophy, and any number of them are doubtless subject to deconstruction. Where the latter disappoints the most is in its suggestion of
truth's connivance with violence, of its violent determination, whereas
in Girard's theory, truth, as incarnate in the victim, is irreconcilable
with violence. Truth survives its every test, hermeneutic and institutional, being the unique criterion by which violence is detected
and repudiated.

The *Cogito* and the Demoniac

In "Plato's Pharmacy," Derrida uncovers the properly tragic origins of
philosophy in the fearful symmetry between logos and its other, its rival model and obstacle in whose expulsion logos originates. As Girard

writes with explicit reference to Derrida's essay, "philosophy, like tragedy, can at certain levels serve as an attempt at expulsion, an attempt perpetually renewed because never wholly successful" (*VS* 297). It is to the renewal of that attempt with Descartes, as explicated by Derrida in "Cogito and the History of Madness" (*Writing and Difference*, henceforth *WD*), that I now turn my attention, for here again Derrida's notions display a rigorous homology with Girard's theory and a significant resonance with Scripture.

In this essay Derrida reviews Michel Foucault's *Histoire de la folie à l'âge classique*, where Foucault argues that in Western culture madness has undergone a process of exclusion, of silencing, of internment. This is witnessed in the form of "le grand enfermement," whereby mad people were rounded up and placed in newly organized asylums in seventeenth-century France. The closure is no less manifest in the form of the categorical exclusion of madness from philosophical discourse in the pages of Descartes's *Meditations*. Reason is put on trial by Foucault. Juridical language scarcely masks the thematics of sacrificial expulsion that run throughout his essay, and they appear regularly in Derrida's commentary on it as well: "Madness is expelled, rejected, denounced in its very impossibility from the very interiority of thought itself" (*WD* 47; see also 35). Through a complicity of the rational with the political order, madness is silenced and kept captive by an institutional discourse that presumes to objectify it. Not only philosophy, then, but professional psychiatry as well is heir to sacrifice. This is not Foucault's word for it, or Derrida's either, but in a review of this story its fundamental dynamics emerge.

If the prescription for classical philosophy is wonder, *thaumazein*, modern philosophy begins with doubt as a method to ensure certainty in the form of clear and distinct ideas. And this begins, according to the histories of the discipline, with the idea of a self who exists every bit as much *because* of its doubt as in spite of it: *cogito*, or *dubito, ergo sum—ergo sum res cogitans*. Self-doubt itself is proof for the existence of a self. But Descartes's minimal hypothesis for clear and distinct ideas, as deployed in his *Discours de la méthode*, is in fact the fruit of a far more radical, far more extravagant exercise in the *Meditations* (whose title, incidentally, is reminiscent of a genre of religious literature).

Here Descartes hypothesizes the existence of an alien other, a "malin génie" to whose deceptive agency all his certitudes may be prey. This imaginary being is the grandsire of all the brains-in-a-vat and Alpha Centauri hypotheses of radical skepticism entertained by analytic philosophy. Derrida's paraphrase emphasizes the universality of this hypothesis, its totalizing dimension:

> Now, the recourse to the fiction of the evil genius will evoke, conjure up, the possibility of a *total madness,* a total derangement over which I could have no control because it is inflicted upon me—hypothetically—leaving me no responsibility for it. Total derangement is the possibility of a madness that is no longer a disorder of the body, of the object, the body-object outside the boundaries of the *res cogitans,* outside the boundaries of the policed city, secure in its existence as thinking subjectivity, but is a madness that will bring subversion to pure thought and to its purely intelligible objects, to the field of its clear and distinct ideas, to the realm of the mathematical truths which escape natural doubt. (*WD* 52–53)

Derrida shows that the *cogito* is immune to this "mad hyperbole," for its emergence in no way depends on any postulation or determination of the subject's sanity or rationality: "The Cogito escapes madness only because at its own moment, under its own authority, it is valid *even if I am mad,* even if my thoughts are completely mad. There is a value and a meaning of the Cogito, as of existence, which escape the alternative of a determined madness or a determined reason. . . . Whether I am mad or not, *cogito, sum.* Madness is therefore, in every sense of the word, only one case of thought (*within* thought)" (*WD* 55–56). Derrida goes on to show that the rationality of the *cogito* emerges with its reflection, with its representation, in short, with the word, that encloses and excludes madness, to which the *cogito* in its own right is "most hospitable." (*WD* 58) "For if the Cogito is valid even for the madman, to be mad . . . is not to be able to reflect and to say the Cogito, that is, not to be able to make the Cogito appear as such for an other; an other who may be myself. From the moment when Descartes pronounces the Cogito, he inscribes it in a system of deductions and protections that betray its wellspring and constrain the wandering that is proper to it so that error may be circumvented. At bottom, leaving in silence the problem of speech posed by the Cogito, Descartes seems to imply that thinking *and* saying what is clear and distinct are the same thing" (*WD* 58–59). Language expels madness as its originary other, closing it out and shutting it up in a manner analogous to the seventeenth-century asylums whose violent sequestering is the target of Michel Foucault's thesis: "For if the Cogito is valid even for the maddest madman, one must, in fact, not be mad if one is to reflect it and retain it, if one is to communicate it and its meaning" (*WD* 58). It is language that punctuates the disquieting continuity of madness and reason—which is madness itself—within the amorphous realm of thought. Language temporalizes the *cogito*, giving it its historical existence and giving existence to history, or history to existence:

> From its very first breath, speech, confined to this temporal rhythm of crisis and reawakening, is able to open the space for discourse only by imprisoning madness. This rhythm, moreover, is not an alternation that additionally would be temporal. It is rather the moment of temporalization itself as concerns that which unites to the movement of logos. But this violent liberation of speech is possible and can be pursued only in the extent to which it keeps itself resolutely and consciously at the greatest possible proximity to the abuse that is the usage of speech— just close enough to say violence, and just far enough to live and live as speech. Due to this, crisis or oblivion perhaps is not an accident, but rather the destiny of speaking philosophy—the philosophy which lives only by imprisoning madness, but would die as thought if a new speech did not at every instance liberate previous madness while enclosing within itself, in present existence, the madman of the day. It is only by virtue of this oppression of madness that finite-thought, that is to say, history, can reign.(*WD* 60–61)

What is expelled by the *cogito* as language is madness as indifferentiation. The emergence of the *cogito* as language, as rationality, as philosophy, consists in the rejection of the violence it performs, in the performance of the violence it rejects. Language is the representation of the violence, the chaos, the indifferentiation it rejects; in its oblivion, in forgetting or erasing the traces of its violent origin, it emerges from crisis and perpetuates itself as philosophy. The erasure, the oblivion, must never be total, lest reason lose the sense of its identity, which it owes to the non-sense it expels. "Language being the break with madness, it adheres more thoroughly to its essence and vocation, makes a cleaner break with madness, if it pits itself against madness more freely and gets closer and closer to it" (*WD* 55).

This simultaneous mindfulness and forgetfulness of an originary violence is precisely the paradox that Girard uncovers in sacrifice, as well as in the myths and rituals that grow up around it. The destiny of madness, of the "malin génie"—which is monster enough to merit ritual expulsion—is that of the sacrificial victim: "Sacrificial substitution implies a degree of misunderstanding. Its vitality as an institution depends on its ability to conceal the displacement upon which the rite is based. It must never lose sight entirely, however, of the original object, or cease to be aware of the act of transference from that object to the surrogate victim; without that awareness no substitution can take place and the sacrifice loses all efficacy" (*VS* 5). The substitution of animal for human in sacrifice thus follows on the substitution of one for the violence of all. The surrogate must remain close enough to be named as violence and far enough to be named as violence of the other, as a violence other than the one that expels it.

According to Foucault's theory, it is the role of both asylums and discursive institutions, philosophy among them, to effect a like substitution regarding madness and to conceal the effects of this substitution by the psychiatric discourses that objectify madness. Reason prevails, in Derrida's words, "by excluding its contrary, that is by *constituting* its contrary as an object in order to be protected from it and be rid of it. In order to lock it up" (*WD* 40). Derrida questions in turn the juridical, that is, sacrificial, tenor of Foucault's inquiry, according to which "the victims of whom he speaks are always the bearers of sense, the *true* bearers of the *true* and *good* sense hidden and oppressed by the *determined* 'good sense' [an allusion to Cartesian *bon sens ou raison*] of the 'division'—the 'good sense' that never divides itself enough and is always determined too quickly" (*WD* 57). Thus, Foucault is seen as sacralizing madness to victimize psychiatry.

Foucault's trial of reason cannot inculpate psychiatry without engaging in the sacrificial practice of scapegoating, whereby a unique offender is judged to cover up a more massive complicity. This symmetry emerges in a lengthy passage wherein Derrida pronounces his eloquent *tu quoque*, which I intersperse with attention to its sacrificial resonance: "Does it suffice to stack the tools of psychiatry neatly, inside a tightly shut workshop, in order to return to innocence and to end all complicity with the rational or political order which keeps madness captive? The psychiatrist is but the delegate of this order, one delegate among others. Perhaps it does not suffice to imprison or to exile the delegate, or to stifle him; and perhaps it does not suffice to deny oneself the conceptual material of psychiatry in order to exculpate one's own language" (*WD* 35). For *delegate* we may substitute the word *surrogate*, thus viewing psychiatry within a process, a *procès*, a trial characterized by an oceanic complicity in violence: "All our European languages, the language of everything that has participated, from near or far, in the adventure of Western reason—all this is the immense delegation of the project defined by Foucault under the rubric of the capture or objectification of madness. *Nothing* within this language, and *no one* among those who speak it, can escape the historical guilt—if there is one, and if it is historical in a classical sense—which Foucault apparently wishes to put on trial" (*WD* 35).

The argument of *Violence and the Sacred* (chap. 1) that law is the mystified heir to sacrifice and to its contradictions—the violent expulsion of violence—finds its validation in Derrida's following objection: "But such a trial may be impossible, for by the simple fact of their articulation the proceedings and the verdict unceasingly reiterate the crime" (*WD* 35). If the law is put on trial, its judgment—if it is to be lawful—must be incriminated in turn. Its interdiction engages a structural contradiction interesting for the way it resembles the contradictory structure of the ritual process, wherein the community enjoins the very prohibitions whose enforcement serves to constitute it as a community. As Girard writes, "the universal spread of 'doubles,' the complete effacement of differences, heightening antagonisms but also making them interchangeable, is the prerequisite for the establishment of violent unanimity. For order to be reborn, disorder must first triumph; for myths to achieve their complete integration, they must first suffer total disintegration" (*VS* 79). According to Derrida's reading, this is what happens in Foucault's text, where reason puts reason on trial in the name of a silence, an indifferentiation, that it cannot champion without recourse to a discourse that oppresses this silence: "If the *Order* of which we are speaking is so powerful, if its power is unique of its kind, this is so precisely by virtue of the universal, structural, and infinite complicity in which it compromises all those who understand it in its own language, even when this language provides them with the form of their own denunciation. Order is then denounced within order" (*WD* 35). Foucault, then, does not demystify reason but assists in its properly mythical reconstruction.

This is not a fortuitous coincidence in my view. The crisis of order, the crisis of reason as the crisis of the difference between madness and reason, serves to define philosophy as a sacrificial crisis: "To define philosophy as the attempt-to-say-the-hyperbole is to confess—and philosophy is perhaps this gigantic confession—that by virtue of the historical enunciation through which philosophy tranquilizes itself and excludes madness, philosophy betrays itself (or betrays itself as thought), enters into a crisis and a forgetting of itself that are an essential and necessary period of its movement. I philosophize only in *terror,* in the *confessed* terror of going mad. The confession is simultaneously, at its *present* moment, oblivion and unveiling, protection and exposure: economy" (*WD* 62). This is the very economy of sacrifice, which engages violence against violence, which evokes terror only to forget its origin, which ritually exposes the community to violence to protect it from violence. The violent decision separating madness from reason as nonmeaning from meaning is a "division on whose basis, after which, logos, in the necessary violence of its irruption, is separated from itself as madness, is exiled from itself, forgetting its origin and its own possibility" (*WD* 62). The "*confessed* terror of going mad" is that of indifferentiation, and its oblivion regenerates a properly mythical order. No wonder, then, that Derrida likens philosophy to a white mythology, a metaphor suggested to him by Anatole France's *Jardin d'Epicure.* The flowers of rhetoric that philosophy effaces to germinate and establish its own turf are "*les fleurs du mal.*" When Derrida describes Focault's critique as "order . . . denounced within order," he is reading him as philosophy's and psychiatry's "*hypocrite lecteur.*"

This primal scene of reason, this creation of the *cogito* as reason and history out of the originary expulsion of its madly undifferentiated other, resembles nothing so much as the mythic scene of creation out of chaos as recorded in the first chapter of Genesis. It is the Babylonian myth, as all the commentaries remind us, adapted by the ancient Hebrews. The process of dividing light from dark, water from firmament, and so on, is one that adapts the notion of creation as the victory over the undifferentiated, which in the prior version took the form of the chaos-monster, Rahab the dragon, according to Isaiah (51:9). The monster is ever the form of the unformed, of the undifferentiated, of violent doubles, whose social form, as Girard has shown, is unanimous violence. For Michel Serres as well, this is the origin of every *genèse:* "The *turba* of Lucretius, the stormy mass of diverse elements in disorder, given over to the shocks, the clashes of the mêlée, the chaos given over to the jolts [*cahots*], is the crowd, the mob [*cohue*]. The physical chaos of the circumstances, in which the first *turbo* is rooted, is, so to speak, isomorphic with the furious crowd of the Bacchantes, geared up for the *diasparagmos*, with the crowd at Rome or elsewhere. Chaos makes the same noise as the social mob" (*Genèse* 164). Primo Levi shares the same intuition of the *social* structure insinuated by the cosmic metaphors of Genesis when he evokes the leveling pathology of the Lagers as "an atavistic anguish whose echo one hears in the second verse of Genesis: the anguish inscribed in everyone of the 'tohu-bohu' of a deserted and empty universe crushed under the spirit of God but from which the spirit of man is absent: not yet born or already extinguished" (*The Drowned and the Saved* 85).

Creation is sacrificial in its primary instance, being the victory of the sacred over violence that comes about as man's sacralization of violence. The story of the flood is the same tale, in which ubiquitous human violence ("Now the earth was corrupt in God's sight, and the earth was filled with violence" [Gen. 6:11]) is terminated by divine violence. The fact that the flood narrative is attended by a system of classification, such as we find with Adam in Eden, marks it as a foundation myth. It is the function of myth, as Lévi-Strauss has argued, to account for difference, for discontinuity in the real. Its more primal function, according to Girard, is to disguise mimetic, ubiquitous violence, to cover up violent indifferentiation, for such a misunderstanding is necessary to elect a scapegoat in which difference is perceived as such and from which all subsequent differences derive.

In Descartes's *Meditations*, madness is the form of this primal indifference, in which madness and reason are rival doubles within the amorphous realm of the *cogito*. If it is true that "madness is a case of thought (*within* thought)," it is likewise true that thought is a case of madness if it does not know whether it is mad or not. If the fusion or confusion of madness and reason is madness itself, is the very definition of madness and nonmeaning, it is reason that says so. But where will reason draw its definition, its determination, if not from the expulsion, the oblivion—however irrational—of the madness coterminous with it? Madness and reason oscillate, gyrate in a tangled hierarchy where they alternate as names for a class of which they are both members.

If the salt loses its savor, wherein shall it be salted? How is reason to emerge from this crisis "in which reason is madder than madness—for reason is nonmeaning and oblivion—and in which madness is more rational than reason, for it is closer to the wellspring of sense, however silent or murmuring" (*WD* 62)? At a certain point, thought decides, as language, what is mad and what is not. This, according to Derrida, stems from

> the recognition of an essential and principled truth: to wit, if discourse and philosophical communication (that is, language itself) are to have an intelligible meaning, that is to say, if they are to conform to their essence and vocation as discourse, they must simultaneously in fact and in principle escape madness. They must carry normality within themselves. And this is not a specifically Cartesian weakness (although Descartes never confronts the question of his own language), is not a defect or mystification linked to a determined historical structure, but rather is an essential and universal necessity from which no discourse can escape, for it belongs to the meaning of meaning. (*WD* 53)

Up to that point, however, in the undecidability of thought and madness, we are dealing with rival doubles whose mimesis is incarnate in the *"malin génie"* presiding over this illusion—as illusion. This properly imaginary monster is the rival, model, and obstacle to the discourse that seeks to dispel illusion. Descartes's decisive *fiat*—this is Derrida's word for it (*WD* 38)—creates anew the world of reason, the world of philosophy, as well as the world *in extenso,* as *res extensa.* But according to the terms and dynamics of Derrida's own reading, this is not accomplished without re-creating the myth of creation in all its originary violence.

Every myth is a foundational myth, and when philosophy returns to its origins, its genesis, it repeats the essential dynamics of ritual sacrifice. The divine fiat is a *decision* that masks a *"dicession,"* a *"dissension . . .* une division de soi" (*L'Ecriture et la différence* 62); it punctuates chaos in the same manner that language separates the *cogito* from itself and enthrones it as reason. Thereafter, Descartes can easily proceed, like Adam in the garden, with his classifications of body and soul, animate and inanimate, and all the rest. Where phylogeny recapitulates ontogeny, it is a case of ontotheology recapitulating mythology. The argument of the *Meditations* is a white mythology; rational demonstration proceeds as de-monsteration.

"The quite national incapacity of the French to get rid of the Cartesian cogito," to which Girard has alluded in a lighter moment ("De la folie" 62), arises from their incapacity, and ours as well, to come to terms with the violence of origins—whence Derrida's renewal of the project with Hegel ("The Pit and the Pyramid" in *Margins of Philosophy*), with Husserl (*La Voix et le phénomène*), and with Heidegger ("Ousia and grammè" in *Margins of Philosophy*), where he uncovers essentially the same operation.

Derrida, who is somewhat the "malin génie" as regards the French language, invented the term *différance* to come to terms with violent origins. This anathememe expresses, and performs as well, the difference of the self from itself within itself, *"une division de soi,"* which produces subsequent differences of every kind and which subsequent mythical narratives occlude. The violence of interpretation is heir to an originary expulsion that interpretation conceals even while reenacting it. Order and difference, such as that between land and watery chaos or light and dark in Genesis, but between madness and sanity as well in Descartes, are born of this originary violence, to which they remain close enough to name and far enough to name as other—indeed, wholly other: madness, chaos, violent indifferentiation.

This proximity and distance of violence, of madness, is that of the sacred, of the divinity who, as Girard states, "will be as benevolent from afar as he was terrible in propinquity" *VS* 134). What seventeenth-century asylums did, according to Foucault's historical thesis, was to institutionalize just that proximity and distance of madness that ritual sacrifice accomplishes with respect to violence. Thus, Girard's further remark about the expulsion of violence is of interest for the study of madness as institutionalized in the form of psychiatry: "It is the knowledge of violence, along with the violence itself, that the act of expulsion succeeds in shunting outside the realm of consciousness" (*VS* 135). Substituting the word *madness* for *violence* in this sentence yields a précis of Derrida's reading—not only of Descartes but of the entire history of philosophy as a perpetual crisis of reason: "this crisis has always begun and is interminable" (*WD* 62).

The expulsion of madness by its representation, by language, is not definitive in Descartes. On the contrary, reason requires its proximity, its enclosure, to guard its own identity, to assert itself as reason. Reason not only takes it in, shelters it, hospitalizes it, but also alienates it, all for the sake of its own identity. The definitive expulsion of madness does not serve the aims of reason any more than the definitive expulsion of the sacred serves the aims of culture as a hierarchy of differences. "Religion, then, is far from 'useless.' It dehumanizes violence; it protects man from his own violence by taking it out of his hands, transforming it into a transcendent and ever-present danger to be kept in check by the appropriate rites appropriately observed and by a modest and prudent demeanor. Religious misinterpretation is a truly constructive force, for it purges man of the suspicions that would poison his existence if he were to remain conscious of the crisis as it actually took place" (*VS* 134–35, trans. modified). Religion is described here as a remedy to violence but also as a poison, chiefly for the veil it draws over consciousness: a *pharmakon*.

Modern culture, which is synonymous with sacrificial crisis as the dissolution of differences (*VS* 188), translates religion unequivocally as poison, as an opiate it seeks to expel. The rationalist expulsion of religion is properly sacrificial, however, as the latter is defined by mistaking the effect of violence for its cause. According to Derrida's reading, this is how philosophy treats (its own origin in) madness (the parenthetical phrase designating just what is expelled and veiled at once). Reason operates sacrificially, exposing madness to view while concealing its resemblance to it. It is just this paradoxical structure that Girard discovers in the narrative of the Gerasene demoniac in the synoptic Gospels (Mark 5; Luke 8; Matt. 8).

Jesus is confronted by Gerasenes who complain of a madman who is possessed by demons and inhabits the tombs, existing between the living and the dead. His indifference to living and dead, to the difference between them, constitutes the difference of this creature from the rest of the community. The demoniac is a *phantom* creature whose structural resemblance to writing as portrayed by Derrida is noteworthy: neither living nor dead, the madness of the demoniac embodies indifferentiation, the same crisis of difference that Derrida portrays when he evokes "the sense of *krinein*, the choice and division between the two ways separated by Parmenides in his poem, the way of logos and the non-way, the labyrinth, the *palintrope* in which logos in lost; the way of meaning and the way of nonmeaning; of Being and of non-Being" (PP 62).

Girard identifies this demoniac as a sacrificial victim: he is given to autolapidation, imitating in his own person the sacrificial practice of the community toward its victims; that is, he simulates the destiny allotted to victims, whose stoning incarnates the violence at a distance on which every community depends. He gives his name as "Legion," whereby he bears witness to the unanimous, mimetic violence of the crowd: "In describing the unity of the multiple, the Legion symbolizes the social principle itself, the type of organization that rests not on the final expulsion of demons but on the sort of equivocal and mitigated expulsions that are illustrated by our demoniac, expulsions which ultimately end in the coexistence of men and demons" (*The Scapegoat* 182). When the demons ask Jesus that they not be expelled from the country, they are permitted to invade a flock of pigs, which subsequently hurl themselves over a cliff. The cliff symbolizes a classical locus of ritual execution; like Rome's Tarpeian rock, it offers violence at a distance. The gregarious, that is, unanimous, self-destruction of the pigs symbolizes the mimetic violence of the community. The demoniac is consequently found to be sane by the Gerasenes, who ask Jesus to leave their territory. The demons ask not to be expelled from the country for the same reason that the Gerasenes ask Jesus, on curing the demoniac, to leave the country: the community relies on the proximity of the demons for the perpetuation of its sacrificial order.

It is ordinary human reason, still mimetically dependent on the incarceration of its other, its double, still in the grips of mimesis, that expels Jesus: "Since all coexistence between Jesus and the demons is impossible, to beg him not to chase away the demons, when one is a demon, is the same as begging him to depart, if one is from Gerasa" (*The Scapegoat* 182). In the eyes of the community, Jesus replaces the madman as indifferent to the difference on which the community is founded: "These unfortunate people fear that their precarious balance depends on the demoniac, on the activities they share periodically and on the kind of local celebrity their demoniac had become" (181). In this "espèce de célébrité locale qu'est devenue leur possédé" we recognize "*le fou du jour*" cited by Derrida, "the madman of the day" (*WD* 61), whose enclosure, whose attenuated expulsion, is necessary to the life of philosophy. The madman is the truth of the community, though not so as to warrant the romantic celebration of madness that runs from Dumas père (*Kean ou Désordre et génie*) through the contemporary Nietzcheans, whose latter-day praise of folly holds up madness as a sort of countercultural (i.e., metaphysical) ideal. This is the superior sense that Derrida detects in Foucault's vision of the insane as "*true* bearers of the *true* and *good* sense hidden and oppressed" (*WD* 57)—and before whose "*confessed* terror" (*WD* 62) Derrida somewhat quixotically flourishes his pen as well.

The demoniac figures as a guarantee of Gerasene order that his definitive expulsion menaces. This order resembles philosophical, Cartesian order, for it creates an alien form whose expulsion is what constitutes it as reason. The analyses of both Derrida and Girard reveal madness as the truth of the community, but once again, not in such a way as to ensure a stable relation between truth and falsehood as simply exterior to each other. Madness is not a truth that transcends the lie of reason, for that would merely reverse a hierarchical order without challenging the violence of the hierarchy on which order is founded. Madness does not differ from reason or from the community from the outside, whereby it can just as well be romantically divinized as damned. It is the difference of reason and of the community from itself, within itself; it is their differance, their originary *polemos.*

Philosophy or Anthropology?

Although further examples of a homology between Derridean and Girardian analyses can be adduced, it is doubtless more appropriate at this point to say where all this is going, for by no means are Girard and Derrida going in the same direction. To the contrary, Derrida's suggestion, at the close of *Glas,* that it is "time to perfect the resemblance between Dionysus and Christ" (291a) clearly indicates the radical difference between them. Girard has argued strenuously against any such resemblance, insisting that the Judeo-Christian logos is the victim and that it differs fundamentally from both pagan mythos and philosophical logos. This is indeed the foundational—and redemptive—import of what he calls "the anthropology of the Gospels": "If you understand the old sacred as a closed system, and if you understand the Gospels as a revelation of how that system works, then the Gospel cannot come from within the closure of violence" ("The Logic of the Undecidable" 16; see also *THFW* 264–76). The properly hermeneutic role of Scripture is to reveal the originary violence that myths occlude and philosophy, in its wake, bleaches out. Perhaps it is only as a revelation of violence within the text of philosophy that Derrida can be of interest for Girardians, but that interest is not to be underestimated.

If Derrida can be said to have an adversary, it is not so much theology as our philosophic tradition, which persists in its blindness to its own theological predisposition and orientation, which is ever "heliocentric," moving toward the rising sun as toward the *"fons et origo"* of truth and light, as he argues in "White Mythology." Derrida's work regularly demonstrates that the explicit rivalry between philosophy and theology is in fact an implicit fraternity. They are in fact *frères ennemis*, enemy twins whose failure to recognize their identity, their role as polemical doubles, their mimetic rivalry for ascendancy, is just what ensures their conflict.

Derrida has concisely analyzed this "conflict of faculties" in an essay on Kant's work bearing in part that very title ("Mochlos, ou le conflit des facultés"). Kant's efforts to demarcate between higher and lower faculties (between theology and philosophy) as between what is inside and outside the university, between *savoir* and *pouvoir*, merely reveal their *"marges envahissantes,"* their undecidable *"parasitages."* Theology assumes what philosophy questions, but only in quest of the founding authority claimed by theology. In its rivalrous quest for an irreducible ground, for a transcendental signified governing the play of signifiers, philosophy does not so much differ from theology as from itself and within itself, once again as differance. Philosophy and theology emerge as accomplices, with Derridean emphasis on the *pli*, the fold, whose outer edge forms an inner lining—whence the properly improper figure of invagination (see "Parergon," in *La Vérité en peinture*, and "Living On,") by which Derrida marks his structurally offscene and somewhat obscene activity with respect (or rather dysrespect) to philosophy as a foundational discourse. In "Mochlos, ou le conflit des facultés," the same chiasmic paradox configures the relations of power and knowledge, of action and truth, as they compose "sets which are somehow always greater than themselves and always encompass the whole of which they should only comprise a part and a subset" (46). It is ultimately inconsequential whether such a foundation bears the name of God or nature, matter or perception, pragmatism or metaphysics, or experience or structure itself, at least to the extent that any or all such terms function, in Kenneth Burke's handy phrase, as "God terms" (*The Rhetoric of Religion* 3).

It is indeed difficult to conceive a way out of this vicious circularity, in which every quest for origins, as for an *ens realissimus*, ultimately reveals itself as theological in its origin—unless it proceeds, with Girard, as an anthropological inquiry into the origins of the theological, of the religious, of the sacred itself. Even Derrida appears to sanction this inquiry, however unwittingly: "My discourse here is not one which is very respectful with regard to the sacred, it is a discourse which says: we are going to explain how sacralization happens, it's all over the place [il y en a partout] and here is how it happens"

("L'Oreille de l'autre" 197). But whereas for Derrida it always happens as a *petitio principii*, for Girard it begins with the victim, as revealed, for instance, in John's Gospel: "In principio erat verbum," where *verbum* translates *logos*, and *logos*, victim. Deconstruction will not allow philosophy to pursue its rational vocation innocently—that is, in ignorance of the violence of its origins—but it will not pursue the anthropological implications of this discovery: violence and origin are one. Confounding discourse with the violence that discourse defers, it tends to condemn language to a vicious circle whose center is everywhere and circumference nowhere. This is true, but only in the sense of a nuclear relation to the victim. As Girard observes, "if there is really 'something' to Derrida, it is because there is something else: precisely a deconstruction which broaches the mechanisms of the sacred but which stops short of the surrogate victim" (*THFW* 64, trans. modified).

For Derrideans, of course, Girard's genetic hypothesis, along with what he argues as its scriptural basis, must appear as yet another instance of a deluded quest for foundations, as something inscribed within the nostalgic pathos of origins. For Derrida, the quest for origins is mythologocentric in its primary instance, there being no valid or rationally plausible point of departure from which to postulate the generation of signs or concepts. As he says in *Of Grammatology*, "the genetic root system refers from sign to sign. No ground of nonsignification—understood as insignificance or an intuition of a present truth—stretches out to give it foundations under the play and the coming into being of signs" (48). We naturally tend to think that there were things before signs; there were things and then signs of things at the beginning of culture. According to Derrida's conception, it is as if there were no things before signs, as if, as he says via Peirce's semiotics, "*the thing itself is a sign.*" Derrida does not argue nonsensically that there were signs before things; it is the "before" he contests, the notion of precedence, of the presence of things before signs. It is a notion we must abandon in favor of the untraceable play of signs, which we have to count among the things we place before them. We cannot account for signs, at least not for their origin (anyway, not without an anthropological hypothesis, which is the burden of the next chapter). In the beginning there were signs, though we are able neither to postulate an other than theocentric origin, nor, consequently, to say, in good philosophical conscience, "in the beginning." Derrida is indeed the bad conscience of philosophy as a foundational discourse; for just that reason he may serve as a goad to anthropological research, particularly as it concerns, as does Girard's work, the origin of myth.

If Derrida is correct in arguing that logocentrism is mythocentrism, then Girard offers a decisive supplement to such a view when he argues that the absent center of myth is the victim whose traces mythology is devoted to covering up. In the texts of philosophy and mythology alike the erasure of origins bears witness to the primacy and omnipresence of mediation, that is, of desire, which is mimetic in its primary instance. As Eric Gans argues in his elaboration of Girard's hypothesis, desire is born of deferred appropriation of the victim (*The Origin of Language* chap. 2). This deferral is necessarily collective and mimetic, for it is inspired by the fear of succumbing to the unanimous violence that, by mimetic contagion, centered on the victim in the first place.

In the beginning was the victim, whose designation, or deferred appropriation, was the first sign. To designate the victim as desirable and taboo is one and the same. The sacred, the holy, and the accursed, as identical and irreducibly bivalent, are born in the same moment as is desire. And so is humankind, the infinitely desiring subject, the subject whose desires are infinite because their object is ultimately only a sign of another's desire. Because Girard's hypothesis postulates mimesis at the origin of our species, it can accommodate a poststructuralist critique of origins without succumbing to an infinite regression, to a "renvoi infini," to the aporetics of an origin that by definition is "always already in search of itself" (Gans, *The Origin* x). It can do this because it argues that origin and deferral are one. To show this in detail, and so engage Derrida's text in and with the victimary hypothesis, is the project of the next chapter.

For Girardians, the Derridean critique of origins, like that of representation itself, can be read as a crisis of difference. It is too often perceived as a nefarious one, for it engages a crisis of meaning. Sense and nonsense, like reason and madness, fail to separate; we seem encouraged to entertain nonsensical propositions such as "the second is the first," or "signs come before the things they signify," whereupon such elemental notions as first and second, before and after, or sign and thing simply lose their meaning. Everything is text, there is nothing outside or beyond the text, and the text is not about any "thing" that precedes it ontologically. Everything is text, and the text is *strictu sensu* meaningless. We are lost in a labyrinth of signs of which we are both the makers and the products. This has inevitably occasioned the charge of cynicism, nihilism, and even opportunism, because deconstruction seems to favor complacency in the academy and in society as a whole (see, e.g., Fischer, *Does Deconstruction Make Any Difference?*). It is consequently viewed as rather more conservative than radical, there being no motivation to challenge values or institutional structures if that challenge results only in the reduction of all values to signifiers whose signifieds have no referents in the "real" world—which itself exists only as the interminable play of differance. That a certain "wild" deconstruction (as discussed by Dasenbrock, *Redrawing the Lines* 15) can lead, indeed has led, to such conclusions is undeniable; there are texts to this effect. But this is not inevitable.

In fact, this crisis can be read as salubrious to the extent that it challenges the foundational claims of philosophy. True, philosophy has always done this, but usually in the name of a better philosophy. Derrida's challenge is expressly poised within and without philosophy by focusing on what it excludes: the unruly law of the letter. If philosophy is born (and reborn) of sacrifice, as Derrida's reading of Plato (and Descartes) more than suggests, then Derrida irreversibly and irretrievably points beyond philosophy. The crisis is doubly salubrious for anthropological research if it reveals a sacrificial dynamic at the origin of the philosophical text, one that is homologous to the crisis in which representation originates according to the victimary hypothesis. This is just what I have been attempting to demonstrate, that Derridean deconstruction, rather because than in spite of its leveling effects, clears a path for Girardian exegesis. If values are reducible to signs, we may interrogate the origin of signs in the designation of the victim as the origin of values, all other values, in the ethical sense, being ultimately reducible to the relation to the victim. That has not changed. It is a matter of showing that deontology recapitulates semiology once the logos of the sign is traceable to the victim. This would serve to demonstrate the point that Eric Gans has tucked away in a footnote to his theory of culture, namely, that "in Derrida's work, philosophy renders up its final insights to anthropology" (*The End of Culture* 315n).

But the opposite—Girard leading to Derrida—is not the case if it is true that the victim is the underlying and irreducible fact of even philosophical institutions—as the fate of Socrates, to mention a cardinal instance, seems to imply. Girard's critique of culture as a mystified hierarchy of differences and representations of differences has a dangerously leveling effect, as he has acknowledged, but it does not lead to meaninglessness or to any structural indifference between what is true and false or good and bad. On the contrary, it is rooted in the irreducible difference between victim and persecutor. This difference has an indelible moral claim on our consciousness that we must reconcile with our cognitive impulses to form a unified theory of culture. In *Violence and the Sacred* this necessity is posed by and as the alternative "between total destruction and the total renunciation of violence" (240), the totalizing ambitions of this theory being warranted by the scientifically calculable prospect of total violence.

Plato has written somewhere that every man is born with "a memory of justice," a fact that I glean from the epigraph to Marcel Ophuls's documentary film by that title. The film deals with the Nuremburg trials as they concern more recent atrocities (Algeria for the French; Vietnam for the Americans). For Derridean deconstruction such a memory is perhaps but a metaphysical postulate. From a Girardian perspective it should be traceable to a concrete fact, to an arbitrary, sacrificial victim of injustice. It is difficult to conceive of a memory of justice as emanating from any other source, especially for a Plato, especially Derrida's Plato, who writes "from out of the death of Socrates" and whose academy is born of just the sort of crisis that Socrates' death precipitates (see Voegelin, *Order and History III: Plato and Aristotle*). Protagoras attributes justice to Zeus, who sends Hermes to install it equally in all to prevent humanity from destroying itself amidst ubiquitous, arbitrary violence (*Protagoras* § 332–23a). Derrida in fact likens writing to the messenger god—"sly, slippery, and masked, an intriguer and a card, like Hermes, he is neither king nor jack, but rather a sort of *joker*, a floating signifier, a wild card, one who puts a play into play" (PP 93)—though with no reference to the sacrificial role of the trickster in culture (I return to this role in the conclusion). Hermes is indeed a good figure for philosophy as hermeneutic, as interpretation, but also as hermetic, closed, blind to the violence that produced it, blind to its own sacrificial origins. From an anthropological perspective we are inclined to view the Hermes myth the other way around: it was humanity who sent a message, in the form of a messenger, to Zeus, or rather as Zeus, the victim as sacralized divinity, a surrogate of human violence. Hermes' notorious slyness figures his cryptically mediating role between humans and a violence they divinize. Hermes, the victim, is the god's messenger, his mediator, and the message, the medium, is violence. Derrida goes on to describe "this god of resurrection" as "less interested in life or in death than in death as a repetition of life and in life as a rehearsal [*répétition*] of death" (PP 93). This is just how Girard describes the efficacy of sacrifice: "simultaneously good and evil, peaceable and violent, a life that brings death and a death that guarantees life" (*THFW* 102).

Every crisis, no matter what its terms, is ultimately a crisis of difference, that is, a crisis of order and meaning in terms of the difference between good and bad as between true and false. That these *values* emerge only in retrospect, as the consequence of a violent decision that resolves the crisis, is common to the reasoning of both Girard's originary hypothesis and Derrida's critique of origins. For Girard, the victim is an effect in which the notion of causality originates in the same way that for Derrida the exclusion of writing or madness is an effect on which the very notion of origin depends. Whether we may assign a concrete origin or a definitive term to this process is where Girard and Derrrida differ, but they differ sharply and clearly. Derrida can only perpetuate and extend this crisis, disseminating its recognition by uncovering it in even the most apparently benign forms of cultural representation: in philosophy and in the academy. Girard proceeds to argue for a nonviolent, nonsacrificial resolution of the crisis: identification with the victim, whereupon no mystified expulsion, communal or global, is operative.

This identification with the victim is not reducible to moral sympathy. That is important, but it is not rationally decisive. Rather, it is justified, logically warranted, by the victim's arbitrary selection from the community. It is the logic of "there but for the grace of God go I." The statement is reputed to have originated on the scene of a public execution, whose sacrificial function, amidst a jeering mob, is ably summarized by Robert Calasso: "It is significant that we say *Law and order*—and not merely *law* or *order*. In fact *order* does not repeat nor does it confirm the meaning of *law*. *Order* is what *law* cannot achieve all by itself. *Order* is *law* plus sacrifice, plus the perpetual supplement, plus the perpetual surplus which must be destroyed in order for *order* to exist" (*La Ruine de Kasch* 188). Translating "the grace of God" as the mimetic desire of the community, which is how I translate *polemos*, endows the logic of this apothegm with anthropological confirmation rather than sentimental bathos. Perhaps it is only in a world governed by a policy of Mutually Assured Destruction (nimbly abbreviated by the originators of this policy as MAD), whose sacrificial vocation is writ large in terms of nuclear holocaust ("wholly burnt offering") and from whose arbitrary selection no one is immune, that a theory of sacrifice has any prospect as a science of man (see chap. 4).

At the very least it contributes to possibilities for a properly moral philosophy, one that would overcome the notorious fact/value impasse, by which I mean the classical Humean statement of moral relativism as it concerns the questionable deduction of an "ought" from an "is." For all we know, according to Alasdair MacIntyre, Hume intends only that such a deduction "needs great care" (*A Short History of Ethics* 174; see also Bernard Williams, *Ethics and the Limits of Philosophy* 120–31). The mimetic hypothesis significantly contributes to such care. If a cognitive error as to the origin of violence can be established as a fact, it logically compels identification with rather than alienation from and expulsion of the victim—indifference being complicitous with the victimizers. Moreover, Hume's declaration that "tis not contrary to reason to prefer the destruction of the whole world to the scratching of my finger" (*Treatise of Human Nature* 416) is contrary to reason to the extent that the "whole world" includes his finger along with whatever or whoever scratches it. In a nuclear world of absolute danger, which is perhaps only amplified or multiplied by the destabilizing effects of current ideological implosion, a moral judgment against victimization is likewise a practical one, for what is obliterated is the difference laid down by Hume between ostensibly incommensurate calamities. Hannah Arendt's reflections are pertinent here: "The [philosopher's] moral imperative is actually never imperative. Even if the philosopher wishes to impose his reasoned demands on those who do not reason— as, for instance, in Plato. In Kant you deal with a basically nonreligious morality, which is based on the absolute autonomy of human reason. Kant's morality is simply practical reason. The real imperative underlying the categorical imperative is: don't contradict yourself. And this is clearly the basic law of thinking, or a command of reason" (in Young-Bruehl, *Hannah Arendt* 366). The conclusion that this situation logically entails a choice for the victim issues, I think, from an imaginary dialogue with skeptics and nihilists, who find themselves in a situation analogous to that of the radical idealist. But rather than kicking a stone to prove matter or motion, we have to imagine, with George Orwell, the philosopher's boot in the skeptic's face. In lieu of such a dialogue, I refer the reader to the appendix, where I review a reported dialogue on ethics, the law, and the victim.

Of course, a plea for a nonviolent solution to differences among humans is something that, like Cartesian "*bon sens*" of yore, strikes us as "la chose du monde la mieux partagée," that which "is of all things in the world the most equally distributed," as Descartes says of it. For who, among powers, principalities, and professors, does not endorse such a plea? The victimary hypothesis concerning the violent origins and the mimetic nature of humankind stands out, nonetheless, for proposing a scientific, anthropological foundation for this solution. Scripture scholars will have to grapple with the claim that this hypothesis originates in the Bible (see Schwager, *Must There Be Scapegoats?* and *Semeia 33*) if only to explain to the common reader why the end of our species, which is so clearly and calculably within our grasp as the definitive revelation of human violence, should remind us of what we read in the Bible. What I have tried to show is that even profane literary critics, who are concerned with the effects of writing and with the prospect for its science as a grammatology, will have to grapple with what appears to be the sacrificial origin of these effects.

3

Violence and the Origin
of Language

Pretexts

An investigation of the question of origins might well begin with
Jean-Jacques Rousseau in the eighteenth century, for that is where
the problematic quest for origins begins, with the discrediting of
biblical authority and scriptural orthodoxy, in terms of which origins,
being divine, are by definition no problem. This in part is the point
of Rousseau's insistence near the beginning of his *Discours sur l'origine
de l'inégalité parmi les hommes* that "we must begin by discarding all
the facts" (*Oeuvres complètes* 3:132). The context of this remark clearly
suggests that he is sidestepping the authority of biblical narrative, "la
lecture des livres sacrés," which at least officially represents the facts
for his culture. This in turn appears to pose no problem for our reso-
lutely profane, scientific culture, though part of my argument will
concern a relation to the sacred informing and deforming our own
quest for origins.

For Jacques Derrida, Rousseau's works provide the occasion for a
radical critique of both the notion of origin and our commonplace—
and philosophical—notion of representation as the representation of
being, of being present, or of being as a presence in which representation originates. It is the idea of language as a copy of reality, as a
mirror of nature, an idea Richard Rorty (*Philosophy and the Mirror of
Nature*) has examined in the history of philosophy and somewhat *as* its
history. At issue in Derrida's critique is the capacity of language to refer to anything outside itself, to represent a "reality" that is not always

already a representation, indeed, a *supplement* to writing. For writing is conceived in our culture, the most writerly, bookish culture of all, as a mere technical supplement to language, an arbitrary representation of representation that veils or distorts our access to reality, the thing itself; whereas for Derrida writing represents a "supplement of origin" that replaces an origin, a presence that never took place. At issue in this regard is the possibility of true representations, and therefore of knowledge, of science itself, along with the notions of truth and value with which every scientific quest is invested. As Derrida states toward the very beginning of *Of Grammatology,* "The idea of science and the idea of writing—therefore also of the science of writing [grammatology]—is meaningful for us only in terms of an origin and within a world to which a certain concept of the sign (later I shall call it *the* concept of the sign) and a certain concept of the relationships between speech and writing have *already* been assigned" (*OG* 4).

In *Of Grammatology,* Rousseau provides the occasion to challenge this concept, to reveal its internal contradictions. It is these very contradictions that interest me for exploring other possibilities in the human sciences, possibilities for a science that is rooted in people's relations not primarily with signs but with others, as well as in their relations with what they deem to be wholly other, the sacred. I do not mean anything theological by the sacred, for in the anthropological perspective of this chapter the sacred is but the name that people give to their own violence; indeed, it is the name by which people misrepresent their own violence. In so using the term I am drawing from the "fundamental anthropology" advanced by René Girard, principally in *Violence and the Sacred* and *Things Hidden since the Foundation of the World.* The contradictions in Rousseau's texts are especially interesting for what they both reveal and disguise, mark and erase, about the violence of human origins in its relation to desire. I argue that the contradictory logic of the sacred, as it originates in a desire of untraceable origin, conforms to the contradictory logic of the supplement that Derrida uncovers in Rousseau: the supplement of an origin that never took place, the supplement that takes the place of the origin.

Rousseau's desire for origins, to recover or retrieve them in nature, with a mother, or in a self harmonious with a mother/nature, is legible throughout his works. The preface to his *Confessions* announces the definitive revelation of an absolutely original self that he declares can serve as the "primary basis of comparison for the study of men, which has yet to begin" (*Oeuvres Complètes* 1:3). By the third paragraph, he summons the Last Judgment to testify to the integrity of his portrait and its model, and the penultimate paragraph of this work holds its challengers liable to death by smothering. It is readily apparent how such claims testify to a desire bearing the marks of the sacred as it originates in violence. I could analyze at length how what Derrida might call Rousseau's "overlordly" or "apocalyptic tone" (see "D'un ton apocalyptique adopté naguère en philosophie") links his project of original self-definition to definitive violence, but for the present, Rousseau serves as but the occasion, the pretext, to relate Derrida's critique of origins to Girard's originary hypothesis. I return to Rousseau at the end of the chapter, however, as he offers a certain paradigm of the way a sacrificial scenario is realized in history, heralding terrors discussed in subsequent chapters.

Throughout all this discussion I make no effort to pursue the natural scientific dimensions of Girard's hypothesis as it beckons research in ethology and physical anthropology concerning stimulus response, matching behavior, and motor mimicry among animate life forms. This is not to deny the importance of this research, even its temporal and etiological priority—far from it. Such research represents "the way down" from Girard's theory through the study of antecedent causal conditions that might support or undermine its plausibility. Amidst parsimonious data, natural scientists and philosophers rightly debate where it is appropriate or legitimate to speculate and hypothesize. The argument advanced here reflects a choice to proceed, so to speak, across elements of Girard's originary hypothesis, that is, through aspects of Derrida's critique of origins that correspond to it. I proceed thereafter upward, however obliquely, through aspects of culture and history that are illuminated by their correspondence. This commitment engages a further option in favor of Eric Gans's "formal theory of representation," as developed in *The Origin of Language*, even though it urges a significant reorientation of what it styles as Girard's "institutional theory." Gans is the only one to pursue Girard's relatively inchoate speculation on language origins in a coherent and systematic fashion, and from the first he has insisted that his work differs less from Girard's, by another order of magnitude, than from theories about language and culture from which questions of origin are excluded as a matter of principle.

Tracing the Victim

> Every enhancement of life enhances man's power of com-
> munication, as well as his power of understanding. Empathy
> with the souls of others is originally nothing more but a
> physiological susceptibility to suggestions: "sympathy" or
> what is called altruism, is merely a product of that psycho-
> motor rapport which is spirituality (*induction psycho-motrice*,
> Charles Féré thinks). One never communicates thoughts:
> one communicates movements, mimic signs, which we then
> trace back to thoughts.
>
> —Nietzsche

What first takes place, according to Girard, is violence, and what then takes its place is the sacred. Both require a victim. The victim is the issue of violence and the origin of the sacred; it comes after nature and before culture, which originates in the sacred, that is, in the deference paid to the victim. The victim in this conception serves to bridge the gap between nature and culture and to mark their definitive rupture. And the difference between nature and culture issues from the primordial difference between the human and the sacred, which is inhabited from the beginning by what Derrida neologizes anarcheologically as *differance*.

In the beginning, before the beginning of humanity, there was violence among hominids. It is aboriginal, it is predatory. According to ethological theory, violence is especially prevalent in advanced species, whose dominance patterns are fragile and susceptible to breakdown (in Hamerton-Kelly, *Violent Origins* 123–25, henceforth *VO*), so that intraspecific aggression becomes lethal. It is the mimetic violence of all against all, having its origin solely in another's violence, which it imitates. In the beginning is imitation, not an origin. In the beginning are violent doubles, multdoubles. When the violence of all against all becomes the violence of all against one a victim is produced, which is likely to happen when a difference, a weakness, marks out a single member of the mêlée for destruction. So in a sense we can say with Derrida that in the beginning was the mark, the trace of a violence that has no origin except in another's violence, a trace of nonorigin or an arche-trace. I will say just that when I have traced the cultural destiny of the victim, for the victim is the trace of a violence that has no origin except in "itself," that is, in another's violence.

In the beginning, consequent to natural violence, is the victim. Around the victim is poised a circle of violent predators, each bent on appropriating its remains. There is nothing more natural than to appropriate the victim for oneself and carry it off. This impulse to violent appropriation is natural to all. It is what produced the victim in the first place, and all participate in it—except, in the end, the victim, who represents a difference prior to any identity. But it is just as natural to hesitate before appropriating the victim, lest one fall victim in turn to the unanimous violence that produced it in the first place. It is important to insist here, following the minimalist norms of scientific hypothesis, that no thinking or reflection is required at this stage of developments, only reflex action. Hesitation is a structural necessity, as Girard observes in conversation with Walter Burkert: "As I imitate my neighbor, I reach for the object he is already reaching for, and we prevent each other from appropriating this object" (*VO* 123).

It is here that Girard hypothesizes a first moment of "noninstinctual attention" focusing on the victim. It issues from the "maximal contrast" between the unanimous mêlée that produced the victim and the calm that succeeds its destruction: "Since the victim is a common victim it will be at that instant the focal point for all members of the community. Consequently, beyond the purely instinctual object, the alimentary or sexual object, or the dominant mate, there is the cadaver of the collective victim and it is this corpse which constitutes the first object for this new kind of attention" (*THFW* 99). Whether this attention is grounded in the spectacular frustration of instinct or the clash of rival instincts, the result is the same. Willy-nilly, all those surrounding the victim are guarantors of this calm and of the attention informing it.

In *The Origin of Language,* Eric Gans refines Girard's hypothesis to suggest how this moment coincides with the emergence of the first sign. The natural act of appropriation is a reflex on the part of all; it thereby becomes a gesture, indeed, a sign, for it designates the victim as desirable—and as forbidden. All imitate this movement toward the victim because all desire the victim, if only out of reflex imitation of movement toward the victim prior to anything like desire. It is the confluence of these movements that ensures the victim's inaccessibility, indeed, that makes the victim an object of desire in the first place—or rather in the second place, every desire being a second to another. The object that all desire is perforce the one that none dares appropriate. To designate the victim is to designate it as both desirable and taboo in one and the same movement or moment. The sacred, in all its foundational ambivalence—as infinitely desirable and as infinitely accursed, dangerous to approach—is born in and as this same movement or moment of desire.

This moment is contradictory but not incoherent; rather, it is "contradictorily coherent," as Derrida writes of the structural center in "Structure, Sign and Play in the Discourse of the Human Sciences": "And as always, coherence in contradiction expresses the force of a desire" (*WD* 279). Desire is central to Girard's hypothesis, but only as a force that is concentric and eccentric at once.

The victim is holy, sacralized by its deferred possession, which alone accords peace to the group. The victim is not desired for its own sake; all its value emanates from the desires it animates and magnetizes. And its value is contradictory, antithetical—whence the "antithetical sense of primary words" that so fascinated Freud (*Standard Edition* 11:153–62) and that etymo-ethnological research on a word like *sacer* has born out (Beneveniste 452–56; Kerenyi 108–11). Gans's formal theory enables us to conceive the movement from the natural to the cultural, which is to say first and foremost the sacred, in this originary deferral. The act of seizing the prey becomes a gesture designating the victim but deferring its appropriation because that act appears manifestly dangerous to any attempting it, the possessor of the prey quite naturally being in danger of falling victim in turn to the other predators. And this deferral is *naturally* contagious, mimetic, for all predators designate the object at once as desirable and taboo: it is taboo because desirable, its possessor risking destruction by other predators, and desirable because taboo, every abortive seizure, every mimetic gesture, designating it as desirable, *performing* its desirability. This results in a properly uncanny moment in which an object signifies only to the extent that it signifies symmetrically opposite values: attraction and repulsion, each by the other. Any word designating this object will be double, self-contradictory, antithetical. Sacred words differ from all others in that they differ from themselves from within themselves, designating what is attractive and repulsive, holy and accursed. They differ, that is, in the mode of differance, as Derrida describes it in *Positions:*

> First, *différance* refers to the (active *and* passive) movement that consists in deferring by means of delay, delegation, reprieve, referral, detour, postponement, reserving. In this sense *différance* is not preceded by the originary and indivisible unity of a present possibility that I could

reserve, like an expenditure that I would put off calculatedly or for reasons of economy. . . . *Second*, the movement of *différance*, as that which
produces different things, that which differentiates, is the common root
of all the oppositional concepts that mark our language, such as, to take
only a few examples, sensible/intelligible, intuition/signification, na-
ture/culture, etc. (8–9).

Girard says no less when he attributes to the delay, the postponement, the deferral affecting the victim, the root of all subsequent
differences:

> Because of the victim, in so far as it seems to emerge from the com-
> munity and the community seems to emerge from it, for the first time
> there can be something like an inside and an outside, a before and after,
> a community and the sacred. We have already noted that the victim ap-
> pears to be simultaneously good and evil, peaceable and violent, a life
> that brings death and a death that guarantees life. Every possible sig-
> nificant element seems to have its outline in the sacred and at the same
> time to be transcended by it. (*THFW* 102)

The verb form in which the victim "appears" in French is *se pré-
sente*. It might be cited as an instance of how " 'everyday language,' "
according to Derrida, "is not innocent or neutral. It is the language of
Western metaphysics," viz., the language of being as presence (*Positions* 19). Nonetheless, the presence or appearing present of the victim
in Girard's text depends entirely on abstinence or deferral. It is not
ontological presence that is posited here, still less ontotheological
presence, but its antithesis: a hallowed illusion, a quid pro quo by
which abstinence constitutes presence. The only presence is that of
the community to itself as mediated by the victim. Girard's hypothesis
in this regard is not one in which the concept of the sign, as sign of a
presence, is "already *assigned*." On the contrary, and in accordance
with deconstruction, he writes that "the philosophical attitude that
still dominates the various methodologies of the human sciences cannot accommodate a hypothesis of this kind. Everything is still subject
to the ideal of a mastery that arises immediately and intuitively, from
direct contact with the data—this is perhaps one aspect of what we
nowadays refer to as the 'metaphysics of presence' " (*THFW* 437,
trans. modified). As the dictionaries remind us, a hypothesis is a conditional proposition subject to empirical verification. The point is that
nothing in Derridean deconstruction serves to falsify it. Girard does
not exploit the ambiguity of language as Derrida does, and this formal

difference has substantial implications that remain to be examined. Suffice it for the present to observe that where Derrida's critique of the sign is transposable to or translatable in ordinary language, it beats a path to Girard's hypothesis. This is not fortuitous. Differance designates the structure of desire.

The relation of the victim to the community, as described by Girard, is irreducibly—Derrida would say "undecidably" (*Positions* 42–43)—active and passive: the community comes out of the victim no less than the victim comes out of the community. It is transcendent in that it is the matrix of differences and values (life/death, good/bad, and true/false as they depend on being in- or outside the community), which are in no wise antecedent to the power of attraction and repulsion emanating from the victim. "The substitute does not substitute itself for anything which has somehow existed before it" (Derrida, *WD* 281), such as a community. This magnetic power is expressed in Derrida's notion of "the generative movement [of *différance*] in the play of differences," which he evokes in contradistinction to a static structuralism:

> [Differences] are neither fallen from the sky nor inscribed once and for all in a closed system, a static structure that a synchronic and taxonomic operation could exhaust. Differences are the effects of transformations, and from this vantage the theme of *différance* is incompatible with the static, synchronic, taxonomic ahistoric motifs in the concept of *structure*. But it goes without saying that this motif is not the only one that defines structure, and that the production of differences, *différance*, is not astructural: it produces systematic and regulated transformations which are able, at a certain point, to leave room for a structural science. The concept of *différance* even develops the most legitimate principled exigencies of a "structuralism." (*Positions* 27–28)

Differance is neither genetic, except in the sense that it generates all structures and governs their transformations, nor structural, except that no principled structuralism is possible without it. It corresponds to Girard's demand for a human science that is both genetic and structural (*Job* chap. 15; *VO* 108) without privileging either the differences composing a structure or a chronology imposed by a unique, selfsame origin, a hieratic or hierophanic center that would escape the play of differences, the play, that is, of rivalrous desires. What Derrida objects to in the concept of a "centered structure" is the concept of a "foundational immobility" that, bearing the name of God, man, nature, substance, consciousness, and the like, would be "beyond the reach of play" (*WD* 279–80). At the center for Girard is "une méconnaissance proprement foundatrice" originating in and as desire; it is this misunderstanding that "opens the way for difference itself," "la Différence en tant que telle" (*THFW* 44). At the center is the victim, but it's centrality does not let it "escape the play and the order of the sign" (*WD* 292), for the victim is a sign of the interplay of desire.

The origin is double, a relation of mimetic doubles to an object of desire that is antithetically double in its significance, its value. "Everything begins with structure, configuration, relationship," as Derrida paraphrases Lévi-Straussian structuralism in "Structure, Sign and Play in the Discourse of the Human Sciences" (*WD* 286). So too for Girard, with the decisive difference that the victim makes: all structure emanates from the originary relation to the victim.

The victim is decisive in its very undecidability; it is a homicide and deicide at once—from which the notions of "homo" and "deus" subsequently derive their meaning. The gods created humankind; so says mythology. Humankind created the gods; so say our human sciences. We have to conceive of the origin of the gods and of humanity in the same moment, with the gods being constructed retrospectively, belatedly—Derrida would say "*après coup*," "nachträglich" (*WD* 210)—out of the deference paid to the sacralized victim, which is but the deference desire must pay to an object desired by so many others. The victim is not a "transcendental signified," which Derrida describes as "*a concept signified in and of itself,* a concept simply present for thought, independent of a relationship to language, that is of a relationship to a system of signifiers," and which "in and of itself, in its essence, would refer to no signifier, would exceed the chain of signs and would no longer itself function as a signifier" (*Positions* 19–20). Rather, Girard describes the victim as "transcendental signifier" whose signified is "all actual and potential meaning the community confers on the victim and, through its intermediacy, on to all things" (*THFW* 103). Meaning as diacritical difference, subject to all manner of oppositions and displacements (paradigmatic or syntagmatic, as in cat/hat or cat/dog), does not precede the victim, not is it even proper to or possessed by the victim, except as a signifier of the difference between meaning and nonmeaning.

The victim functions as does the art that in the developing course of culture will come to represent and replace it (for the esthetic relation to the victim, see Gans, *The Origin* 185–96). Like art for us today, the victim is not a simple object of observation by gazing subjects. Because of the power (falsely) sensed as radiating from it, the victim transmits a subjective dimension, a dimension of conscious or willing agency, for the victim is experienced as the subject of an ambivalent power of which it is the object, the mediator and the sign. The victim's power to fascinate its beholders, to bind (whence *fasciare*) them in a state that allows neither forward nor backward movement—not stasis but hypostasis—issues from the double bind affecting the object of desire as it says "take/don't take me." All those surrounding the object reinforce this bind.

The victim's power to fascinate is one with its power to mediate signification. The victim is accordingly the mana of the system of cultural differences; its function, as described by Lévi-Strauss, whom Derrida quotes, " 'is to be opposed to the absence of signification, without entailing by itself any particular signification' " (*WD* 290). It is for just this "antinomial" character (which is the character of a written character, of a letter, such as the anomalous *a* in differance) that Derrida likens mana to writing, as the mark or representation of a meaning that is in no wise present in it. Derrida does not thematize writing at this point of his discussion, but rather the supplement, which is what writing represents in our culture: a signifier in excess of an original meaning that it travesties or perverts. This is what writing represents to Lévi-Strauss in the wake of Saussure and of Rousseau before him, and this is why, as Derrida amply demonstrates in *Of Grammatology*, they condemn it. Their veritable expulsion of writing repeats Plato's gesture in the *Phaedrus*. For Derrida, however, "it could no doubt be demonstrated that this *ration supplémentaire* of signification is the origin of the *ratio* itself" (*WD* 290). For Derrida, writing represents the "supplement of origin," the mark or excluded member in which language originates. It is in and as the dead letter, which is what writing represents for Rousseau, that we find the origin of language: "The death of speech is therefore the horizon and origin of language. But an origin and a horizon which do not hold themselves at its exterior borders. As always, death, which is neither a present to come nor a present past, shapes the interior of speech, and its trace, its reserve, its interior and exterior differance: as its supplement" (*OG* 314). We must locate the origin of language not in the mark itself, which means nothing, but in its exclusion as the exclusion of nonmeaning, of nondifference. This is where Girard locates the victim, from whose exclusion meaning is thereafter free to proliferate. The victim is the supplement of an origin that is constituted only by the victim's expulsion. I am not speaking here of a historical reconstitution, which Girard recognizes as impossible (*THFW* 44, 64; *VO* 89), but of a generative principle whose very erasure accounts for properly mythological reconstitutions.

It is in terms of the ritual imperative, the need to re-create the foundational murder from which the newborn community derives and perpetuates its existence, that we can understand this proliferation of meaning:

> There is no difficulty in explaining why ritual is repeated. Driven by sacred terror and wishing to continue life under the sign of the reconciliatory victim, men attempt to reproduce and represent this sign; this attempt consists first of all in the search for victims who seem capable of bringing about the primordial epiphany, and it is there that we find the first signifying activity that can always be defined, if one insists, in terms of language or writing. The moment arrives when the original victim, rather than being signified by new victims, will be signified by something other than a victim, by a variety of things that continue to signify the victim while at the same time progressively masking, disguising, and failing to recognize it. (*THFW* 103)

Any sort of thing can substitute for the victim precisely because the victim is always already a substitute, a signifier, a mark, in Derridean terms, of a deferral. The sacrificial origin of money as a substitute for the object of desire has been plausibly argued by Michel Aglietta and André Orléan (*La Violence de la monnaie*). From substitute to substitute, from disguise to disguise, from a mark to a model that is already a mark, the ritual imperative is the place where appropriative mimesis leads, cedes, or *defers* to ontological mimesis; it is where behavioral mimesis leads to imitative representation, or esthetic mimesis; it is where the representation of desire is wed to the desire for representation. The representation of another's desire becomes the representation of the object of desire. This is what Roberto Calasso summarizes as "l'immense astuce sacrificielle: la substitution": "By sacrificing something *which takes the place* of another, we put into motion the very machinery of language and of algebra, of digitality triumphant. The deception by which we can butcher a substitute on the altar and not the thing itself elicits an inordinate increase in potential, such that, in its expansion, it will entirely erase from our mind the necessity of sacrificial offering. Pure exchange, which systematizes substitution, slowly suppresses the object's uniqueness, a memento of the primordial victim" (*La Ruine de Kasch* 210).

It is the double and ever-ambiguous vocation of language, as serving both reverence and reference (Gans, *The Origin* 63), that generates the sacred and profane institutions of culture and hence the possibility of both constative-scientific and performative-ritualistic utterances. As Girard summarizes it, "the victim must be the first object of non-instinctual attention, and he or she provides a good starting point for the creation of sign systems because the ritual imperative consists in a demand for substitute victims, thus introducing the practice of substitution that is the basis of all symbolizations" (*VO* 129). This "practice of substitution" is representation—substituting a word for a thing, different words for different things, one word for another (metaphor), and so on—and results in the fragile construct of language. Its deconstruction shows that ritual sacrifice is a supplement to divine presence, to which, in the expulsion of the victim, it only defers, which it only displaces. Representation is preferred to presence as the representation of violence is preferred to a violence in which all symbolization dissolves (*VS* 97–99).

The ambiguity or undecidability of this distinction between constative and performative utterances, as laid down by J. L. Austin (and already "deconstructed" by him before Derrida and others took it on), requires no comment here other than that the former seeks its realization in maximal though never total distance from the referent, as in the "purely" formal representation of mathematics, whereas a "purely" performative utterance seeks maximal proximity to its referent; indeed, it seeks to be its own referent, as in the statement, "this meeting will begin." Culture evolves in and as the differance between these two extremes.

Derrida's description of the logic of the supplement in Rousseau provides an apt description of the ritual imperative. Rousseau describes masturbation as a "dangerous supplement" to sexual possession (*Confessions* 108–9), though he confesses that "*jouissance*" would be the death of him:

> Are things not complicated enough? The symbolic is the immediate, presence is absence, the nondeferred is deferred, pleasure is the menace of death. But one stroke must be still added to this system, to this strange economy of the supplement. In a certain way, it was already legible. A terrifying menace, the supplement is also the first and surest

protection; against that very menace. This is why it cannot be given up. And sexual auto-affection, that is auto-affection in general, neither begins nor ends with what one thinks can be circumscribed by the name of masturbation. This supplement has not only the power of *procuring* an absent present through its image; procuring it for us through the proxy [*procuration*] of the sign, it holds it at a distance and masters it. For this presence is at the same time desired and feared. The supplement transgresses and at the same time respects the interdict. This is what also permits writing as the supplement of speech; but already also the spoken word as writing in general. Its economy exposes and protects us at the same time according to the play of forces and of the differences of forces. (*OG* 154–55)

The economy Derrida is describing here exhibits that of sacrifice, thus allowing the substitution of that word for *supplement* throughout the passage.

The parallel is not as fortuitous as it may seem at first glance: masturbation for Rousseau is the representation of the satisfaction of desire, its ostensibly immediate satisfaction as rape. This fantasy accordingly communicates with Rousseau's literary fictions, toward which he is analogously ambivalent, as witnessed by the second preface to *La Nouvelle Héloïse,* which stages an unresolved debate about the novel's morality. Sacrifice similarly represents to the community the forces that generate it and whose untrammeled release threatens to dissolve it. The economy of sacrifice simultaneously exposes and protects the community. Derrida's last sentence also suggests why sacrificial representation is always attended by dread concern for ritual purity. The concern for exact repetition is the greater for the fact that its exact significance escapes its participants. Moreover, there is also the concern lest the play of forces representing and disguising originary violence explode into that violence itself, lest the representation of sacrifice lead to a sacrificial crisis, the mimetic violence of all against all against which ritual sacrifice is intended to protect.

The sacred is perceived as present in the victim, though it prevails only in what the victim represents, in what represents the victim: the saving, peaceful, mimetic presence of the community to itself. And the self, ego, or self-consciousness, as the consciousness of a self that desires (Gans, *The Origin* 50), is not at the origin of representation, but is its by-product. Desire, in a word, is differance as described by Derrida in the essay bearing this improper, anarchical anticoncept as its title: the becoming space of time, the becoming time of space: "An interval must separate the present from what it is not in order for the present to be itself, but this interval that constitutes it as present must, by the same token, divide the present in and of itself, thereby also dividing, along with the present, everything that is thought on the basis of the present, that is, in our metaphysical language, every be-ing, and singularly the substance or the subject. In constituting itself, in dividing itself dynamically, this interval is what might be called *spacing*, the becoming-space of time or the becoming-time of space (*temporalization*)" (*Margins of Philosophy* 13).

The Girardian subject as homologously divided, as differance, as desire, is constituted in the space-time of deferred appropriation in which notions of presence and absence originate. As Derrida writes of it in *Of Grammatology*, "this means that differance makes the opposi-tion of presence and absence possible. Without the possibility of dif-ferance, the desire of presence as such would not find its breathing space. That means by the same token that this desire carries in itself the destiny of its non-satisfaction. Difference produces what it forbids, makes possible the very thing that it makes impossible" (143). The word *desire* can substitute for *differance* in this last sentence because the antithetical structure of differance operates according to the struc-ture (or as Derrida will later have it in *The Post Card*, the "stricture") of the double bind in *Violence and the Sacred:* "Man and his desires thus perpetually transmit contradictory signals to one another. Neither model nor disciple really understands why one constantly thwarts the other because neither perceives that his desire has become the reflec-tion of the other's" (*VS* 147). The crux of this analysis is that Girard's originary scenario does not conflict with a poststructuralist critique of origins because it posits that origin and difference are one, that rep-resentation is the by-product of an originary differance, of mimetic de-sire, rather than the representation of any kind of origin or originary presence. Concomitantly, origin and indirection, obliquity, are one: the gesture of representation is a by-product of the aborted act of ap-propriation. And origin and misrepresentation, or misprision, are one to the extent that the victim is accorded a power owing to represen-tation alone.

The victim is the source of ambivalence for the members of the newborn community. It is in this sense that the victim represents the community, for it represents the ambivalence of each and all toward each and all, an ambivalence originating in desire. Each and all are at once rival, model, and obstacle with regard to the object of desire. Each member is the source of the others' ambivalence toward the victim, and it is this ambivalence that the victim represents for the community. Thus, both victim and members are the originary source of ambivalence, though it is important to see, as the members do not, exactly how the victim represents the community: truly and falsely at once. Truly because the community originates in the representation of the victim, who represents singly the violence of all; falsely because the feelings of the desiring subjects are projected onto the desired object. The victim is the source of ambivalence and ambivalence is the source of a properly human community.

This has not changed even today. What we identify as social tensions reflect institutional needs as the latter work to channel ambivalence, mediate hostile rivalries, and succor victims, and institutional needs just as inevitably generate hostility and, indeed, produce victims.

Because I am examining this hypothesis in the context of eighteenth-century literature, let me note in passing that the human community is born neither out of sympathy among its potential members or between any two of them (Rousseau) nor out of any symmetrical antipathy (Hobbes), but out of both at once. The explanation of neither Rousseau (*Discours sur l'origine de l'inégalité parmi les hommes*) nor Hobbes (*Leviathan*) is sufficient. Both are necessary, for Rousseau represents the origin of human culture from the point of the victim, and Hobbes, from the point of view of the violent community.

Everything in this scenario moves along the bias, in the very same "oblique and perilous movement" by which Derrida styles the task of deconstruction (*OG* 14); everything is at acute angles of which the victim is the hinge. The angles form the triangle of desire bounded by the relation of rival subjects toward the object of desire, whose study in the novel—*as* the novel—composes Girard's first book, *Deceit, Desire and the Novel*. Novels by Cervantes, Proust, Dostoyevsky, Flaubert, and Stendhal demonstrate that desire originates neither in us nor in the object but in others who, be they parents, peers, or subordinates, serve as a model for the selection of the object. Social relations precede object relations and determine them. Deconstruction is continuous with this analysis to the extent that it uncovers mediation everywhere that immediacy is postulated. Representation is destined to indirection, that is, mediation, for it is the representation not of an object but—via the object—of another's desire. The object is the sign of another's desire, which is itself the mimetic sign, the repetition, reproduction, and representation of another's desire, and so on ad infinitum in the seemingly infinite proliferation of cultural representations. It is this structure that generates the seemingly endless supplementarity by which one object of desire substitutes, stands in for, and supplants another.

Nothing (but desire) takes place at the sacred center, which is why anything can take its place, hence the manner in which Rousseau describes taking Thérèse Lavasseur as his common-law wife: she is a supplement to "Maman," Mme de Warens, who is herself a supplement to Rousseau's natural mother, who died at birth, who is herself a supplement to nature—unless nature is a supplement to her:

> A little intimacy with this excellent girl, a little reflection upon my situation, made me feel that, while thinking only of my pleasures, I had done much to promote my happiness. *To supply the place of* my extinguished ambition, I needed a lively sentiment which should *take complete possession of* [literally "fill"—*remplit*] my heart. In a word, I needed a successor to mamma. As I should never live with her again, I wanted someone to live with her pupil, in whom I might find the simplicity and docility of heart which she had found in me. I felt it was necessary that the gentle tranquility of private and domestic life *should make up* to me for the loss of the brilliant career which I was renouncing. When I was quite alone, I felt a void in my heart, which it only needed another heart to *fill.* Destiny had deprived me of, or at least in part, alienated me from that heart for which Nature had formed me. From that moment I was alone; for *with me it has always been everything or nothing. I found in Thérèse the substitute [supplément] that I needed.* (cited in *OG* 157)

There is a vertiginous play of substitutions, whereby the desiring subject ("I wanted") becomes desired object ("heart she found in me"), so that Thérèse becomes a replica of a lost mother and of a self possessed, of auto-affection. The mother signifies an irreplaceable locus of intimacy—though on the other hand that place is filled as readily as one signifier displaces another. Derrida's comment on this "chain of supplements" not only "deconstructs" Rousseau's declared desire for presence, it also explains the cultural role of signs as they issue from desire: "Through this sequence of supplements a necessity is announced: that of an infinite chain, ineluctably multiplying the supplementary mediations that produce the sense of the very thing they defer: the mirage of the thing itself, of immediate presence, of originary perception. Immediacy is derived. That all begins with the intermediary is what is indeed 'inconceivable [to reason]' " (*OG* 157). "il n'y eut jamais pour moi d'intermédiaire entre tout et rien": between everything and nothing there is nothing—that is, there is the signifier whose function is to display the difference between everything and nothing, between the thing itself and all cultural mediations. Rousseau's obsessive critique of the signifier, of the letter, was bound to bring its central role into view.

But something else here comes plainly into view, something that Derrida, in his preoccupation with formal structures, never discusses: Rousseau's "extinguished ambition," his "brilliant career." Immediacy is derived above all in the sense that it is the residue of social ambitions never gratified and never entirely renounced. This is especially evident in Rousseau's last writings, the *Rêveries* and the *Dialogues*, where society plays the role of monstrous double to Jean-Jacques's archly hieratic and ultimately vengeful solitude.

> While he is occupied with himself, they are also occupied with him. He loves himself and they hate him; he is what everybody is occupied with; he is also everything for himself, he is also everything for them; for as to them, they are nothing in themselves, neither for him, nor for themselves, and provided that J. J. be miserable, they require no other happiness. Thus everybody, he and they each from their own quarter, has two great experiences to deal with; they, with all the grief that it is possible for men to heap on the soul of an innocent being, and he, with all the resources that innocence can draw from itself to bear it. (*OC* 1:860)

"Il n'y eut jamais pour moi d'intermédiaire entre tout et rien"; where "tout" and "rien" are "lui" and "eux," except that each is the mediator of the other's desire—for everything, "tout." Rousseau's inflated imagination of himself as sacrificial victim and foundation of social cohesion strongly suggests that his skewed ontology, as analyzed by Derrida, recapitulates Girard's sociology. This is not surprising, for Rousseau's undisputed contribution to theory is the ethical superiority he claims for the victim (see Gans, "The Victim as Subject"). The claim is valid regardless of whether Rousseau has unique title to it. The importance of Rousseau's individualism is that he places the victim at the center of culture, making the unique position of marginality the central question for modern society, where the individual person is elevated to the rank of an institution (O'Keefe, *Stolen Lightning* 387).

In a sense, Rousseau democratizes the marginality of the victim; it is now a position for which theories, including deconstruction, compete in their claims for superiority.

Tracing Institutions

> I call the basic truth of every genus those elements in it the existence of which cannot be proved. As regards both these primary truths and the attributes dependent on them the meaning of the name is assumed. The fact of their existence as regards the primary truths must be assumed; but it has to be proved of the remainder, the attributes.
>
> —Aristotle

The experience of the sacred as divine presence is born of a maculate conception; it is illusory but efficacious. Or rather, it is efficacious because it is illusory. The links (or macula) that bind a community as a religion are forged by abstention from the object of desire. If the etymology of *re-ligare* is to believed, the ties that bind the community are double, issuing from a double bind that ensures the sacred its foundational role. The sacred is nothing and nowhere, it is only the force of attraction and repulsion attending the object of a desire sufficiently intense to inspire another desire that in turn is sufficiently intense to render appropriation dangerous or dreadful. The object, the victim, becomes only a signifier of desire. The sacred is nothing but this mortal opposition, this resemblance of desires, which is why anything, any object, can represent the sacred: the sacred does not exist except as the signifier of desire's ambivalence. Thus, anything can represent the sacred, even writing, especially writing as the mark of an absence, of an abstinence prior to any awareness of presence or absence. From this notion comes the properly victimary status of writing for Rousseau, of whom Derrida cannily observes that "what he excluded more violently than another must of course have fascinated and tormented him more than another" (*OG* 98). This combination of fascination and torment generates Rousseau's writings, propelling him to a tormented and fascinated view of himself as victim. This could hardly be otherwise if, following Derrida's analysis, writing is the double of an origin it supplants.

Thus, we can say with Derrida that in the beginning is the trace, the body of the victim being the trace of a violence that, being mimetic, does not originate with it or with anyone. The origin of this violence, improperly attributed to the victim whose destruction ends violence, is properly unrepresentable; it is proper only to the rivalry of combatants, to their mimetic conflict. The sacralization of the victim erases this nonorigin—the nonoriginal but only repetitive, mimetic origin of violence—when it enshrines the victim as the origin of the community. What Derrida writes of the arche-trace thus describes the victim in Girard's scenario:

> The value of the transcendental arche [*archie*] must make its necessity felt before letting itself be erased. The concept of arche-trace must comply with both that necessity and that erasure. It is in fact contradictory and not acceptable within the logic of identity. The trace is not only the disappearance of origin—within the discourse that we sustain and according to the path that we follow it means that the origin did not even disappear, that it was never constituted except reciprocally by a nonorigin, the trace, which thus becomes the origin of the origin. From then on, to wrench the concept of the trace from the classical scheme, which would derive it from a presence or from an originary nontrace and which would make of it an empirical mark, one must indeed speak of an originary trace or arche-trace. Yet we know that that concept destroys its name and that, if all begins with the trace, there is above all no originary trace. (*OG* 61)

The adverb *reciprocally* translates *en retour,* which is something else again as it signifies the retroactive constitution of the origin by the trace. This is just how Girard describes the origin of the human community in its active and passive relation to the victim. In Girard's scenario, all begins with the sacred, which destroys its name in the same way as described by Derrida—in the same antithetical way that interested Freud, but more importantly, more decisively for the nascent human community, in the way it erases the traces of human violence. As Girard observes in the context of a discussion of Derrida to which I will return, "Western thought continues to function as the effacement of traces. But the traces of founding violence are no longer the ones being expelled; rather, the traces of a first or second expulsion, or even of a third or fourth. In other words, we are dealing with traces of traces of traces, etc." (*THFW* 65).

These traces are legible in the institutions that culture develops with the repetition, proliferation, and complication of ritual sacrifice. I can do no more here than sketch some examples of institutions traceable to sacrificial practices in order to suggest the generality of the latter and the corresponding theoretical parsimony of the victimary hypothesis:

• Animal husbandry issues from the need to keep animals to substitute for human victims (*THFW* 68 ff.).
• Kingship emerges from the divided identity of the victim, for it bifurcates the function of the victim as founder and savior of the community from the equally necessary destruction of the victim (*THFW* 51 ff.). Of course, the literature on the sacrificial role of kingship, from Shakespeare through Frazer, Hocart, and Kantorowicz, is superabundant. The value of the victimary hypothesis is for the coherence it lends to such massive data.
• Theater represents a sacrificial crisis that it no longer comprehends or from whose comprehension it shrinks back (*VS*, especially chaps. 3 and 5).
• Literary criticism begins with Aristotle's efforts to protect dramatic poetry from Plato's canny expulsion of it (*VS* 292–95; *THFW* 7–10); for tragedy represents a violence whose symmetry belies differences on which culture depends. The reliance of critical theory today on *polemos* requires no elaboration (for its relation to violence, see Siebers, *The Ethics of Criticism*).
• Narrative literature in general begins with the epic hero's destruction of a monster, that is, of an unnatural, inhuman, and consequently sacred violence whose nonetheless saving power is invested *en retour* in the figure, the fiction of the hero. There is no hero without a monster to slay who is but the double of the hero, whose bad violence is doubled by the hero's good violence.
• The law accords to the city a monopoly on violence in quest of the right victim, the culpable origin of violence (*VS* chap. 1 and chap. 5 of this book). And the procedures of the law, as heir to sacrifice, do not fail to display a dramaturgical structure that issues in turn from and remains party to a more primitive liturgical imperative; it is precisely when proper juridical procedure appears designed more to satisfy the demand for ritual purity than to meet transcendent goals of justice that the law is, as it seems now, in crisis (Denvir 825–26). According to what is identified as a "structural theory" of crime, our entire political economy is one that generates crime, such that criminals are

reinterpreted as being victims of an established order (Elias, *The Politics of Victimization* 90–91, 235). Later, I discuss the issue of a "general economy" of sacrifice, engaging the dynamics of money, competition, and exchange.

• As a profession historically replete with mystified expulsions, psychoanalysis betrays sacrificial dynamics, as has been admirably scrutinized by François Roustang in *Dire Mastery: Discipleship from Freud to Lacan*. The theoretical origins of psychoanalysis in the misrecognition of mimesis have been analyzed by Mikkel Borch-Jacobsen in *Le Sujet freudien*. The repression of violence by its sexual (mis)representation is the topic of Tobin Siebers's reading of Freud and Lacan in *The Ethics of Criticism*.

• Sports betray an agonal structure that depends entirely on the mimetic symmetry essential to many sacrificial rites. Their role as a representation and displacement of communal violence is patent. Their patently *totemic* character in this country, with our Bulls, Bears, Cubs, Hawks, Eagles, Lions, and the like, representing various metropolitan clans, reflects properly mythic residues. Luc Routeau's detailed analyses of games (see "Au Cirque" in *Esprit* and "Le bouz-kashî" in Dumouchel, ed., *Violence et Vérité*) in primitive and modern cultures lends anthropological depth to such evidence. There is scarcely a game whose rules and goals are not traceable to ritual sacrifice.

• The sacrificial meal has long been the focus of anthropological inquiry. Eric Gans (*The End of Culture*) and Michel Serres (*Le Parasite*) explore its relevance to the victimary hypothesis.

• War has already been mentioned. I deal with it at greater length farther on.

This list is by no means exhaustive. It is intended to promote an agenda for further study in the human sciences, with the practical aim of uncovering relations to human violence that go largely unnoticed, indeed, relations that institutions, beginning with and as sacrifice, serve to cover up.

Among cultural institutions, those devoted to representation are especially high on the agenda for future research. There is philosophy, and the academy born of its ambiguous relation to *polemos*, as I have argued in chapter 2. I have mentioned theater, but film, both popular and high-cultural, is crucially important for study in what we call the media age. Popular film and television are massively devoted to expelling the monster, to chasing bad violence with good: to perpetuating mythology in sacralizing violence. Nathanael West's *Day of the Locust* powerfully evokes the dynamics of mob violence informing the Hollywood "star system," and Mark Crispin Miller's critique of television, *Boxed In*, exposes the victimary dynamics propelling televised comedy. *Vox populi, vox dei:* we see pop culture to be religious through and through once we recognize the religious as the sacrificial. So-called escape literature and entertainment are transparently scapegoating, though what escapes is just that transparency. On the other hand, high-cultural cinematic productions, at their best, perform the same service as great novels in revealing dialectics of desire, mimesis, and violence that other institutions exploit (Livingston, *Ingmar Bergman and the Rituals of Art*). Whereas sacrificial violence is a structuring principle in pop-cultural adventure narrative, we rightly award critical acclaim to works where it is a theme to be recognized and renounced.

And then there are books. They interest us as institutions not merely because our hugely bookish culture derives in part from comment on and subsequent rivalry with the Bible, the good book, the God book (McKenna, "Biblioclasm: Joycing Jesus and Borges" and "Biblioclasm: Derrida"), but also for reasons advanced by Derrida when he seeks to "put in question . . . the unity of the book, and the unity 'book' considered as a perfect totality, with all the implications of such a concept." "And you know," he continues, "that these implications concern the entirety of our culture, directly or indirectly" (*Positions* 11). This global phrasing—"le tout de notre culture, de près ou de loin"—is not atypical of Derrida's discourse as it seeks out the implications of differance everywhere. It is a warrant for the comparisons and correlations being pursued in this book, as it clearly suggests that the range and scale of Derrida's detotalizing ambitions are in no way incommensurate with that of Girard's "unifying theory" of culture. The victimary hypothesis thinks the religious through rather than simply siding with religion or attacking it.

Derrida's deconstructive target is the book as an institution that confides in the capacity of signifiers to represent signifieds that are ultimately independent of them; he aims at the book as the exemplary institution of logocentrism. As he writes in *Of Grammatology*'s first chapter, "The End of the Book and the Beginning of Writing," the idea of the book is the idea of a totality, finite or infinite, of the signifier; this totality of the signifier cannot be a totality, unless a totality constituted by the signified preexists it, supervises its inscriptions and its signs, and is independent of it in its ideality. The idea of the book, which always refers to a natural totality, is profoundly alien to the sense of writing. It is the encyclopedic protection of theology and of logocentrism against the disruption of writing, against its aphoristic energy, and, as I shall specify later, against difference in general. If I distinguish the text from the book, I shall say that the destruction of the book, as it is now under way in all domains, denudes the surface of the text. That necessary violence responds to a violence that was no less necessary. (*OG* 18)

Derrida's pro-gram for this disruption accordingly adopts a fragmentary title (*De la grammatologie*), recalling the earliest tradition of the codex (as in *De amicitiae* and *De senectute*; see Ong, *Ramus, Method and the Decay of Dialogue*) This tactic is inscribed in the title of *Positions*, the plural marking an animadversion to a single, unitary *stance* or thesis, "the very idea of a thetic presentation, of positional and oppositional logic, the idea of position, of *Setzung* or *Stellung*" (Derrida, "The Time of a Thesis" 38). Elsewhere this tactic is marked in the title of *Margins of Philosophy*, the first work to exhibit the irregular columns of parallel texts that compose the strategy of Derrida's *Glas*, tolling the death knell for the book. Denuding the surface of the text, tracking the book's operations back to the expulsion of writing that institutes it, and uncovering that erasure constitute the task of deconstruction as pursued across the writings of Rousseau (as of Husserl in *La Voix et le phénomène* and of many another in various essays).

Derrida's mention of violence here is neither fortuitous nor hyperbolic. He has the same understanding of its complex structure and its sacrificial effects as does Girard. As he says, "the structure of violence is complex and its possibility—writing—is no less so" (*OG* 112).

Books are the building blocks of Western culture, which everybody, Derrida and Girard included, rightly observes is quickly becoming a planetary culture (*OG* 3, 10). Derrida sometimes plays on the phonemic vicinity of tome and tomb to emphasize books' monumental status; it is that of a funerary monument, such as a pyramid in which a body is encrypted. What is encrypted in the book is the letter, as is the letter *a* in differance, which we pass over in silence when we read it aloud: "The *a* of differance, therefore, is not heard; it remains silent, secret, and discreet, like a tomb. . . . It is a tomb that (provided one knows how to decipher its inscription [la légende]) is not far from signaling the death of the king" ("Differance" in *Margins of Philosophy* 4, trans. modified; see also "The Pit and the Pyramid" in the same vol.). The legends of Oedipus and Pentheus as told by Girard (*VS* chaps. 3 and 5) and the legend of Romulus as told by Michel Serres (*Rome: Le Livre des fondations*) are the one Derrida tells of the letter, the legend of a murder that lies at the foundation of the city and whose inquest threatens its stability. The silence surrounding the letter, the space it marks prior to signification, lies at the origin of language; this is what Derrida concludes, in resoundingly sacrificial terms, from his analysis of Saussure's demonstrably violent exclusion of writing from the field of linguistics: "Then one realizes that what was chased off limits, the wandering outcast of linguistics, has indeed never ceased to haunt language as its primary and most intimate possibility. The something which was never spoken and which is nothing other than writing itself as the origin of language writes itself within Saussure's discourse" (*OG* 44). This is to locate writing, for all intents and purposes, at the origin of culture as a system of differences and the representation of differences. That is what culture is: the institution of difference whereby language is possible and that language makes possible. It is the letter that represents—indeed, embodies or incarnates—this institution, that of the sign in its arbitrary relation to a natural environment: "The very idea of institution—hence of the arbitrariness of the sign—is unthinkable before the possibility of writing and outside of its horizon. Quite simply, that is, outside of the horizon itself, outside the world as space of inscription, as the opening to the emission and to the spatial *distribution* of signs, to the *regulated play* of their differences, even if they are 'phonic' " (*OG* 44). Writing properly represents culture as it is conceived here, as a hierarchy of differences and representations of differences, including the difference between nature and culture, which the latter alone inscribes and institutes. For Saussure and Rousseau, however, writing improperly represents language, distorting its " 'natural bond, the only true bond, the bond of sound,' " displacing " 'le cri de la nature,' " " 'le cri de la passion' " (*OG* 35, 36).

As it did with Plato before him and Saussure and Lévi-Strauss after, this "rupture with nature" (*OG* 36) leads Rousseau in turn to accuse writing of "the *forgetting* of a simple origin," which it displaces, supplements, usurps. "Writing, a mnemotechnic means, supplanting good memory, spontaneous memory, signifies forgetfulness," and it is for this "violence of forgetting" that writing is liable in turn to expulsion (*OG* 36). What is expelled in and as writing is the "double" of representation whose simple origin in nature it supplants. What is expelled with writing is the notion of a nonsimple origin, an originary parricide or fratricide; what is expelled, as I have shown with reference to Plato, is the violence of doubles, or violence itself. The structure of violence is complex because it is violence itself that expels another violence, the violence of doubles that it expels to (re)institute, "*en retour,*" a simple, nonviolent origin. "There is not an origin, that is to say a simple origin," for Derrida (*OG* 74) because the latter is constituted only by repeating the violence it expels, by dissimulating an originary violence, for it dissimulates its own violence in the violence it expels. The simple origin is accomplice to the nonsimple origin, the violence of doubles it expels. This "complicity of origins," as the violence that dissimulates itself in the expulsion of its other— its other self, its rival double, its true violent origin, the origin of its truth as violence, as constituted "by a desire for speech displacing its other and its double and working to reduce its difference" (*OG* 56)— this is what Derrida calls "arche-writing": "This complicity of origins may be called arche-writing. What is lost in that complicity is therefore the myth of the simplicity of origin. This myth is linked to the very concept of origin; to speech reciting the origin, to the myth of the origin and not only to myths of origin" (*OG* 92). There is no simple origin because its recitation requires the erasure of nonsimple origins and the erasure of that erasure. The structure of violence is complex because it is accomplice to its own erasure. Were I tempted to neologize after Derrida, the structure of this complexity might by styled as *violance*, thus encoding the trace, in the mode of the active participle, of its difference from and within itself, encoding its originary dissimulation.

The beginning, the origin, is a myth, being a misrecognition of violence by itself. For Girard, this is the very function of sacrifice: erasing the human origins of violence in the expulsion of the victim, in the sacralization of the victim whose divine violence dissimulates the community's own violence. The victim—like the letter for Derrida— is the fold, "*le pli*" (also for Derrida the hinge, "*la brisure*" [(*OG* 65]), in this structure of violent doubles, this com*pli*city of origins.

This neologistic wordplay and all these chiasmic reversals by which terms, phrases, and propositions turn on themselves, turning themselves inside out, all this syntactic invagination in Derrida's text is variously beguiling and annoying to readers. It is not in any event a gratuitous, formal device, as many adversaries of deconstruction accuse it of being and as many advocates of deconstruction have made of it. It *performs* the skewed relations of outside and inside, margin and center, copy and original, whose dissimulating structure it seeks to manifest. At a certain point of reflection (for example, on language origins, where self-reflection is the rule) such *detours* are perhaps inevitable, especially where difference emerges as a concealed identity. Despite Girard's reservations about such stylistic effects (which I discuss later), he pays implicit tribute to Derrida's discursive strategy when he observes, *à propos* the violent doubles in sacrificial crises, that "being made up of differences, language finds it almost impossible to express undifferentiation directly. Whatever it may say on the subject, language invariably says at once too much and too little, even in such concise statements as 'Each thing meets / In mere oppugnancy' or 'sound and fury, / Signifying nothing' " (*VS* 64). These phrases from Shakespeare's *Troilus and Cressida* and *Macbeth* evoke a violent loss of difference whose misapprehension generates a foundational difference. Derrida has regularly complained of saying less and more than he means and of his own structural complicity with metaphysics in that regard. Another phrase from Shakespeare bespeaks this dilemma. In *A Midsummer Night's Dream* Helena feels persecuted by Lysander's vows of love, although *and* because she is sworn to envy Hermia, Lysander's former lover, for being beloved as well by Demetrius whom she loves desperately. She exclaims, "When truth kills truth, O devilish-holy fray!" (act 3, scene 2, 129). This oxymoron speaks for the whole play insofar as it concerns rival lovers who lose their identity (see Girard, "Myth and Ritual in Shakespeare"). It also expresses the structural contradiction at the scene of origins, *chez* Rousseau and Lévi-Strauss, being examined by Derrida, where violence is a truth that violence expels. There is nothing simple about representing the complicity of violent origins, as Girard himself testifies: "Symbolized reality becomes, paradoxically, the loss of all symbolism; the loss of differences is necessarily betrayed by the differentiated expression of language. The process is a peculiar one, utterly foreign to our usual notions of symbolism" (*VS* 65). This peculiarity surfaces when confronted with a structuralist reading of symbolic violence, which it can oppose only to a mythic nonviolence and not to itself.

The fold or *pli* is what structuralism does not see in its confidence in binary opposition, in differential systems (the raw and the cooked, nature and culture, and so on) that indeed inform our usual notions of symbolism. In seeking correspondences between mythic or kinship patterns and differences in nature reflected in such patterns, structuralism renounces any scientific quest for cultural origins. Poststructuralism may be said to begin as a critique of this properly mythic confidence in difference, in binary opposition, which bears with it a belief in nonviolent origins, in naturally good savages who are living "in a 'state of culture' whose *natural* goodness had not yet been degraded" (*OG* 112). Lévi-Strauss holds writing to be a trademark of this degradation, as he argues in *Tristes Tropiques* (chap. 27, "La Leçon d' écriture"). Reminding us of the obvious fact that ethnographers write, both James Clifford and Renato Rosaldo have engaged deconstructive motifs in analyzing the benignly pastoral illusions that field anthropologists entertain about their object (Clifford and Marcus, eds., *Writing Culture* 96, 113). But the attention of anthropologists to deconstruction has as yet been limited to a critique of representation, whereas Derrida's reading extends to properly sacrificial motifs explicitly examined by Girard.

In reviewing Lévi-Strauss's efforts to elicit from Nambikwara children their proper names, which they are forbidden to reveal (*Tristes Tropiques* chap. 26), Derrida uncovers a scenario of violent origins of the kind that Girard has uncovered elsewhere in the anthropologist's structural reading of myth (*VS* chap. 9; *DBB* chaps. 8 and 9). Lévi-Strauss succeeds by coaxing one child to tattle on another, who had previously struck her, whereupon the others follow suit in reprisal, "*en guise de représailles*": "From then on, it was very easy, although rather unscrupulous, to incite the children against each other and get to know all their names. After which, having created a certain atmosphere of complicity, I had little difficulty in getting them all to tell me the names of the adults" (*Tristes Tropiques* 279; cited in *OG* 111). The taboo affecting the proper name prohibits revealing an order of classification, "the inscription within a system of linguistico-social differences" (*OG* 111); namely, culture itself in its difference and differentiating activity from nature.

It is here that Derrida observes that the "structure of violence is complex." There is first a violence in separating nature from culture, "the originary violence of language which consists in inscribing within a difference, classifying, in suspending the vocative absolute." It is accordingly labeled "arche-writing, arche-violence, loss of the proper, of absolute proximity, of self-presence." There is then a second violence, consisting in the taboo affecting the names; it is "reparatory, protective," concealing and thereby confirming this arche-violence, thus being "the effacement and obliteration of the so-called proper name which was already dividing the proper." Finally, there is a third violence, instigated by the anthropologist, which reveals the concealment and therefore the original rupture whose violence the concealment functioned to expel from consciousness. "It is on this tertiary level, that of the empirical consciousness, that the common concept of violence, (the system of the moral law and of transgression) whose possibility remains yet unthought, should no doubt be situated" (*OG* 112).

Each level of violence repeats the former in its dissimulating structure, each is a *mise en abîme* of originary violence, which culture functions to conceal—and not least in the person of the anthropologist. He acknowledges himself as the culprit, *"le coupable"* (*OG* 112), in instigating the mimetic violence of this "guerre des noms propres," as Derrida calls it. How should we regard him? He figures as the god presiding over this war, which he instigates and authorizes, but he also figures as the victim, as what the victim represents to culture—"the culprit," the excluded member, the insider outside, the origin of a violence that the community in no wise conceives as its own.

But the violence does not end here, for Derrida's role is not to be discounted. Tobin Siebers has astutely commented on Derrida's spectacular failure, a failure amounting to a concealment, to appreciate the fact that the revealing of names is instigated by empirical violence, in the form of one child striking another. Further violence is thereafter averted by being channeled into representational forms; it is deferred in and as revealing the name of the victim's adversary. As Siebers observes, "the 'Battle of Proper Names' illustrates with perfection the notion of 'differance,' but only if we understand that the object of deferral is violence. Here the system of writing hinders the escalation of physical aggression. The transgression defers the blow into a representational domain. The difference between the blow and the transgression is the reduction of violence in the latter" (*The Ethics of Criticism* 86). In sum, "violence is contained through representation" (92), that is, through language, and above all, language representing language,

language about names. This is no small accomplishment, no slight advantage over the endless reciprocity of blows. This is indeed how, with Derrida's help on the logical con-tortions of representing the victim, I have hypothesized the origin of language: in the mimetic designation of a victim whose mystified agency and consequent sacralization generates *homo sapiens* as a symbol-using animal. My discussion of ritual sacrifice as the periodic regeneration of culture has attempted to show that symbolization is indissociable from the concealment and alienation of human violence. It does no good attacking symbolic violence or the violence of symbols if their destruction leaves no space between violent antagonists (recall language, writing, and culture-as-writing as spatialization). For that is what the victim affords: the space of representation. To blame writing for a violence it serves to defer is a classically sacrificial gesture whereby "the containment is mistaken for cause." Siebers goes on to observe that "whatever dissipates violence and is identified as its last resting place is always seen as its source" (92). To mistake the victim for the violence, the effect for the cause, is the essence of scapegoating.

Thus Siebers's analysis poses serious problems, not for my correlation between Girard and Derrida, which sustains itself at the (post-) structural level, but for deconstruction as a critique of violence, for the properly sacrificial role of deconstruction itself as an institution. I return to these problems in the conclusion.

Indifferance

> ... on ne pratique pas impunément la duplicité de pensée, la pensée (du) double.
>
> —Borch-Jacobsen

Far from being one and indivisible for Girard, the origin is, to cite his only neologism, "interdividual" (see *THFW* part 3) as it proceeds from the mimetic rivalry of doubles whose violence is erased in the expulsion/sacralization of the victim, from a violence whose human origin is erased in the difference that divinity makes. Following Derrida, I spell this difference, that of the sacred, with an *a*, as differance, to represent the sacred as the difference of human violence from and within itself and as the dissimulation of that difference. The victim is the originary trace or the arche-trace of this violence, and it destroys its name as sacred, as antithetically holy and accursed. It destroys itself as value in the same way, in the same sense that arche-trace destroys itself as arche-. The victim has no value; all values derive from its expulsion in the same way that, though the letter has no value, all linguistic value, all meaning as representation, derives from its entombment or what its entombment represents: ob-literation of originary violence.

The sacred destroys its name in the same way that difference, as from an origin or as selfsame identity different from others, self-destructs, or deconstructs, as differance. As I mentioned earlier, it destroys its name in precisely the antithetical way that intrigued the author of *The Interpretation of Dreams*. For Freud this antithetical sense is important for understanding the language of dreams (see the *Standard Edition*, vol. 11, 162), for a science of dreams that are the representation of wish fulfillment. Dreams, he declares, are the "royal road to the unconscious," the path we must trace to formulate the science of desire that goes by the name of psychoanalysis. In *Le Sujet freudien*, Mikkel Borch-Jacobsen argues extensively—and I do not hesitate to say definitively as to the occluded agency of mimesis in psychoanalysis—that Freud's own desire for originality blinded him to the originality of his own discovery about dreams, that in his rivalry with Jung for scientific precedence and ascendancy he did not sufficiently attend to the mimetic origin of desire that is encoded, distorted, and misrepresented in dreams. From the viewpoint of this essay, Borch-Jacobsen's stunning analyses have the further, not to say decisive, interest of being a reading of Freud that combines—indeed fairly synthesizes—Girardian and Derridean perspectives. Perhaps the only thing the author leaves for me to do is to thematize his book's hermeneutic achievement, its unique critical gesture: to thematize, that is, the remarkable correlations between Girard and Derrida so as to argue, for instance, for concrete possibilities in the human sciences that Derrideans, perhaps more than Derrida himself, are apt to dismiss.

Nothing Derrida advances by way of his critique of origins or of representation as the representation of an original presence, nothing that goes by the name-that-erases-its-name of supplement, arche-trace, differance, and so on (or, by another name, *pharmakos*, as I argue in chapter 2)—nothing thus suggested is proof against Girard's anthropological hypothesis of human origins as rooted in the dynamics of mimetic desire. On the contrary, a "principled" critique of structuralism, a deconstruction of ontotheology (or ontotheologocentrism, as it is sometimes monstrously labeled), is one that clears a path to a genetic hypothesis that postulates the "complex" and accordingly undecidable origins of desire and the sacred, of the human and the holy as they issue in turn from a relation to a crypt, a corpse, a dead letter, a pure signifier.

The origin, or at the origin, is a repetition for Derrida. Girard's hypothesis argues no less. Thus, when Derrida paraphrases some verse of Edmund Jabès, an expatriate Egyptian Jew preoccupied with books and holocaust whose victimary thematics fairly predestined him a place in Derrida's canon, he produces a seemingly uncanny paraphrase of everything analyzed in this chapter: "Death is at the dawn because everything has begun with repetition. Once the center or the origin have begun by repeating themselves, by redoubling themselves, the double did not only add itself to the simple. It divided it and supplemented it. There was immediately a double origin plus its repetition. Three is the first figure of repetition. The last too, for the abyss of representation always remains dominated by its rhythm, infinitely. The infinite is doubtless neither one, nor empty, nor innumerable. It is of a ternary essence" (*WD* 299). These are not merely beguiling paradoxes; they repeat the structure of the scene(s) I have just reviewed, the scene of the foundational murder (Girard) and the originary scene of representation (Gans), which Borch-Jacobsen (*Le Sujet freudien* 149) incisively labels the "other scene as beyond the scene, the proscenium of originary mimesis" ("autre scène comme outre-scène, avant scène de la mimésis originaire") and of which the letter, as a repetition, is the mark and model. Three, not two, is the original figure of repetition for the same reason that it is the ultimate figure of infinity and of circularity, eternal return, and *Wiederholungszwang*, the compulsion to repeat—namely, because there is no object for a subject (as there is no nature for a culture) prior to another subject that designates it as an object of desire and because that subject in turn is constituted only by the other subject's desire, and so on, infinitely and undecidably. The origin of desire is undecidable, being ever only, or "always already" in deconstructivese, the copy, the repetition of another desire. It is always another subject that institutes a subject in its "undecidable identity" (Borch-Jacobsen, *Le Sujet freudien* 65). It is in virtue of this "recurrence that is originary" that the subject is forever "en retard sur son origine" (147): "The other was always already at the origin (without origin) of the individual and everything had already begun—everything, that is to say: history—in a *pre*history that is *prei*ndividual" (286).

Desire is the origin of this undecidability as it bears on a victim whose attraction ensures its repulsion; thus, it is also true that undecidability, as attraction-repulsion, is the origin of desire. These two statements do not contradict each other; rather, they are themselves undecidable. In this sense, then, undecidability is truth, as deconstructionists claim, but this is not grounds for conclusions about our inability to know anything, as some have argued. On the contrary, it is grounds for understanding desire as what makes us human, and never more so than when we dissimulate its origin and its power by locating them in the object. It is also grounds for understanding our desire for truth, for understanding what makes truth desirable, namely, the victim, as I argue further in the next chapter.

The victim is the origin of an indecision, the focus of an originary indecision, an irreducible ambivalence, in which our species is born along with the sacred. Desire is the origin of the sacred, which is only the erasure of the mimetic (non)origin of desire; the sacred is the originary *dis-simulation* of violence in the original sense of the word, which is that of concealing a resemblance. The logic of desire is contrary to the logic of identity and difference, of identity and noncontradiction, both as to its origin and as to its signification. A culture develops according to principles of identity and difference as long as it succeeds in masking that resemblance. It develops in differentiating between good and bad victims as between others and one's self, one's own.

Today we apprehend that culture is in crisis (as perhaps all great writers have seen: "Qui la ramène à son principe," Pascal said of it, "l'anéantit."), and not least because of activities like deconstruction, whose problematic of difference we may regard as "a new name for some old ways of thinking." This, of course, is the way William James characterized pragmatism, whose alliance with Derrida has been suggested by Richard Rorty in *Consequences of Pragmatism* (90–109), though the full consequences of this "postphilosophical" juncture await elaboration. This way is at least as old as the Enlightenment insofar as it detects false dichotomies and illusory differences, such as man and Moslem or human and Hottentot, as did Montesquieu, Voltaire, and Diderot. It would be erroneous to reduce deconstruction to Enlightenment demystification, but it would be equally so to deny its continuity with that tradition just because it questions in turn the ontology of the latter.

This is not to say that nothing has changed, that history is illusory or that no progress is probable or possible. The progressively *leveling* effects of modern culture, as intuited by Pascal and Tocqueville, are real. These effect are legible in and as deconstruction itself, which is but a symptom of a widespread crisis of difference. Technological progress is indubitable, both for weal and woe, and deconstruction offers real intellectual progress when it traces technological progress to our peculiarly writerly culture, to the *technè* of formal marking that attracted and repelled Plato. Deconstruction is necessarily ambiguous about its own progress over metaphysics, which it cannot oppose without becoming accomplice to the latter's binary habits of construction. Being able neither to destroy nor ally itself with our philosophical tradition, it advertises itself as its variously dangerous or playful supplement, in which the violence of metaphysical oppositions is displayed. Its very playfulness is its danger as it issues in a formal critique of difference, of representation, from which nothing remains but language, text, writing—whose prestige is just that it does not represent anything. (Well, not quite, for according to the analyses being conducted here, it represents, stands in the place of, and conforms to the destiny of the victim.) Critics have had a field day with that, as deconstructionists gleefully played the goat, giddily flaunting its textual excesses to what was discovered or invented as an oppressive, theologocentric humanism—and the humanists went for the bait. *Polemos* is kingmaker in criticism.

That game is pretty much over, and perhaps there is little enough to show for it. Not much is left of the differences in which philosophy and culture confide. Little enough remains, but that little is precious enough. What remains is the victim, and that is the rock on which the entire cultural edifice can be reconstructed with a sense of the truth of its differences. Here, a moral imperative is indissociable from cognitive deduction.

It is because of deconstruction, rather than in spite of it, that perhaps only one difference now remains. (I say "perhaps" because there is of course sexual difference. On the one hand, this difference is hotly disputed by those who see its determinations as an effect of language; on the other, its critical focus, the manifold oppression of women, is aligned with the difference being argued here [see Siebers, *The Ethics of Criticism* chap. 8]). But it is irreducible, "uncircumventable," or "unbypassable," as the French word *incontournable* in Derridean texts is variously translated. It is a good word; it means you cannot get around it. It is the difference between victim and persecutor, in the name of which the quest for truth as opposed to sacred or sacralized authority is decided. These decisions are being made every day in our institutions; in our schools, our law courts, and our councils of power these decisions are increasingly called into question as the difference between good and bad victims becomes increasingly problematic in the face of revealing traces of violence that all disown—disown, that is, as one's own violence, for we are always prepared to confront another's violence as violently as you please. As Girard observes, it is victims themselves that we hurl at each other in our denunciations of violence (*VO* 140). They have become trajectories in a battle of words, an alibi for further violence. As a consequence, they are victimized a second time, for being passed over by a desire on its predestined route to violence. What Girard wrote in 1962 of masochism, of a perversely self-confident suffering as a principle of justification, is equally true of terrorism today: "Compassion is never a principle but a result. The principle is hatred of the triumphant wicked. Good is loved in order that Evil be hated more. The oppressed are defended for the sake of overwhelming the oppressors" (*DDN* 189). Sacrificial dismemberment will out. The victim, shorn of its referential status, has become a signifier of truth, of moral ascendancy in modern culture, a fact that some critics trace to none other than Rousseau (Gans, "The Victim as Subject"; Kavanagh, *Writing the Truth*).

But the transcendence of this signifier in Rousseau's case is debatable. Every persecutor sees him- or herself as a victim (of poisoned wells, a stab in the back, etc.), and the vengeful strain in Rousseau's writings is unmistakable: "Born sensitive and kindly, carrying pity to the point of weakness, and feeling my soul exalted by all that is akin to generosity, I was humane, benevolent, charitable from taste, from passion even, so long as my heart alone was concerned; I should have been the best and the most clement of men if I had been the most powerful, and in order to extinguish in me all desire of vengeance, it would have been enough to have the power to avenge myself" (*Rêveries du promeneur solitaire* VI, in *OC* 1:1053). Even taking Rousseau at his word here, his claim is enunciated in the conditional contrary to fact, whereby we are entitled to conceive his vengeance as endless.

Disowning one's own violence as another's, as being the other's, as originating with the other, is the surest means of its perpetuation. It is the functional, effective—and not merely formal—equivalent of dissimulating the other's desire as our own, of claiming as one's own the other's desire.

So the wheel goes round, but decidedly not infinitely. In the age of nuclear proliferation—or in Derridean terms, "dissemination," which could be shown to have to same aboriginal, anarcheological structure as both nuclear fission and strategic deterrence—the victim is the focus of a decision from which humankind cannot distract its attention, for the wrong decision would prove definitive for the species.

The game is not endless, not *simply* because of our lethal technological progress, as if it were an accident of history ready to befall us at any moment, but in a complex way that the very notion of differance helps us to understand. It is not in spite of differance but just because of it that the game appears to be up. For there is no "free-play of differences," no *"jeu libre des différences,"* that is not bound by temporal constraints, whereupon we are obliged to conclude that the game is not free. And this is just because of what differance is: the temporalization of space, the spatialization of time, which is just what disallows any confidence in a metaphysics of presence. As Cesareo Bandera has observed, the free-play would be endless *"if the game were immune to time,* if time were not also involved in the game, if a blank were not also a pause, if *la différance* were not also a deferring of the differences. As it is, we cannot possibly talk about the deferring of the differences without talking about the time involved in such deferring" ("Notes on Derrida" 321). Because time is irreversible, the game is structurally bound to accelerate with the erosion of differences, with their inevitable deconstruction, with the closure of metaphysics, for no sooner is a difference postulated than it is liable to be deconstructed and demythologized, shown to inhabit, inform, and enfold its other. The result has been ably summarized by Bandera:

> The point is that, as the game accelerates, there will be more and more differences in less and less time. And since the reciprocal differentiation depends on the duration of their deferring, the shorter this duration becomes the less distinctly different will they be from one another. Which means that beyond a certain time threshold *la différance* begins to work in reverse, against itself, actively promoting a state of general undifferentiation, for there will be a diminishing number of differences

capable of making any difference whatsoever. Beyond such a point *la différance* turns into *l'indifférance*. In other words, the game that Derrida has uncovered in his deconstruction of metaphysics cannot be postulated as endless—not because there is anything external to it that would stop it or destroy it, but because it can generate its own destruction *in time*. ("Notes on Derrida" 322)

I can scarcely imagine a better argument for the historical relevance of deconstruction, or even perhaps for its scientific relevance. One imagines a cyclotron, where atoms of meaning, constantly bombarded by the gramm, accelerate and split explosively. What has become infinite and limitless from the human, historical perspective is the potential cycle of violence, or the violence of the game itself, for there is nothing outside it, no king or divinity, to arrest the play of its differences, to inhibit "this conflictuality of differance" (Derrida, *Positions* 44).

Deconstruction does not generate this crisis of difference, which I have identified as the sacrificial crisis. It is only symptomatic of its acceleration, which it enhances and magnifies by its demonstration that *"there is nothing outside of the text* [there is no outside-text; *il n'y a pas de hors texte]" (OG* 158), that there is nothing outside the game, no stable center to the structure, no transcendental signified that can anchor or arrest the substitution and displacement of signifiers. Contrary to the jubilation of deconstructors, who rejoice in "the vertigo of seeing meanings resolve endlessly into other meanings" (Schneidau, "The Word against the Word," in *Semeia 23* 17), this is not grounds for celebration, for what is in play is mimetic desire as it leads to violence. This is not an interpolation on my part but rather Derrida's own lucid vision of this chain reaction, this *"enchainement déchainé"*:

This process of substitution [that of Theuth, the god of writing, for the king-god Ra], which thus functions as a pure play of traces or supplements, or, again, operates within the order of the pure signifier which no reality, no absolutely external reference, no transcendental signified, can come to limit, bound, or control; this substitution, which could be judged "mad" since it can go on infinitely in the element of the linguistic permutation of substitutes, of substitutes for substitutes; this unleashed chain is nevertheless not lacking in violence. One would not have understood anything of this "linguistic" imminence" if one saw it as the peaceful milieu of a merely fictional war, an inoffensive word-play, in contrast to some raging *polemos* in "reality." It is not in any reality foreign to the "play of words" that Theuth also frequently participates in plots, perfidious intrigues, conspiracies to usurp the throne. He helps the sons do away with the father, the brothers do away with the brother that has become king. (PP 89)

The "madness" of this substitution is its infinity, so that no meaning can be arrested or come to rest but is always only, or "always already," the "*restance*" of its polar opposite—but only "in the element of the linguistic permutation of substitutes." In "reality"—that is, in history, in the global village that is our polis—the quotation marks come off, the madness is literal. As if providentially revealed by history, it is evidenced in the name of Mutually Assured Destruction, in which appears the historical form of our crisis of difference. It is immanent in history as the history of ever-accelerating violence. As the difference between matter and energy erodes, empirical violence knows no material limits. As the difference between totally destructive strategies erodes, the likelihood of apocalypse, its historical immanence, scares the hell out of everybody concerned, and all are concerned. By its own internal laws, differance, which rules that the external is internal, leaves no space, least of all outer space, between violent antagonists.

So we have had mimetic policies of deterrence, which we might also spell with an *a*, as *deterrance*, for at least two reasons: it invites us to recall both the terrain it protects and the terror (from *de-terrere*) it perpetuates and in which it originates. For deterrance is nothing but the deference we pay to the sacred, to absolute violence, in its difference from itself, or its differance as it originates in mimetic dissimulation and menaces and protects undecidably.

No one is immune to that violence, which Winston Churchill was perhaps the first to evoke in a language replete with the dynamics of our sacred origins: "Safety," he said to the House of Commons in 1955, "will be the sturdy child of terror, and survival the twin brother of annihilation" (cited in Schell, *The Fate of the Earth* 197). Here again, language is very telling. The genius of Churchill's chiasmic formulation pinpoints the structural indifference of safety and annihilation, of survival and terror; they have functioned as rival twins whose alternation makes the world go round in the form of alter nations whose differences, however real, dissolve in the face of the violence that both threatens and protects them.

While I am citing "literary" references to history, let me recall Hölderlin's verse for its resonance with Churchill's oratory: "But where danger is, / grows the saving power also." Heidegger cites this text along with the statement that "poetically dwells man upon this earth" to conjoin philosophy with art. He concludes with this paraphrase: "The closer we come to the danger, the more brightly do the ways into the saving power begin to shine and the more questioning we become. For questioning is the piety of thought" ("The Question concerning Technology," *Basic Writings* 317). But just as Hölderlin has observed, the saving power never goes without the danger, whose shining power radiates from the explosive proliferation of solar (nuclear) energy on the planet. Heidegger is fond of contrasting the radiance of the Greek temple over the shimmering waters of the Mediterranean to the industrial power station polluting the air and water of the Rhine, without ever reflecting that the Greek temple was first and foremost a power station, being the locus of sacrifice to the divinity's saving power. The danger in our day consists in any such resolute piety, in sacralizing questioning, the question of being, or philosophy itself. What is passed over in silence throughout Heidegger's writings is the victim (see Caputo, "Heidegger's Scandal: Thinking and the Essence of the Victim"), whose call (*"rufen"*) is not heard in "Questions concerning Technology," though its vertiginous career is foreseeably closed by our very proximity to the origins of piety: the holy, the sacred, violence by name. Heidegger's thinking is shrewdly intact when he resists any identification between the Greek tradition of logos and its Johannine formulation as victim (see *THFW* 264–75). Churchill and Hölderlin for their part echo what Girard writes of the sacrificial god, Dionysus by name, but Titan, Saturn, Minuteman, or any other will do: "He will be as benevolent from afar as he was terrible in propinquity" (*VS* 134). It is the same violence, its propinquity or distance being its differance, its difference from itself. Derridean analysis helps show how the Girardian sacred is the origin of propinquity and distance, of presence and absence, of a time before and a time after. Girardian analysis protects us in turn from the delusion that originary differance favors complacency about our temporal and spatial finitude or that it destines us to infinite meaninglessness, for the finite end of meaning, as between life and death, is within palpable reach. Indeed, Girard lends a meaning and a value to deconstruction that its adherents at times seem only too anxious to elide or ignore.

We have grown accustomed to thinking that we inhabit a world from which absolute values are absent, and have been absent since the French Revolution—or the Enlightenment, or Cartesian epistemol-

ogy, or Galileo (whose status, by the way, as a victim of sacralized persecution accounts as much as anything else for the destabilizing
import of his scientific discovery: as narrated by Giorgio de Santillana
in *The Crime of Galileo*, his trial has all the marks of a "botched kill,"
"la structure d'hallali manqué," which is how Girard leads us to see
the trials of Job [*Job* 26]). Nonetheless, much of our presumed relativism is nonsense. We inhabit a world of absolute values; for proof we
need only regard the violence that attends the imposition of or rivalry
between these values. Violence is nothing if not the signifier of the
absolute, the form and substance of absolute desire. The absolute is
alive and well among us; the question is whether we can live it down,
or outlive it, survive it. It is a question of "living on," "*survivre*," to
borrow from the title of the Derrida essay discussed in the next chapter. The indecision attending this question is a scandal to our ordinary
powers of rational deduction. Yet, it should not surprise us if we read
Girard correctly, for our desire to live on hinges on decisions that desire, being what it is (the other's, allogenetic), does not make.

Girard's conception of desire, which according to *Deceit, Desire and
the Novel* is revealed by our greatest writers, accounts for the seemingly
derealizing effects of deconstruction as it undermines our confidence
in such concepts as subject and object, substance, referent, and so
on—the entire host of metaphysically derived concepts that we take to
be percepts or realities. In the Derridean critique of ontology, these
are to be inscribed within an economy of differance: "Nothing—no
present and in-*different* being—thus precedes *différance* and spacing.
There is no subject who is agent, author, and master of *différance*, who
eventually and empirically would be overtaken by *différance* [which *différance* would take the place of, "*surviendrait*"]. Subjectivity—like ob-
jectivity—is an effect of *différance*, an effect inscribed in a system of
différance" (*Positions* 28). This is indeed how I have described desire,
in its "active *and* passive movement," as it produces an object producing subjects desiring it. In fact, I can substitute the word *desire* for
differance in every instance of this text, which goes on as follows:

> This is why the *a* of *différance* also recalls that spacing is temporalizing,
> the detour and postponement by means of which intuition, perception,
> consummation—in a word, the relationship to the present, the refer-
> ence to a present reality, to a *being*—are always *deferred*. Deferred by
> virtue of the very principle of difference which holds that an element
> functions and signifies, takes on or conveys meaning, only by referring

to another past or future element in an economy of traces. This economic aspect of *différance*, which brings into play a certain not conscious calculation in a field of forces, is inseparable from the more narrowly semiotic aspect of *différance*. It confirms that the subject, and first of all the conscious and speaking subject, depends upon the system of differences and the movement of *différance*, that the subject is not present, nor above all present to itself before *différance*, that the subject is constituted only in being divided from itself, in becoming space, in temporalizing, in deferral; and it confirms that, as Saussure said, "language [which consists only of differences (JD)] is not a function of the speaking subject." (*Positions* 28–29)

Indeed not, for language is a function of desire precisely as difference. The subject's "being divided by itself" is its mimetic constitution, what Girard calls its interdividuality. Conceiving difference as desire, whose objects are but the signifiers or traces of another desire, shows the ontologically decentering import of Girard's displacement of both subject and object by desire "itself": "If desire is the same for all of us, and if it is the key to the system of relationships, there is no reason not to make of it the real 'subject' of the structure—a subject that comes back to mimesis in the end. I avoid saying 'desiring subject' so as not to give the impression of relapsing into a psychology of the subject" (*THFW* 303).

As there is for Derrida "no economy without *différance*," which is "the most general structure of economy" (*Positions* 8), there is for Girard no economy—not even in the "restricted" sense, the one Derrida calls "classical"—without desire. To fully demonstrate this homology, one need only correlate Derrida's discussion of Georges Bataille, entitled "De l'économie restreinte à l'économie générale" (in *WD*), with the several works of a decisively Girardian stamp devoted to this topic by Georges-Hubert de Radkowski (*Les Jeux du désir: De la technique à l'économie*), Michel Aglietta and André Orléan (*La Violence de la monnaie*), Paul Dumouchel and Jean-Pierre Dupuy (*L'Enfer des choses: René Girard et la logique de l'économie*), and Eric Gans (*The End of Culture: Toward a Generative Anthropology*), who acknowledges the economic import of differance while further engaging the socioeconomic theories of Marvin Harris, Marshall Sahlins, and Jean Baudrillard. Pending extensive, doubtless book-length elaboration, suffice it for the nonce to observe that according to Girard's conception, and as filled out by the analyses just mentioned, everything passes by the detour and postponement of desire, which functions and signifies like the elements described in Saussurian linguistics, "above all else opposing, relative, and negative entities" (Saussure, *Course in General Linguistics* 119).

The Subject (of) Violence

> There is a definite social relation between men, that assumes, in their eyes, the fantastic form of a relation between things. In order, therefore, to find an analogy, we must have recourse to the mist-enveloped regions of the religious world.
>
> —Marx

> If we look at the most enlightened portion of the world, we see the various States armed to the teeth, sharpening their weapons in time of peace the one against the other.
>
> —Kant

Economic com-petition is ruled by mimetic desire, which is not ruled, governed, or mastered in any way by a value emanating from the object, the commodity, but controlled only by another desire. The advertising industry exploits this fact when it regularly focuses less on the object of consumption than on the image, that is, the imitation, of its hierophantically self-possessed consumers. Thus too, from the present perspective, Marx's genially droll analysis of the commodity fetish approaches its comic apex when it describes the "metaphysical subtleties," the "theological niceties," as a "necromancy that surrounds the products of labor as long as they take the form of commodities" (*Capital* 71–76). For these and still other religious figures express the sacralization of the product in its "social form," whereby "the process of production has the mastery over man, instead of being controlled by him" (81). Necromancy suggests a corpse whose interpretation governs the economy, which for Marx means that something, a product of labor, is transformed into nothing, "a social hieroglyphic" (74). Notwithstanding Marx's efforts to revive that corpse by demystifying its producers, what is germane to my project is the simultaneous religious inflation and ontological nullity of the object in its social form. The two always go together; indeed, they reinforce each other as the mimetic nature of competition and conflict works to ensure "son néant ultime d'objet": "Nothing is more difficult than to admit the fundamental nullity of human conflict. For the conflicts of others, no problem; but for our own conflicts, it is almost

impossible. *All* modern ideologies are huge machines which function
to justify and legitimate just those conflicts which these days could
put an end to mankind's existence. Man's entire madness is right
there. If we don't admit the madness of human conflict today, we will
never admit it. If the conflict is mimetic, the equally mimetic resolution leaves no residue; it purges the community entirely precisely
because *there is no object*" (*THFW* 31; see also 310–11). Neither the
subject nor the object takes precedence in this "Discours sur le peu
de réalité." This is how Girard, taking the phrase from the surrealists,
styles the genius of Flaubert, whose *Bouvard et Pécuchet* attacks "science and ideology—the very essence of the bourgeois conception of
reality all-powerful at the time" (*DDN* 151; on Flaubert's symbolic discourse on violence as the latter issues from an erosion of differences,
see McKenna, "Allodidacticism" and "Flaubert's Freudian Thing").

What takes precedence to subject and object alike, and to all ontological determinations, is desire—precisely, the desire for precedence. This is not to deny the reality of objects, as somewhat averred
by Borch-Jacobsen (114–15), but to trace their derealization by the increasingly violent desire of rival subjects. Just where people insist
most vehemently on the originality of their desire, or on its real objective origin (remember Molière), is where desire is most liable to become mimetic. Originality becomes the object of desire, displacing its
former object, however discrete or appetitive to begin with. It is still
ontological desire, as it were, if it is conceived as a desire for being that
the other unknowingly transmits to the self, with which the other con-
*tam*inates the self (according to the undecidable structure of the "*en-
tame*," another trace word in Derrida): "Once his basic needs are
satisfied (indeed, sometimes even before), man is subject to intense
desires, though he may not know precisely for what. The reason is
that he desires *being*, something he himself lacks and which some
other person seems to possess. The subject thus looks to that other
person to inform him of what he should desire in order to acquire that
being. If the model, who is apparently already endowed with superior
being, desires some object, that object must surely be capable of con-
ferring an even greater plenitude of being" (*VS* 146). The terms of ontological plenitude, of ontotheology as critiqued by Derrida, are in
place; indeed, they have been so since *Deceit, Desire and the Novel*,
which evokes the delusions of desire as "ontological sickness," as "ontological scission" (137)—in a word, as differance. What Derrida's

critique lacks is any intersubjective dimension, any focus on the mimetic rivalry that generates these terms, these conceptual illusions. As this rivalry intensifies, violence itself becomes the object of desire (*VS* 145), displacing the initial object—the other's object or the other's very being as an object of desire—until things heat up to such an intensity that violence will displace desire altogether as subject. This is where we have found ourselves today, as we contemplate the rivalry for the disposition of total violence, of "total and remainderless destruction," as Derrida characterizes it in his contribution to "nuclear criticism" ("No Apocalypse . . ." 27). This essay, to which I will return momentarily, thematizes the previously mentioned temporal acceleration of violence, above all by its title: "No Apocalypse, Not Now (full speed ahead, seven missiles, seven missives)."

According to Borch-Jacobsen, the prospect of total war is always already *present* with the dual emergence of subjects, of mimetic doubles. It is the original and ultimate destiny, the eschatology of our ontological project, as is clear in this Hegelian paraphrase (or hyperbole) of Girard:

> The rage which takes hold of me at the sight of my neighbor does not come from the fact that he dispossesses me of something, but rather that he steals me, inexplicably, from myself. Whence the total, totalitarian character of the war in which we are engaged and which no satisfaction can pacify: "It's him or me." . . . There is a violence inherent to the very *appearance* of the other; all empirical violence testifies to it; it has no other "reason" than desire (*that is to say self-consciousness*) which seeks its own self in the other and wishes to exist for its own self, independently and close by itself in its self-possession [*dans sa propriété:* as its own property, etc.]. Desire is violence because it is desire to be one's own self, [*désir d'être propre*],desire of propriation and, as such, a desire that is allergic, murderous. (Borch-Jacobsen, *Le Sujet freudien* 115)

For Borch-Jacobsen, this *désir d'être propre* engages all the ambiguities of property, of author- and ownership, that Derrida explores in "White Mythology" as undecidable (in *Margins of Philosophy*). "Le désir est un désir impropre du propre—mimésis de propriation" (*Le Sujet freudien* 115).

But we need not accede to the a priori bleakness of this radically metaphysical depiction of intersubjective rivalry, for it virtually denies to mimetic conflict the existence of any object other than "reconnaissance." The same problem emerges in Borch-Jacobsen's interpretation of Lacan (*Lacan: Le Maître absolu*), whose thinking is traced to Alexandre Kojève's reading of Hegel, where man = desire = desire of the other's desire = desire of nothing = desire of death—whereby Borch-Jacobsen appears to rejoin certain Freudian postulates (*Todestriebe*, or death instinct) that his reading of Freud genially disqualifies. In my view, Girard rightly insists that the object is initially essential to appropriative mimesis, whence the institution of taboos affecting such natural desirables as women and food, which are inherently liable to foment rivalry (*THFW* 27f). The theory of appropriative rivalry is accordingly not devoid of an economic, material foundation, whose erosion is the work of mimetic desire in a more complex culture. But here again Borch-Jacobsen differs far less from Girard than from all the uncritical readings of Freud and Marx that, ignoring the role of mediation, merely repeat their theories and attempt to apply them to history. This is why I urge attention to Eric Gans's effort to complete the institutional theory with his formal theory of representation, which accounts for both reference and reverence, for physical and metaphysical desire. Both dimensions are clearly active on the scene of history: humankind certainly does satisfy simple appetitive needs and just as clearly embarks on fantastical and fantastically sanguinary adventures, of which the prospect of total war is the perfection, the consummation. What unites Girard, Gans, and Borch-Jacobsen against most research in literature, philosophy, and the social sciences is the heuristic fecundity of the mimetic hypothesis, of mimetism as the key to cultural interpretation. Nietzsche boasted that with the "will to power" he held the key to history. I make the identical claim in these pages for one or another variant of Girard's mimetic hypothesis as a goad to similarly oriented research in natural science, economics, and political culture. Our intellectual climate remains resistant to "metanarratives" in favor of thick descriptions, regional ontologies, and uniquely local histories. But Marcel Gauchet, whose project for a religious history appears concordant with Girard's own, provides the warrant for such inclusive research in *Le Désenchantement du monde: Une Histoire politique de la religion:*

It is not a question of revoking the demands for information and proof which the new disciplines concerning man in society have developed over the last century. But it is no longer possible to dispense with the kind of theoretical and philosophical questioning with which the latter thought they had broken. We must go beyond these disciplines while conserving what they have taught us in content and method to reforge links with the "speculative" and "totalizing" tradition that they did not really succeed in interrupting—proscription and anathema (of a Freud, a Durkheim) spring from a deception: Montesquieu or Rousseau, Tocqueville or Marx continue to tell us more about society than the whole of sociology put together. (xxii)

Internecine war does not happen every day, not ostensibly so. We have institutions whose exact purpose is to mask the violence informing relations between self and other, to deflect it away from the community. Nevertheless, we know that they are breaking down, that they cannot withstand the deinstitutionalizing, deritualizing impulses of Western culture, which is perhaps that of all culture (Gans, *The Origin of Language* 227), which we have called Enlightenment and which today goes by the name of deconstruction, and which Nietzsche, anticipating Girard on this point as well as others, ascribes to the relentless truth-seeking impulse of Christianity itself: "*What*, in all strictness, has really *conquered* the Christian God? The answer may be found in my *Gay Science* (section 357): 'Christian morality itself, the concept of truthfulness taken more and more strictly, the confessional subtlety of the Christian conscience translated and sublimated into the scientific conscience, into intellectual cleanliness at any price' " (*On the Genealogy of Morals* 160). The refined linguistic sensibilities of deconstruction reflect this impulse even as it attacks the scientific conscience, as when it archly deconstructs the Enlightenment (*Of Grammatology*, passim). Where Girard differs from it is in his anthropological focus on the victim as the origin of our truth seeking and as revealed in Scripture (*THFW* part 2; *VO* 109–45; *The Scapegoat* chap. 15; *Job* passim. For deconstruction's "genealogy" in Nietzsche, see Schrift, in Silverman and Welton, eds., *Postmodernism and Continental Philosophy;* for Girard and Nietzsche on the victim, see Siebers, *The Ethics of Criticism* ch. 6).

According to this view, the breakdown of institutional Christianity is the legacy of the crucifixion narrative, which is one with the Hebrew Bible's denunciation of overtly sacrificial institutions, indeed, of all forms of victimization. In our day this denunciation is pandemic in its extension to covertly sacrificial institutions, uncovering victimization everywhere from law (Unger; Denvir; Norris chap. 7; Elias) to philosophy, whose arbitrary differences no longer protect us from a violence we have to own up to. This is especially the case with the forlorn institution known as war, which in the nuclear age is *"fabulously textual*, through and through" (Derrida, "No Apocalypse" 23) for being unwinnable, unwageable, unthinkable—or at least *"inénarrable*," as it leaves no witnesses to represent it. For Derrida, the ontological implications are unambiguous, for war finally resolves our crisis of representation:

> The only referent that is absolutely real is thus of the scope or dimension of an absolute nuclear catastrophe that would irreversibly destroy the entire archive and all symbolic capacity, would destroy the "movement of survival," what I call *"survivance*," at the very heart of life. This absolute referent of all possible literature is on a par with the absolute effacement of any possible trace; it is thus the only ineffaceable trace, it is so as the trace of what is entirely other, *"trace du tout autre*." This is the only absolute trace,—effaceable, ineffaceable. The only "subject" of all possible literature, of all possible criticism, its only ultimate and a-symbolic referent, unsymbolizable, even unsignifiable; this is, if not the nuclear age, if not the nuclear catastrophe, at least that towards which nuclear discourse and the nuclear symbolic are *still beckoning:* the remainderless and a-symbolic destruction of literature. Literature and literary criticism cannot speak of anything else, they can have no other ultimate referent, they can only multiply their strategic maneuvers in order to assimilate that unassimilable wholly other. ("No Apocalypse . . . " 28)

Derrida does not name this "wholly other" as the sacred; he does not have to, for that is what philosophers since Hegel have named it. But Derrida exceeds the imaginative reach of philosophers in naming its referent as absolute violence. If it is the "subject" of all literature and criticism—indeed, of all possible cultural discourse—it is because violence, as Girard argues, is the true subject, the active and passive agent, the agendum and dilendum, of all cultural institutions, of institutional formation and dissolution. Whereas for Derrida literature consists in deferring this total dissolution, for Girard it has the superior merit, in its greatest moments, of referring directly to it—recall the foundational and universal significance he attaches to Heraclitus's dictum, as it appears at the beginning and the end of *Violence and the Sacred:* "Strife [*polemos*] is the father and king of all. Some it makes gods, others men; some slaves, and others free" (*VS* 88, 318). In the final analysis, to which nuclear war's finality fairly impels us, the category of reference appears to be more imposing, more revealing for literary studies than that of differance—not in spite of Derrida but just because of what he says about "the only 'subject' of all possible literature, of all possible criticism," the "ultimate referent": violence. In answer to the question about the seemingly "hypostatic," personified role of violence in his discourse, Girard asserts that "violence, in all cultural orders, is always in the final analysis the true *subject* of every structure that is ritual, institutional, etc." (*THFW* 210, trans. modified).

The "etc." here is peculiarly expressive, for it marks a pleonasm: what institution, on examination of its origin, structure, and dynamics, is not to some degree ritual? I attempted to show this earlier in sketching out the (admittedly masked) continuity of a number of Western institutions with sacrificial practices. In his nearly encyclopedic survey of institutions, D. L. O'Keefe has argued seriously, and I think successfully, for seeing the ritualistic character of the social sciences themselves (*Stolen Lightning* 104–8). This is not a mere facile irony, a self-mocking ploy of academic journalism. Western history, particularly in the form of scientific progress, has proceeded apace with a process of desacralization, of deritualization, but only by the transfer, the displacement, of ritual practices from one institution to another. As this process becomes more conscious of itself and accordingly more transparent, it inevitably results in the process of deinstitutionalization with which history and progress began. This is the theory of Eric Gans's *Origin of Language*, which built on Girard's originary hypothesis and was destined to issue in a theory about the end of culture, the end being a theory of cultural self-understanding, "a genuinely scientific anthropology" that owes nothing to ritual practices (*The End of Culture* 52). Science replaces culture, which is a good thing if it means that knowledge replaces sacrificial practices. Whether this expectation is premature or preposterous is open to debate. What is not open to debate is the correlate processes of desacralization, or deritualization, and deinstitutionalization, as shown by our institutional crises everywhere from the law courts to literature, whose self-divisive strategies have begun to invade law journals (see Rose, *Dialectic of Nihilism: Post-structuralism and Law*).

Our aggressive secularization does not for all that fail to betray its continuity with religious institutions, as Girard shows when he continues his reflections on violence as the true subject: "From the time when the sacrificial order begins to come apart, this subject can no longer be anything but the *adversary par excellence*, which combats the installation of the Kingdom of God. This subject is the devil named by tradition, precisely the one whom theology declares to be the subject and whom it nonetheless declares not to exist" (*THFW* 210, trans. modified). Not to exist, that is, as an unambiguous substance, a principle incarnate. For the devil, even according to theological tradition cited here, does not *simply* exist, but doubly. Its duplicity is ontological. The duality of the devil is redoubled in itself; it is not the Antichrist incarnate, the traditional rival double of the savior; its *adversity* is that of a being whose power issues from its not being, as being only the illusory being of the other. Its violence is "the exercise of the illusion of difference" (Dumouchel, "Différences et paradoxes," in Deguy, ed., *René Girard et le problème du mal* 218).

Girard's reference to theology is anything but traditional. He reverses the theological conundrum wherein the devil's ruses extend to persuading us that he does not exist so as to persuade us that evil does not exist, such duplicity ensuring the even greater sway of evil among us. For Girard, the ruse of the devil is to persuade us that he does exist in person, substantially, whereby the evil that people do is expelled, projected outside them and into the agency of an incorrigibly ill will that is the alien rival of human good will.

This explains our ineluctable and irreducible ambivalence toward Rousseau, whose affirmation of his own good will is one we cannot dissociate from "*la Terreur*" and every revolutionary purge since then. Jean Starobinski ably suggests the link: "Did Robespierre get his unshakable belief in his own goodness from Rousseau? It was a belief they shared, with similar consequences in each case; since evil exists, they both held that it only exists elsewhere. It is fomented by others, by conspirators, by evil souls. Because that fear was not groundless in every case, it led them to generalize their mistrust to the point of losing touch with reality. Limitless suspicion brought limitless punishment" ("Rousseau in the Revolution" 50). This is the sacrificial—or logocentric—principle, as formulated by Eric Santner, that "evil remains that which intervenes from the outside into an otherwise pure and innocent inside" (*Stranded Objects* 6).

But to reify evil and personify the devil in this way is to mask the role of the mimetic double, of the violent rival of a will that is ill for being but the transposition or transfer of the other's desire. The devil does not exist except as this qui pro quo of mimetically violent doubles, as this rivalry of non-entities: "The genius of the novel rises above the oppositions that stem from metaphysical desire. It tries to show us their illusory character. It transcends the rival caricatures of Good and Evil presented by the factions. It affirms the identity of the opposites on the level of internal mediation. But it does not end in moral relativism. Evil exists . . . and it is metaphysical desire itself—deviated transcendency—which weaves man's thread in the wrong direction, thus separating what it claims to unite and uniting what it claims to separate. Evil is that negative pact of hatred to which so many men adhere for their mutual destruction" (*DDN* 192). The devil is merely the name of this *coincidentia oppositorum*, though its definitive role in history, its role as the absolute subject and the absolute referent of history, is nonetheless ensured as long as we cling to this ontological delusion.

The devil is duplicitous, being our hallucinatory double. The devil is our madness, as he owes his existence to our incapacity to see ourselves in our rival double. Dostoyevsky accordingly casts Ivan Karamazov's archrival, his hallucinatory double, the devil, in the role of an imitator, a literary hack (for more on this duplicity, with reference to Baudelaire and deconstruction, see McKenna, "Double Talk"). The devil is evil incarnate according to tradition, but only, according to my reading of human relations, as violence incarnate, which is what violence becomes when we misrecognize it, alienate it, and incarnate it in others—other selves, rival doubles, or, much the same thing, the devil himself. This is the essence of the fantastic, of superstition itself, which Tobin Siebers has analyzed as "the representation of identities as differences" (*The Romantic Fantastic* 12). The seeming autonomy of evil, its hypostasis, is the inevitable result of this qui pro quo, which Ronald Aronson defines as madness when madness is defined as violence "organized in such a way as to keep itself out of touch with its origin":

> With the mad destructiveness of those who hold state power but have no effective power [over power, over violence] we are approaching, in our secular world, the meaning of this force that must apparently remain central to our lives for generations to come—evil. The characteristic of madness we have neglected so far is its *unreachability;* it yields a praxis out of circuit in relation to the world which generates it. Evil is the human out of touch with itself, driven there by extreme circumstances out of its control, finding the power to strike blindly even while unable to strike truly. It is mad, frozen, impotent human praxis, striving to lose touch with its source. (*The Dialectics of Disaster* 202–3)

In the end is the double, as "it" "was" from the very beginning when, as the story goes, man and woman first ate of the apple to be like gods in the knowledge of good and evil. Today we have this knowledge as never before—unless, as Girard urges, we include the likes of Cervantes, Dostoyevsky, Shakespeare, and Proust in the ranks of our human scientists: "Only a pseudo-science runs counter to the greatest works of our literary heritage. A real science will justify their vision and confirm their superiority" (*DRR* 78). It is absolute knowledge, being knowledge of the absolute, as even Derrida allows. All the rest is literature. Culture has survived to this day through denying this knowledge, as Girard writes of our sacrificial crisis:

> Violence will come to an end only after it has had the last word and that word has been accepted as divine. The meaning of this word must remain hidden, the mechanism of unanimity remain concealed. For religion protects man as long as its ultimate foundations are not revealed. To drive the monster from its secret lair is to risk loosing it on mankind. To remove men's ignorance is only to risk exposing them to an even greater peril. The only barrier against human violence is raised on this misconception. In fact, the sacrificial crisis is simply another form of that knowledge which grows greater as the reciprocal violence grows more intense but which never leads to the whole truth. (*VS* 135)

Well, now we know the truth, and no radical critique of origins can dispell it. To deny violence the last word may depend on our understanding the first word, the "*Überworte*" (Freud), as it names a victim whose place is taken by the sacred, thus marking a divine origin that never took place. This cannot go on, there being no place for violence if absolutely everyone is to be its victim. This is not merely a moral determination, as when we say "there is no place for that sort of behavior here," but also an ontological determination, there being literally no place for violence to exercise its sovereignty over subjects, however deluded as to their origin, who no longer exist.

4

Postmodernism: The Victim Age

The question whether objective truth can be attributed to a human thing is not a question of theory, but is a *practical* question. In practice man must prove the truth, that is, the reality and power, the this-sidedness of his thinking. The dispute over the reality or non-reality of thinking which is isolated from practice is a purely *scholastic* question.

—Marx

Post-isms

It has become commonplace to observe that "postmodern" is a slippery term, that from both a historical and an esthetic point of view, in terms of both periodization and formal production, postmoderism is not easily distinguished from what, with Eliot, Joyce, Kafka, Picasso, and Duchamp, we have been calling modernism. That is as it should be. The root meaning of modernism refers to the present time, from the Latin *modo*, "just now." Perhaps labeling as *postmodern* what is but the form of modernity only makes explicit the paradox already informing the notion of modernism itself, which would apply to any self-consciously progressive or avant-garde cultural activity with respect to its own era. Consider, for instance, these remarks, which could easily be directed against deconstruction as a school of criticism: "Moreover, a new type of teaching has lately appeared, or rather a childish way of prating has gained inordinate popularity among certain people who hunt only for the leaves that cover up the fruit. . . . Those who are busy teaching this way seem not to know and not to want others to know the things they pride themselves on teaching. Or perhaps they are anxious to be thought to teach new and bizarre things. I say this because by the weird and revolting novelty of their terminology they do not fear to divulge what they have in mind" (Robert of Melun,

quoted in Chenu 311). It is clear that some sort of neologistic soph-
istry is being criticized here for seemingly awarding attention to surface rather than to depth and for producing flashy and bewildering
stylistic effects. It calls to mind the "opposition farmer/gardener
(fruits/flowers; lasting/ephemeral; patience/haste; seriousness/play)"
that Plato invokes to blame writing and Derrida to salvage it (Derrida,
PP 151). The fact that the author is inveighing against the *modernitas*,
the *modo docendi*, emerging among Biblical scholars in the mid-twelfth
century encourages doubts about the novelty of contemporary critical
conflict. It is one that many regard favorably and others unfavorably as
but a new version of "la querelle des anciens et des modernes" that
erupted at the end of the seventeenth century.

It remains to be seen, however, whether a notion like the postmodern harbors a deeper paradox, whether it has weightier implications for
the present time, which it curiously designates as somehow past or
"post." In this chapter, I argue that it does, making special reference
to certain writings by Derrida and Girard.

First Derrida, because he has done so much to render problematic
any sense of temporal presence, of being as presence. For this fact
alone he might be deemed the philosopher of the postmodern. Furthermore, he is somewhat the philosopher of "what remains," of
the marginal as both the liminal and the residual, as both originary
and outlandish. This is archly exemplified by the first and last utterances of his *Glas*, which opens with this fragmentary question on
Hegel, "What remains today, for us, here, now, of a Hegel?" and
which closes, in the column devoted to Genet, in such a way as to
rethematize its own writing as a ruin, a wreck: "What I had feared,
naturally, already, is being reedited. Today, here, now, the ruin of"
(7a; 291b; for *Glas* as a dilapidation of the book, see McKenna,
"Biblioclasm: Derrida").

Second Girard, because his sacrificial theory of culture lends both
anthropological and epistemological reference to the issues raised by
Derrida, most notably by Derrida's text on Shelley ("The Triumph of
Life") and Blanchot ("La Folie du jour" and "L'Arrêt de mort") entitled "Living On." This is a translation from the French text, "Survivre" (in *Psyché*), which was not first made available in French,
doubtless to produce freer speculation on living as a matter of surviving. Published in the heyday of academic controversy over deconstruction, along with other essays by Yale critics (Harold Bloom, Geoffrey

Hartman, Paul de Man, J. Hillis Miller), the text toys with problems of its own translation in a marginalized commentary running horizontally parallel to it. As a consequence, the *"sur"* of *"survivre"* retains a self-referential dimension: the deconstructive text deploys and displays its own division. This antic disposition of critical discourse is no longer so fashionable; it need not survive for us to assess the enduring contribution of deconstruction as it concerns postmodernism, whose own thematic resources are perhaps dwindling. This chapter is nonetheless dedicated to showing the far-reaching yet concrete implications of the postmodern as it thematizes question of survival, of living on after the dead. For demonstrable, historical reasons that bear on the recent past as it affects the possibility of a future, a postmodern consciousness is indissociable from the consciousness of being a survivor, of living on. The consciousness of being as presence as being somehow belated, *nachträglich, après coup,* may be the consequence of our deconstructive activity. It is also, I argue, a matter of decisive historical consequence as it concerns our limitless destructive capacity.

To acknowledge Derrida as the philosopher of the postmodern is to acknowledge that we live, in the felicitous term of one of his commentators, in the "post-age" (Ulmer, "The Post-Age"). We are poststructuralist in the (highly disputed) terrain of literary criticism and philosophy and postmodern in the (perhaps waning) field of literature and the fine arts, owing to the self-devouring irony of so many of our textual and plastic productions. We style ourselves as post-Christian in the domain of religion and (perhaps) of culture as a whole. For Marcel Gauchet, our society is posttheological for having experienced what Max Weber first styled as "the disenchantment of the world." There are still other "posts" by which we mark our sense of belatedness, beginning with that very term, which for Harold Bloom (see *The Anxiety of Influence* and *Agon*) describes the relation of virtually any poet as ephebe to a precursor with respect (or disrespect) to whose glory the ephebe stands in an anxious, fallen, rebellious state. According to Richard Rorty (*Consequences of Pragmatism*), we are, or at least should be, postphilosophical, at least to the extent that, as Derrida suggests, we are past the point where we can legitimately or convincingly distinguish between philosophy and other kinds of writing. According to Gregory Ulmer (*Applied Grammatology*), Derrida's program for a science of writing and consequently of all sign systems as grammatology has, or should have, so transformed our relation to texts and phenomena that we are, as the subtitle of his book suggests, in an era of "post (e)-pedagogy." We are in multiple senses postpostal: for the way tele-communications have supplanted and irrevocably altered our experi-ence of communication-at-a-distance in the media age, and for the way, as already suggested, in which our sense of both historical peri-odization and contemporaneity is transformed by our use and illustra-tion of the term *postmodern*. In *The End of Culture*, Eric Gans argues that we are experiencing a "Copernican revolution" with regard to "the desultory and empirical character" of the humanities and the so-cial sciences, which must give way to the systematic rigor of "a gen-uinely scientific anthropology": "The study of culture is itself a fundamental and urgently required element of culture" (52) with re-gard to which we are, in a sense, postcultural.

There is no need to subscribe to the validity of all these "post" claims, or still others not mentioned here, in order to acknowledge their critical mass as culturally significant. It is a significance to which the philosopher of science Michel Serres (*Hermes III: La Traduction*) lends considerable gravity when he argues that we are balefully posthistorical: in the nuclear age, science has entered its definitive state, that of a thanatocracy, in which its most powerful impulses are working in service to the death instinct.

It is in just this sense that I add that we are, finally and definitively (i.e., historically and anthropologically) postwar. I mean that term in the narrowest and broadest possible senses. First of all, I mean it in the sense in which historians speak of the period beginning in 1945, a period beginning unmistakably, because so spectacularly and cata-strophically, with Hiroshima. Hiroshima marks (and indubitably mars) the end of World War II and the beginning of our era, the era chiefly characterized by the Cold War because no one can afford the all-consuming apocalyptic consequences of a hot one. And so we are post-war in the broadest sense, as Jonathan Schell makes plain in *The Fate of the Earth*, where he shows that war conceived and waged with a view to palpable gains, territorial or ideological, is a thing of the past, that our age-old definition of war no longer applies to what we cannily dub nuclear holocaust in which all is lost, in which all are losers. Consensus on this point is near perfect.

The Future Perfect

Holocaust, it is worth recalling, is a religious term, a properly sacrificial one designating a wholly burnt offering—which all too humanly has loomed as our near future. Indeed, our future, if we are to have one, depends absolutely on the deferral of the absolute violence that has been instituted as the policy of deterrence. As I will show, this policy bears all the structural attributes and contradictions of Derridean differance. In view of this imminent apocalypse, a topic so familiar as to be frequently boring, we must ask, with René Girard, whether our violent culture is indeed pre- or post-Christian. For if, as Girard argues in *Things Hidden since the Foundation of the World* and in *The Scapegoat,* Scripture consists in a critique of sacrificial practices, and if, on the other hand, our crisis is sacrificial, as our commonplace terms for it seem to suggest, then perhaps we need to assume Scripture's message rather than relegate it to some "metaphysic of the book."

I am prompted to this observation by a contemporary writer's somewhat exasperated reflections on the postmodern. After quoting another critic, who excludes from this category what he calls " 'secular news reports,' " meaning novels about everyday middle-class life, John Updike continues, "so whatever postmodern is, it is not secular news reports. Nor is it, one may hazard, sacred news reports" ("Modernist, Postmodernist" 136). But perhaps it is; there is much that we learn from the newspapers and the media that suggests it is, and I can cite further texts by some contemporary writers that further suggest the postmodern as "sacred news reports."

What news of the sacred? In a sense, we ever have only news of the sacred, never its full presence. It is just this notion of full presence, of parousia, that Derrida deconstructs as ontotheological, as theologocentric. Instead of presence, we have *differance:* "It is because of *differance* that the movement of signification is possible only if each so-called 'present' element, each element appearing on the scene of presence, is related to something other than itself, thereby keeping within itself the mark of the past element, and already letting itself be vitiated by the mark of its relation to the future element, this trace being related no less to what is called the future than to what is called the past, and constituting what is called the present by means of this very relation to what it is not: what it absolutely is not, not even a past or a future as a modified present" (*Margins of Philosophy* 13). The present is to be inscribed under erasure; it is but the mark or the trace of a relation to a future and a past that do not exist as modified presents (before and after) but only "divide the present in itself" (ibid.). This explains the relation between the poststructuralist critique of being as presence and the peculiar temporality of the postmodern, of the "just now" and the "after now," as mediation and spatialization, which is incarnate, as it were, in the supposed "secondarity" of writing, the idea that writing comes after speech and represents it—whereas for Derrida writing symbolizes the origin of language as lacking an origin in the sense of an original world that it represents. To speak of the present as of what is always already past is to speak in the mode of the future with regard to it. The postmodern evokes a sense of the present as future and past with respect to itself, never as present to itself.

If the notion of the postmodern has a grammatical tense, it is decidedly not the present but the future perfect, as when I say, speaking of this essay at the present time, that this will have been a discourse on the postmodern; as when Derrida, disclaiming an "intention to *present*" the three essays composing *Dissemination*, says in "Hors Livre," "This (therefore) will not have been a book" (3). The future perfect is in fact the condition that Jean-François Lyotard lays down for identifying a properly postmodern work; it is not necessarily a text from any historical period, but rather one that testifies, without nostalgia, to *"l'imprésentable"*:

> A postmodern writer or artist is in the situation of a philosopher: the text he writes, the work he accomplishes, is not governed in principle by any rules already established, and they cannot be judged by means of a determining judgment, by the application to the text or the work of known categories. These rules and categories are what the work or the text are in search of. The artist and the writer work therefore without rules, and to establish the rules of what *will have been done*. Whence it is that the work and the text have the properties of an event, whence too that they always come too late for their author, or, much the same thing, that their *mise en oeuvre* always begins too soon. *Postmodern* would be understood according to the paradox of the future (*post*) anterior (*modo*). ("Réponse à la question: Qu'est-ce que le postmoderne?" 367)

This is a good description of what Derrida does in "Hors Livre," where he interrogates—and practices—the aporetics of prefacing, "a necessary and ludicrous operation" as he describes it in Hegel (*Dissemination* 7). The preface is the future past of the philosophical system, of the totalizing representation. It is a dangerous supplement to the totalizing integrity of the system because and although its role is to announce that integrity.

Because and although: this paradoxical, double-binding logic is characteristic of self-referential statements. Later on I will examine its relation to the sacred; its interest at present is in the way it characterizes many an artwork, especially literary works. Cervantes and Sterne immediately come to mind, particularly as they are regarded as precursors, or rather performers, of the postmodern. For this logic is especially widespread in the self-conscious literature of our century. *"Vivre ou raconter"*: "You have to choose: live or tell stories," as Sartre's Roquentin observes in an archly postmodern moment of *La Nausée*, contesting alike false beginnings, false endings, and the "total partiel" we make of them (60–61). That this work, which represents itself as a fragment, performs a deconstruction of the novel very much in the mode prescribed by Lyotard is perhaps not something that calls for strenuous argument. It represents itself as the preface, the program of the novel it will have become, or failed to become; perhaps that is undecidable. At any rate, Derrida has handily formulated the dilemma of Sartre's (anti)novel in "Living On":

> *"But who's talking about living?"*: in other words, who can really speak about living? Who is in a position to? Who is already on the other side [*bord*], little enough alive, or alive enough, to dare to speak about living, not about one's life, not even about life, but about living, the immediate, present, even impersonal process of an act of living that nevertheless guarantees even the spoken word that it conveys and that it thus defies to *speak on living*: it is impossible to use living speech to speak of living—unless it is possible *only* to use living speech to speak of living, which would make the aporia even more paralyzing. (78)

Strictly speaking, structurally speaking, only the dead can speak on living; the living can speak only of the dead. In consequence, as Derrida remarks elsewhere, there is an "apocalyptic tone" that invades "the structure of every scene of writing in general"; it is "a transcendental condition of all discourse, of all experience itself, of every mark or every trace" ("Of an Apocalyptic Tone . . . " 87).

It thus appears then that the future perfect, for Derrida and Lyotard, is the temporal modality, or at least the grammatical translation, of historical becoming in all its openness, in all its resistance to false totalizations, which according to this view is a pleonasm. It translates the present in its differance.

Lyotard, for his part, is quite vehement in his opposition to the ideology of representation that informs efforts of totalization, which is falsehood per se and eminently dangerous: "That illusion is paid for at the price of terror. The nineteenth and twentieth centuries have given us our fill of terror. We have paid enough for the nostalgia of the all and the one, of the reconciliation of the concept with the sensible, of experience that is transparent and communicable. Beneath the general demand for relaxing and appeasement, we hear mumbling the desire to recommence the terror, to accomplish the fanaticism of embracing reality. The answer is: war on the all, bear witness to the unpresentable, activate the differends, save the honor of the name" ("Réponse" 367). This is a very problematic text, however. It mimics Adorno in the swashbuckling mode of its abstractions, in what Derrida might call its "overlordly" or "apocalyptic tone." It opposes totalitarianism and its philosophical accomplices, namely, any philosophy confiding in transparent representation, but it is apparently not opposed to violence. Rather, it is transparently and plangently a call to arms.

The glaring symmetry of Lyotard's violent *re*sistance to what he deems terroristic *re*action is far too reminiscent of Victor Hugo's patently rhetorical declaration of "Guerre à la rhétorique" ("Réponse à un acte d'accusation," in *Les Contemplations*) to serve as an alternative to the violence he ostensibly deplores. It conforms all to romantically to the model of human violence enunciated by Sartre's Frantz von Gerlach at the conclusion of *The Condemned of Altona*: "One and one make one—there's our mystery. The beast was hiding, and suddenly we surprised his look deep in the eyes of our neighbors. So we struck. Legitimate self-defense. I surprised the beast. I struck. A man fell, and in his dying eyes I say the beast still living—myself. One and one make one—what a misunderstanding!" (act 5, scene 3). Frantz has already committed suicide, taking his Nazi collaborator father with him in a car crash. His voice comes to us on a tape recorder, so that he addresses us as one who will have been killed. His voice remains, survives him—"après coup." Why the gimmick? Because violent reciprocity is not the rule of historical becoming but the rule of definitive historical closure, which is just how Sartre's character envisions our future: "The thirtieth century no longer replies. Perhaps there will be no more centuries after ours. Perhaps a bomb will have blown out all the light. Everything will be dead—eyes, judges, time. Night. Oh, tribunal of the night—who were, who will be, and who are—I have been! I have been! I, Frantz von Gerlach, here in this room have taken the century upon my shoulders and have said: 'I will answer for it. This day and forever.' What do you say?" (5.3).

Here apocalypse is a real historical possibility. The future perfect is necessarily employed to evoke this total violence, because, as Jonathan Schell reminds us, "extinction is a human future which can never become a human present." Schell's reflections on the peculiar temporality of the postwar era is instructive here, for it draws on Cartesian certitude: "Like the thought 'I do not exist,' the thought 'Humanity is now extinct' is an impossible one for a rational person, because as soon as *it* is, *we* are not. In imagining any other event, we look ahead to a moment that is still within the stream of human time, which is to say within a time in which other human beings will exist, and will be responding to whatever they see, looking back to our present time and looking forward to future times that will themselves be within the sequence of human time. But in imagining extinction we gaze past everything human to a dead time that falls outside the human tenses of past, present, and future" (*The Fate of the Earth* 140). Such a future can never arrive; it is for the imagination alone, so that we can speak of such a time only now, and only in the tense of the future perfect, only as something that will have taken place. Our relation to the present is governed by the tense of the future perfect in an unprecedented manner. It is not only a philosophical issue, but a historical and political one of the first magnitude.

It is doubtless for this reason that Derrida, in his contribution to "nuclear criticism," remarks that "the terrifying reality of the nuclear conflict can only be the signified referent, never the real referent (present or past) of a discourse or a text" ("No Apocalypse . . . " 23). Nuclear war is accordingly for Derrida *"fabulously textual,"* "a fable, that is, something one can only talk about." As if paraphrasing Schell, to whom he alludes only via someone else's book review, he makes this commonsensical observation: "Unlike the other wars, which have all been preceded by wars of more or less the same type in human memory (and gunpowder did not mark a radical break in this respect), nuclear war has no precedent. It has never occurred, itself; it is a nonevent. The explosion of American bombs in 1945 ended a 'classical,' conventional war; it did not set off a nuclear war" (23). To start a nuclear war is to end everything; it is to start a race with time and against time, of which Derrida's title is evocative: "No Apocalypse, Not Now (full speed ahead, seven missiles, seven missives)"—and of which the future perfect is emblematic, pro-grammatic. Thus, his essay begins with *"at the beginning there will have been speed."* It is the speed of the missiles racing toward remainderless destruction and accomplishing therefore what in the end of his essay he describes as "absolute knowledge." I will return to this later. Paul Virilio also identifies "absolute speed" as the essence of our "pure war" (*Pure War* 59).

It is worthwhile to observe the similar structural necessities governing the historical vision of Baudelaire, for whom *"modernité"* was a neologism. He speaks of "The Painter of Modern Life" as a *"revenant,"* a being returned from the dead who keeps *"la mémoire du présent."* When he announces in *Fusées* that "the World is coming to an end," he is constrained thereby to use the future perfect: "Machinery will have so Americanized us, progress will have so well atrophied in us any spiritual portion, that nothing among the sanguinary, sacrilegious or anti-utopian dreams will be able to be compared to these positive results." For Baudelaire too, we are but "living on": "I ask of any thinking man to show me what remains of life?" At the end of his reflections he expresses feeling "le ridicule d'un prophète" (*Oeuvres complètes* 629–30). Similarly, Ulmer remarks that Derrida seeks to "reassess the efficacy of the *prophet*" ("The Post-Age" 53). But prophecy is not only a formal (post)structure for Baudelaire. He envisions real calamities born of an unprincipled competitiveness whose harvest of victims in our century is only too legible: "Do I need to say that the little that will be left of politics will flounder painfully in the embrace of general animality, and that those who govern will be forced, in order to stay in power and to create the phantom of order, to have recourse to means which would make our contemporary humanity shudder, hardened though it be already?" (*OC* 629). What is "ridicule" to Baudelaire is realism for us, indeed, realpolitik in such forms as we shudder even to talk about. As Pierre Pachet shows in *Le Premier venu*, what informs Baudelaire's prophecy is a sacrificial vision of culture of which he construed himself the victim. However much he may have engineered this construction by fostering his own persecution, as Sartre argues, his *position* as victim is what illuminates his vision of history and legitimates it.

This anchors a discussion about prophecy that takes place in an interview with Derrida. Conceding the affiliation of "deconstructive themes" with "a proliferation of prophecies," he goes on to draw a contrast with philosophy: "The search for objective or absolute criteria is, to be sure, an essentially philosophical gesture. Prophecy differs from philosophy in so far as it dispenses with such criteria. The prophetic word is its own criterion and refuses to submit to an external tribunal which would judge or evaluate it in an objective and neutral fashion. The prophetic word reveals its own eschatology and finds its index of truthfulness in its own inspiration and not in some transcendental or philosophical criteriology" ("Deconstruction and the Other" 119). Prophecy is no doubt independent of a philosophical criteriology—else we could institute a school for prophets and compel attendance by statesmen and rulers—but not of objective criteria; Baudelaire to witness, as are all the prophets, according to Scripture, its criterion is the victim (Luke 11:50; Matt. 23:34–35; see Girard, *THFW* 158–67). It is not a neutral criterion, far from it, but it is not hieratically or semiologically self-authorizing, either. In its utter marginality, it is an external tribunal to the violent forces that produce it. So we need not even agree with Derrida's disclaimer about deconstruction having "a prophetic function" if we see that what it deconstructs is the violent rivalry that issues in victimage. The privilege, the *privus lex*, of prophetic voice is that of the victim, and it is with that in mind that I return to the historical question of surviving.

Après Coup

It is not only Hiroshima and the prospect of its planetary repetition that spawn our sense of living on, of being survivors, of being as survival. There are other events that mark 1945 as the beginning of the postmodern. These are events "on the Western front," so to speak, which Maurice Blanchot evokes in a highly allusive manner in *La Folie du jour:* "Shortly afterward, the madness of the world broke out. I was made to stand against the wall like many others. Why? For no reason. The guns did not go off. I said to myself, God, what are you doing? At that point I stopped being insane. The world hesitated, then regained its equilibrium" (6). As Derrida shows in "Living On," this is a work that contests the possibility of story, frustrating what he calls "the demand for narrative"—for instance, in the repetition of the text's beginning near its end: "I had been asked: Tell us *'just* exactly' what happened. A Story? I began: I am not learned; I am not ignorant. I have known joys. That is saying too little. I told them the whole story and they listened, it seems to me, with interest, at least in the beginning. But the end was a surprise to all of us. 'That was the beginning,' they said. 'Now get down to the facts.' How so? The story was over!" (18). But the impossibility of story, to the extent that it depends on a linear notion of time, of a selfsame present ever-bounded by future and past (presents), is linked for Blanchot, as I have already suggested, to certain events that he evokes explicitly in the more recent essay appositely entitled *Après coup*.

In this essay, Blanchot cites Adorno's claim, which I will consult shortly, that there can be no "fictional narrative" of Auschwitz and meditates on its irrevocable claims on our consciousness. Before pursuing this point, let me observe a certain consensus on this claim. It is one that Roland Barthes cites in Brecht (*Roland Barthes* 123) and that is taken up at length by Lyotard as well, for whom Auschwitz is "a cleavage in Western thought," "a crack in philosophical time" ("Phraser après Auschwitz," in *Les Fins de l'homme* 189). Blanchot pursues:

> The necessity of bearing witness is the obligation of a testimony which only could be born, each in its singularity, by the impossible witnesses—witnesses of the impossible—; certain of them survived, but their living on [*sur-vie*] is no longer life, it is the rupture with the living affirmation, it is the attestation that this good which life is (life which is not narcissistic, but for others) has undergone a decisive attack [*atteinte*] which leaves nothing intact any longer. From that point, it could be that all narration, nay all poetry, has lost the basis on which another language would raise itself, by the extinction of this happiness in speaking which is expected in the most mediocre silence. Doubtless forgetfulness does its work and allows for there still to be works. But to that forgetfulness, the forgetfulness of an event in which all possibility foundered, responds a memory which however failing and without recollection, the immemorial haunts in vain. Humanity was to have died [or had to die: *a eu à mourir*] by the ordeal it underwent in some of its members (those who incarnate life itself, almost the totality of a people promised to a perpetual presence.) That death is still going on. Whence the obligation to never again die only once, without its repetition being able to accustom us to the always capital end. (98–99)

It appears that for Blanchot all the living are survivors of Auschwitz, living, as it were, *"après coup."* For them, for us, nothing is left intact, everything is tainted. It is not a matter here of sympathy or empathy with the dead, or of breastbeating, but of a veritable *"trait d'union"* with the dead that faults conventional ontology. The living present is not conveniently or plausibly opposed to a dead past; rather, the past lives on, irrevocably marking the present with its dead. Eric Santner's makes the same argument in his remarkable *Stranded Objects: Mourning, Memory and Film in Postwar Germany*, whose preface concludes that "the postwar destabilization of certain fundamental cultural norms and notions, above all those dealing with self-identity and community, cannot be understood without reference to the ethical and intellectual imperatives of life after Auschwitz" (xiv).

This too is the *structural* effect of Hiroshima, which, as Robert Jay Lifton reminds us, was also "an end of the world," "a new dimension of death immersion" that, in the light of imminent catastrophe, "we all share." And Lifton further observes, as if paraphrasing Blanchot on the problematic of representation, that "impaired formulation is a central problem for survivors" (*Death in Life* 541–42; 526). Impaired formulation is our postmodern condition, our postwar condition. It has ever been our condition of course, according to some advanced theories of indirect representation, "prison house" theories of language according to which it constitutes a labyrinth rather than a labeling process. But now we have to acknowledge this condition, along with Derrida as its philosopher. The illusion, the nostalgia of unimpaired formulation, of transparent communication, is just what deconstruction reveals—as illusion, erasure, forgetfulness, ontotheology, logocentrism, phonocentrism: "'*la folie du jour*,'" the madness of day, the madness of light, which for Adorno, I submit, is the madness of (undialectical, undeconstructed) Enlightenment, of an imperialistic rationalism. "After Auschwitz, our feelings resist any claim of the positivity of existence as sanctimonious, as wronging the victims; they balk as squeezing any kind of sense, however bleached, out of the victims' fate" (*Negative Dialectics* 363).

Yet it is necessary, as Adorno knew and insistently attempted, to make sense here. In the crime's depth and breadth, in its horror and magnitude, we find ourselves at the "limits of the means of expression," as Saul Friedländer, among others, has shown (*Reflections of Nazism* 51, 70). Charles Maier concurs: "The Nazi experience tests the limits of what history can explain" (*The Unmasterable Past* 100). This is a fact that in turn intensifies the "demand for narrative" and for sense. Silence here is utterly reprehensible, for it risks complicity with the scandalous silence of spectators of the crime, a silence requisite to its accomplishment, as its historians regularly point out. It is in just this sense that the "historians' controversy," or *"Historikerstreit,"* over Germany's past is not, as Maier points out, Germany's alone (161). We must view Auschwitz not as beyond thinking but as where thinking must begin. What we rightly regard as unspeakable must be spoken of, a fact that places us in a crisis of representation of the first magnitude.

For Adorno as well, all the living are survivors of Auschwitz, an attitude reflected in this passage, which probably inspired Blanchot's reflections:

> Our metaphysical faculty is paralyzed because actual events have shattered the basis on which speculative metaphysical thought could be reconciled with experience. Once again, the dialectical motif of quantity recoiling into quality scores an unspeakable triumph. The administrative murder of millions made of death a thing one had never yet to fear in just this fashion. There is no chance any more for death to come into the individual's empirical life as somehow conformable with the course of that life. The last, the poorest possession left to the individual is expropriated. That in concentration camps it was no longer an individual who died, but a specimen—that is bound to affect the dying of those who escaped the administrative measure. (*Negative Dialectics* 362)

Adorno locates the obstacle, the challenge, to philosophical reflection in the victim, in the massive and irreducible fact of victimage.

This is not necessarily grounds for an antiphilosophical empiricism, which Derrida has shown to embody its own metaphysics or logocentrism. On the contrary, it warrants a theory that focuses on the victim as an irreducible referent. As Friedländer remarks, "the memory of Auschwitz, that indelible reference point of the Western imagination, forms an obstacle impossible to evade" by any historical revisionism (62). What is indelible is just what cannot be erased, what irrefragably remains. The word *obstacle* retains its original force as well: a stumbling block, a scandal to rationalization. Derrida, as a philosopher of what remains, of what resists the totalizing economy of a system, is discretely sensitive to this affiliation. He has described portions of his *Glas* as a "philosophy of ashes," "une sorte de philosophie de la cendre," while refusing to grant this word any "philosophical dignity": " '[A]sh' " cannot be an essence, a substance, a philosophical sense. It is on the contrary what in a certain way ruins in advance philosophy or philosophical legitimacy. Whence this double gesture of proposing a philosophy of ashes and showing in what way 'ash' prevents philosophy from closing around itself" ("Entretien avec Jacques Derrida" in *Digraphe* 24). For its ontological ambiguity, Derrida notes the resonance of *"la cendre"* with his other anticoncepts—trace, writing, gramm—as it bespeaks without speaking, or attests without testifying: "La cendre n'est pas, cela signifie qu'elle témoigne sans témoigner. Elle témoigne de la disparition du témoin, si on peut dire [Ash is not, which means it testifies without witnessing. It bears witness to the disappearance of the witness, so to speak]" (23). But Derrida only fleetingly historicizes it with reference to "grandes expériences spectaculaires de l'incinération . . . je pense aux fours crématoires," before concluding on "l'incinération comme expérience, comme forme élémentaire de l'expérience" (23).

The ashes of the dead are buried along with everything else in experience. Derrida will not mark or make a difference between victims and other phenomena. His next remarks, concerning his text *Schibboleth* on Celan, lead to my central point: "Ash expresses quite well what there is about the trace in general, about writing in general, that effaces what it inscribes. The effacement is not simply the contrary of the inscription. We write with ash on ash. And not only is that not nihilistic; I would say rather that the experience of ash which communicates with the experience of the gift, of defenselessness, of the relation to the other as interruption of economy—that experience of ash is also the possibility of the relation to the other, of the gift, of affirmation, of benediction, of prayer . . ." (23–24). The ellipsis at the end is Derrida's. By withholding a noun complement to gift, benediction, and prayer, he hovers at the threshold of what the West has stipulated as positive religious values. It is with these possibilities in mind that I turn to Girard, where the obstacle to reasoning becomes a model for the theory of a general economy of sacrifice.

The compelling interest of Girard's sacrificial theory of culture is that it locates a victim at "the foundation of the world." Here is another, very concrete case where the victim provides Derrida's terminology—supplement, *pharmakon*, remnant-*"restance,"* trace, differance itself—with both anthropological and historical reference.

At the beginning Girard's anthropological hypothesis posits the victim, whose vulnerability is what singles it out for unanimous destruction by the group or horde in a mêlée of appropriative rivalry. With the disposition of projectiles or prosthetic devices to implement the kill (which, I submit, constitutes our instrumental continuity with more "primitive" ancestors), there are no instinctual brakes to the intraspecific violence that characterizes the animal world, as the ethological data on dominance patterns among animals demonstrate. Appropriation by any one of the group surrounding the victim now spells danger from each and every one of its members. All share in this apprehension: indeed, all mime it, all insinuate it to one another, so that there is a moment of noninstinctual attention bent on seizing the prey but refraining from it out of self-preservation (out of an originary tactic of deterrence). In one and the same movement and moment of aborted appropriation, all are rival, model, and obstacle for one another. This is the contradictory structure of desire as informed by taboo, which informs desire in turn. This structure results in, as well as emanates from, the sacralization of the object, as that to which one defers infinitely rather than succumb to the mimetic violence that produced it. Here is where I posit the emergence of what is properly human, of the infinitely desiring subject, the subject of infinite desire, of metaphysical or mediated or mimetic desire, whose objects are only the signifiers of others' desires in a chain leading out to the infinite but indissolubly linked nonetheless to the body, the remains of the victim, the first signifier:

> The signifier, that is the victim. The signified constitutes all actual and potential meaning the community confers on to the victim, and through its intermediacy, on all things.
> The sign is the reconciliatory victim. Since we understand that human beings wish to remain reconciled after the conclusion of the crisis, we can also understand their penchant for reproducing the language of the sacred by substituting, in ritual, new victims for the original victim, in order to insure the maintenance of that miraculous peace. The imperative of ritual is therefore never separate from the manipulation of signs and their constant multiplication, a process that generates new possibilities of cultural differentiation and enrichment. (*THFW* 103)

Peace among men, it is important to note, is not the object of desire, not by any stretch of the historical, political, or sociological imagination. Nothing unites a community, with all the good fellowship and cooperation one can imagine, like the external threat of a common enemy. But the threat is originally internal; it is the violent threat of all against all. It is the annihilating threat of this internal difference, or differance, that we have rematerialized in the postwar, postmodern era; as Jonathan Schell observes, "with the world itself at stake, all differences would by definition be 'internal' differences" (*The Fate of the Earth* 229). Further, Michel Serres observes that "war is a state of order, a classic state of lines and of columns, of maps and of strategies"; it is a "remedy to the violence" of the furious, raging multitude. He concludes that "a society makes war to avoid at all costs a return to that state" (*Genèse* 140). This too is the thesis of Carl Schmitt's *Political Theology*, whose implication in the properly sacrificial dynamic of Nazi Germany has resurfaced in debate following its recent translation.

Peace, then, is not the object of desire, but its by-product, the calm to which the deferred appropriation of the victim gives rise. It is a calm logically—that is, necessarily—attributed to the miraculous agency of the victim, thanks to whom for the first time something like a before (war) and after (peace), an outside (sacred) and inside (community), is marked—marked, above all, as remarked, for its experience is necessarily mimetic and collective. The origin is born of mimesis, literally of re-petition: of mimetic seeking. Girard's theory thus survives the deconstruction of origins, for it does not postulate presence but rather a mimetic abstinence and deferral at the origin of the species.

The passage from nature to culture hinges on mimesis, which animals have in common with humans, as even Aristotle could not fail to see. But unlike animals, humans exhibit unbounded mimetic violence. Among animals, mimesis serves appetitive needs; among humans, it generates desires, from the discrete and familial to the fantastical and, as we know, fantastically homicidal. Violence is not instinctual; it reigns in the absence of instinctual brakes to mimesis. What is distinctive to *Homo necans*, as Walter Burkert identifies our species, is this absence of instinctual brakes to intraspecific violence, brakes that characterize the animal world, as the study of dominance patterns among animals demonstrates. Indeed, the conflation of animal aggression with human violence, like belief in instinctual violence among humans, is an archly sacrificial gesture. It mystifies violence; placing the blame on a subhuman species, it substitutes an animal victim for the effect of human mimesis.

That man disposes of language in the absence of instinct, that language is what breaches, or "supplements," our instinctual fault-line, is what necessitates a theory of violence that is also a theory of representation, a theory of linguistic origins as essayed in the previous chapter. For however skewed and indirect current theory shows it to be, representation is mimetic. That linguistic symbols stand in for things and represent them stems from the originary role of the victim as a surrogate for the violence of the community. That other things stand in for the representation of the victim is the story of culture's development and complexification. That culture regularly and ruthlessly returns to sacrificial practices is the story of our century especially.

Truth Stories

Derrida's genial recapitulation, in "Plato's Pharmacy," of the violent origin of philosophy, as of representation itself, in terms of the sacrificial expulsion of writing and the phonologocentric erasure of its originary traces follows the same scenario. The story of philosophy's violent rebirth in Descartes's *Meditations,* as recounted in "Cogito and the History of Madness," recapitulates the same dynamic: the mystified expulsion of madness as the originary other of reason. The story of philosophy from Plato through Heidegger is ever the same story, the story of violent origins, or origin as violence.

Is it a true story? Or to use Derrida's words, although he no doubt uses them with an (un)certain measure of irony, is it "the truth on truth"? Derrida explores Blanchot's "L'Arrêt de mort" as a warrant for radical skepticism: "the truth *about* truth, *on* truth, truth*less* truth *on* truth" ("Living On" 142). But Blanchot's reflections on surviving the dead in our century suggest that history bears the story out—though Derrida's own reflections on *"la cendre"* go no further than to suggest that truth is too important to be left to philosophy. And if philosophy's dedication to truth issues from the sacrificial expulsion of writing, then the victimary hypothesis emerges as the destiny of philosophy. As the prospect of humanity's violent end repeats the dynamics of its violent beginnings, it appears probable that the very possibility of there any longer being anything like truth, positive truth on which, despite all deconstructions and because of them as well, a human science could be formulated and implemented—all that depends on our understanding of that story, its relevance, its revelatory power, its concrete, immediate, and verifiable reference to our postmodern, postwar condition. We can call it, with Girard, our apocalyptic condition, but only in the literal sense of an unveiling: "When I say that modernity is

apocalyptic, I mean that it is revelatory. . . . Our epoch is characterized by the on-going revelation of the *human* origins of violence. I
think there's a kind of systematic logic to it. A world without sacrificial protection will create all sorts of tools, more and more dangerous,
which will threaten those who build them. Technology when applied
to destruction functions this way: it reveals or disconceals the human
origin of violence" ("The Logic of the Undecidable" 13).

Truth is not before us, in the future, lying yet to be measured or
mastered; our mastery of the world has proceeded apace with the production of means of violence that escape our mastery. Truth is not
above us, in the empyrean, awaiting revelation, illumination, or post-
survival representation; it is not behind us either, in our past, awaiting
Platonic recollection. When Derrida states the case for writing against
metaphysics, as against "all dualisms," " all monisms," he states the
case for the victim very well: "The subordination of the trace to the
full presence summed up in the logos, the humbling of writing beneath a speech dreaming its plenitude, such are the gestures required
by an onto-theology determining the archeological and eschatological
meaning of being as presence, as parousia, as life without differance:
another name for death, historical metonymy where God's name holds
death in check" (*OG* 71). When he shows that writing as spatialization,
as differance, is the structural model of language, he impels us to the
conclusion that language is not violence, but rather an alternative to
violence, the deferral of a violence that language in turn covers up in
the name of a transcendental truth, of God, nature, instinct or whatever. But the death of God has been widely celebrated in our time (for
Baudelaire it was already a banality: "Of religion, I think it useless to
speak and to look for its remains, since still taking the trouble to deny
God is the only scandal in such matters" [*OC* 629]); this death means
that nothing holds violence in check. Although language can and has
served to foment violence, its scientific vocation is a representation, a
theory of violence and victimage that owes nothing to the violence of
representation.

Truth is not transcendental; if anything, it is transdescendental, for
it lies beneath us, underfoot, in the victim, or rather, in relation to the
victim. Truth is historical. There is historical truth in just that sense,
for there can be no denial of what daily threatens to be our posthistorical era. It appears probable—I mean provable—that no other notion or form of truth is salvageable from the wreckage of two and a half

millennia of truth seeking, which Nietzsche in *The Genealogy of Morals* (160–61) hailed ambivalently as the work of Christianity and of which deconstruction is the latest phase, perhaps the last phase. No other form or norm of truth appears to remain or be desirable, because, among other things, our desire for truth is explained by our desire to escape victimization. It is around the victim that our cognitive and moral impulses conjoin, that concern for fact and value cease to oppose each other. The victimary hypothesis is an antidote, a true remedy to the cognitive nihilism that has recently beguiled as many theologians and philosophers as literary critics. It confides in the irreducible dichotomy of victim and persecutor, and no critique of difference, however bent on "undecidability," is proof against it, for indifference to that difference sanctions the persecution of all and threatens the survival of all.

This is not to say that desire for truth is immune to mimetic conflict; it can just as easily become the object of desire—that is, a signifier of another's desire—as anything else. All our inquisitions, sacred and (ostensibly) profane, testify to that. It is in the name of the victim that we condemn them, along with the hieratic postulate of truth, the imposture of truth that produces victims. In so doing we implicitly subscribe to a victimary hypothesis as our criteriology, to the victim as *krites*, or judge.

It is a true story, then, that stands the test of deconstruction, above all, that of undecidability: between victim and persecutor no one hesitates to decide the part of right without endangering his or her own right to decide (*krinein*) anything. This is a story that satisfies the truth-seeking impulse of deconstruction itself, its demystifying fervor in the detection of occulted or mystified violence.

The victim is the matrix of difference and the origin of differance, the play of differences: between signifier and signified, sacred and profane, violence and peace, and chaos and community, whose presence to itself as cum-unus is mediated by the designation of the victim and the deferrals of violence that stem from that originary differance. Difference is the matrix of value; that is the epistemological conquest of structuralism as it concerns itself with the play of binary oppositions. And the victim is the matrix of the difference between good and bad and true and false as well, which the critical scientific spirit determines by detecting natural or human causality behind allegedly supernatural causality. This is the thesis of *The Scapegoat* (especially chap. 15), which articulates the epistemological conquest of our post-structural condition when it locates our truth-seeking impulse in concern for the victim.

Structuralism has successfully displaced attention from entities, essences, and objects and refocused it toward relations in human affairs, which are primordially and fundamentally relations of desire. Recent research in the social sciences has shown how these relations govern entire economies, national and global (de Radkowski; Dumouchel and Dupuy; Dupuy). These relations are structurally destined to misunderstanding just because they are relations of desire, just because human reality is structured by desire, which cannot know itself for being the copy of another desire. This self-misunderstanding is structural, not mysterious. The victim is necessarily the key to this misunderstanding, an effect whose reality does not brook contradiction, not by any stretch of the imagination, however derealizing, surrealizing, or otherwise demystifying.

This is the *structural*, or matricial, import of Auschwitz and Hiroshima as well, and if we are to believe Adorno, it is irreversible: "A new categorical imperative has been imposed by Hitler upon unfree mankind: to arrange their thoughts and actions so that Auschwitz will not repeat itself, so that nothing similar will happen" (*Negative Dialectics* 363). Of course, similar things have happened elsewhere, on a different scale, to different peoples, under different administrations, owing to relations between the state and the violence that the state exists to cover up (I will explore this violence in the next chapter).

On the other hand, most people have an abiding sense that there is nothing similar to Auschwitz. There is a host of books and learned journals committed to demonstrating the uniqueness of the Holocaust. There are compelling arguments, dense with historical research, for the view that it stands outside history. But how can it, if not as a purely victimary event, an essentially sacrificial enterprise devoid of any productive alibi, an *economic* dimension in the most general sense of that word—except the economy of sacrifice itself, which is the economy of violence itself? If Judeocide stands outside history, it is nonetheless as its supplement, its inside turned out, the instance of its last judgment, its external tribunal.

Adorno's rephrase of Kant's categorical imperative is not new. Its persuasive force resonates with the Last Judgment cited in Matthew's gospel (25:35–36): "I was hungry and you gave me food . . . I was in

prison and you came to me." It is only through identification with the
victim that all sacrificial practices, all persecutions and exploitations,
are definitively renounced. In the nuclear age the imperative takes on
a renewed urgency, as identification with the victim obeys a structural
necessity so clear as to amount to a banality. This is an opportunity to
examine what is meant by Hannah Arendt's notorious expression,
"the banality of evil," which becomes rationally comprehensible when
we consider its structural matrix in the mystifications of desire.

For all his apparent, that is, logocentric, confusion about something
like "unimpaired formulation," Robert Jay Lifton is right when he observes that truth is a matter of bearing witness. He quotes another author, David Rawicz, on the Holocaust: "The only thing that matters,
that *will* matter, is the integrity of witnesses" (*Death in Life* 528). It is
a matter of witness against victimage, witness against death by administrative measure: witness against sacrifice, against holocaust, against
scapegoating. For Lifton is more right than he knows when he remarks on the "adaptive usefulness" of scapegoating: "Yet a process at
least bordering on scapegoating seems necessary to the formulation of
any death immersion. It enters into the survivor's necessary theory of
causation and his need to pass judgment on people and forces outside
himself to avoid drowning in his own guilt and symbolic disorder"
(528). Primo Levi testifies concisely to this guilt in a fictive dialogue
about the shame of the survivor: " 'What shame?' Line asked. 'You're
ashamed when you're guilty of something, and they aren't guilty of
anything.' 'Ashamed of not being dead,' Francine said. 'I feel it, too.
It's stupid, but I feel it. It's hard to explain. It's the impression that
the others died in your place, that you're alive gratis, thanks to a privilege you haven't earned, a trick you've played on the dead. Being
alive isn't a crime, but we feel it like a crime' " (*If Not Now, When?*
295). The uniqueness of the Holocaust comes to the fore here again.
The fact that the living survive the dead is an utter banality, yet the
fact that some were chosen arbitrarily to die causes living on to appear
arbitrary in a way that is symmetrical to the deaths of others who died
in "their place." Those closest to those dead are closer to a truth that
others can only resurrect historically.

Very much, if not all, of Levi's writings may be regarded as an attempt to articulate, at least to communicate if not to explain, the
"symbolic disorder" induced by the experience of the camps, where
the causal question "Why?" was not allowed: "Hier ist kein warum"

(*If This Is a Man* 35). *The Drowned and the Saved* seeks, among other things, to restore the difference between the prisoners and their custodians amid "a daily struggle against hunger, cold, fatigue, and blows in which the room for choices (especially moral choices) was reduced to zero" (49–50). It would be little enough to say, perhaps, that the demoralization Levi describes again and again constitutes an experience—indeed, a strategy on the part of the custodians—of radical desymbolization. Such a pale abstraction is incommensurate with the experience he narrates, but that only enhances the truth-value of the narrative.

Certain remarks by Adorno and others suggest that meaning does not survive such a story, that truth, not to mention philosophy or metaphysics, is the victim here, that we face "the truthless truth on truth," "a tale told by an idiot, full of sound and fury signifying nothing." No; the victim is the truth of this story, which is why I return to it so insistently: because no skepticism is proof against it. The obstacle to interpretation becomes its cornerstone very much in the way that what is excluded from philosophical discourse—the grapheme— becomes "a non-site or non-philosophical site from which to question philosophy": "My central question is: from what site or non-site (*non-lieu*) can philosophy as such appear to itself as other than itself, so that it can interrogate and reflect upon itself in an original manner? Such a non-site or alterity would be radically irreducible to philosophy. But the problem is that such a non-site cannot be defined or situated by means of philosophical language" (Derrida, "Deconstruction and the Other" 108). For Derrida, as for many another, this nonsite appears to be what we call literature, as exemplified by its rehabilitation of the grapheme, its investiture of writing "as such." Of all the problems that arise here, I will mention only that the contest of faculties between "philosophy and poetry" is, as Plato testifies, an "ancient quarrel" (*Republic* § 607). Indeed, a return to the origin of Western philosophy in Plato uncovers the victim, which is precisely where the question of origins must be situated. If there is "an original manner" in which to interrogate philosophy, it is with the victim, whose voice survives the sense "squeezed," in Adorno's words, out of its oblivion.

In sum, to call history "a tale told by an idiot, full of sound of fury," is to relegate it to the prehistory (and the posthistory) of the undifferentiated chaos antecedent to the sacrificial mechanism in which human culture is born. Alternatively, a theory that traces the origin of meaning and the matrix of truth to the arbitrary victim of undifferentiated violence is the apposite response to the meaninglessness that violence always nurtures. Moreover, such a theory offers prospects of a totalization immune to accusations of totalitarianism, reprehensible for its harvest of victims. The victim is the structuring principle of sacrifice and its totalitarian avatars. It is the interpretive theme of the victimary hypothesis, which accordingly has no stake in occluding its agency.

Identification with the victim obeys a further structural necessity in this context: to escape the symmetrical necessity of identifying with the persecutors, "a trick you've played on the dead." This is the trick the dead have played on us, as intuited by Marguerite Duras:

> If Nazi crime is not seen in world terms, if it isn't understood collectively, then that man in the concentration camp at Belsen who died alone but with the same collective soul and class awareness that made him undo a bolt on the railroad one night somewhere in Europe, without a leader, without a uniform, without a witness, has been betrayed. If you give a German and not a collective interpretation to the Nazi Horror, you reduce the man in Belsen to regional dimensions. The only possible answer to this crime is to turn it into a crime committed by everyone. To share it. Just like the idea of equality and fraternity. In order to bear it, to tolerate the idea of it, we must share the crime. (*The War* 50)

This is indeed a hard saying, for it urges us to identify our essential humanity with sacrificial institutions. It defines our moral and cognitive imperative as averting scapegoating.

This is what is at issue in Germany's (and not only Germany's) "*historikerstreit,*" the failure to mourn the victims of the Third Reich. It is by far the most persistent theme in the epilogue to Eric Santner's *Stranded Objects,* whose final words make a plea for "the human capacity to bear witness to history and to claim solidarity with the oppressed of history, past and present" (160; see also 153, 156). My only quarrel with Santner's analyses is the confidence he displays in Freudian thematics of mourning as it affects the narcissistic identity of the mourner; for his confidence, that is, in a "primitive narcissism" (5) that the mimetic hypothesis lays open to question at the outset (*THFW* 356–82) and that Borch-Jacobsen effectively deconstructs in Freud's own text: "There is no narcissism except of the other. You have to be two (at least) to make a Narcissus, and what we find here is a kind of transcendental illusion which requires the active collaboration of two parties" (*Le Sujet freudien* 142). In short, it is my view that the incapacity to mourn, its consequent admixture with or transformation as melancholy, is abetted by illusions about narcissism, about indivisible selfhood, which such theory perpetuates when it attributes autonomous self-love to "His Majesty the Baby," to beautiful women, and the like.

Paul Fussell's gloss on Duras's text is pertinent in precisely this regard: " 'The only possible answer to this crime is to turn it into a crime committed by everyone. To share it.' Which means that if you can't imagine yourself an SS officer hustling the Jewish women and children to the gas chamber, you need to be more closely in touch with your buried self" (*Thank God for the Atom Bomb* 113). Yes and no, for there is no self buried deeper than the power of mimesis to compel collective behavior, to induce hideous misconduct. A "buried self" is misleading to the extent that it implies the unconscious agency of depth psychology—yet another scapegoat. Once again, Hannah Arendt's insistence on the banality of evil, hence its scandalously lateral dimension, is more to the point: "Evil is never 'radical,' it is only extreme, and it possesses neither depth nor any demonic dimension. It can overgrow and lay waste the entire world precisely because it spreads like a fungus on the surface. It is 'thought-defying,' . . . because thought tries to reach some depth, to go to the roots, and the moment it concerns itself with evil, it is frustrated because there is nothing" (in Young-Bruehl, *Hannah Arendt* 369). I have identified this "nothing" as mimetic contagion, which is nourished only by delusions about selfsame autonomy. In line with Arendt's simile, I could say that evil is a parasite, a nonsite, whose host is a good will that everyone mistakes as his or her own moral center, thereby sanctioning the extermination of other parasites, of others as such. As Michel Serres remarks (*Le Parasite* 25–38), the host is undecidably double, being host and parasite at once, being a host of violent doubles that feeds on its scapegoats for its putative and altogether parasitic identity. "Masse," in a word, "en différence de soi" (Borch-Jacobsen, *Le Sujet freudien* 288).

Scapegoating is the administration of death (distinct from its advent by "natural" means), and the victim is witness against it. Scapegoating, as Girard has argued, is the origin of the symbolic order, and the victim is witness against its structural distortions, which are those of every culture, of human culture as such, as it seeks to expel from its midst a violence that founds it. It is in the victim that our notion of causality originates, and it is by the victim that every finality is judged.

The truth is the victim, and that condition is in our time universal. The post-age is the victim age. The survivor who identifies with the victim, who adopts victimage as his or her truth, as his or her past and future, is a true survivor, a being in whom truth survives and through whom survival is a truth, a genuine human possibility rather than a contingency, alibi, or accident. Such a survivor is the antithesis of the sacrificial mechanism of adaptation by which culture has forged its destiny, "from the foundation of the world" through its certain sacrificial consummation: "a republic," as Jonathan Schell, along with numerous others, prognosticates, "of insects and grass." To restate the proposition in poststructural terms, the victim is the difference that makes for differance, then as now: by then, I mean at the violent origin of our species; by now, I mean any time now, any such time before humankind's future in victimization will have been perfected. At such a time, all difference between victim and persecutor will have been truly obliterated, and Macbeth will have had the last word.

Such a time seems less imminent since the catastrophic collapse of the Berlin Wall, which *Time* magazine (Dec. 13, 1989) cannily dubbed a "Deconstruction"—*sans plus*. It is an accurate designation, for it testifies to the breakdown of a system, a structure, that, for all the real political and economic differences informing it, was essentially propelled by mimetic rivalry in its most baleful portents. The astonishing swiftness of the collapse testifies to the hollowness, the ritualized co-dependence of many of the disparities presumably undergirding it. As a result, both sides have found themselves woefully unprepared to deal with each other or with the world that their mortal opposition served to structure and render luminously—and for many numinously—intelligible. Jubilation over the end of the Cold War has thus been tempered by legitimate concern about its destabilizing consequences, about a loss of difference that seemed to provide such order and predictability to the world for four decades that nostalgia for it has become a central theme of its discussion (see, e.g., Barnet, "Defining the Moment," and Mearsheimer, "Why We Will Soon Miss the Cold War").

What the future holds for a world no longer secured by ideological difference is a topic of anxiety to all concerned, and in the nuclear age all are concerned. With the resurgence of old nationalisms, the incentive for small nations to acquire nuclear arms is the greater for their no longer coming under the tutelage or constraints of superpower alliances and strategies. In such a politically volatile environment, the dangers of terrorism (discussed in the next chapter) are significantly enlarged. Nor should we discount the capacity of so-called great powers, actual and emergent, to squander the benefits of possible reconciliation on improvident alliances and explosive interventions.

In sum, the most dire prognoses are just as plausible as the fulfillment of our best hopes for the species, only now there is no theological cocoon in which to hide from the consequences of our actions. I have argued throughout that much of mimetic theory is borne out by history. History may yet falsify its bleakest apprehensions, but that development could only further gratify its ethical intentions. Mimetism is not determinism but rather a fact of human conduct whose critique I am conducting here. Being subject to representation, it is subject to control; that has ever been the practical vocation of what we revere as science. Its antithesis is human freedom and ethical responsibility, whose possibility is eloquently evoked as a *"pure future"* by Marcel Gauchet. I quote at length from but one passage, whose structural *vision* is borne out by its having been published in 1985, well before anything like a thaw in superpower dogmatisms was foreseeable:

> Our commerce with the future is gradually going to dispense hereafter with divines, with tragic intercessors and sacrificers. For that is its major paradox: it becomes all the more secular as it reveals its invisible provenance. The more it becomes unpredictable, the less it is inevitable; the more it makes us responsible, the more it returns us to the insurmountable and cold assurance that it is we who make it, that it is from the infinitely complex entanglement of our actions that it will be born. And the less it is possible for us to hold it up as an object of superstition, of a cult. And the more certain it will be that we only know one thing about it: that it will be *other* than what we are able to represent it as being—the more that confrontation with our limits obliges us to become authors of a history that nothing nor anyone determines from a point outside of it and that only comprises one enigma: our own. That is a sure sign that we are moving henceforth against the grain of the religious logic of origins: here the ordeal of otherness, eternal matrix of dependency, has become the compelling benchmark of freedom. (*Le Désenchantement du monde* 267–68)

5

State Secrets

Indirections

In past and in some present cultures, the sovereign sway of evil among people is attributed to demonic agency. Although secular states are no longer captive of this idea, the control of violence continues to elude them; our relation to violence is one that largely escapes us, and never more effectively than when we hypostatize it, whether as ill will or instinct. Our misunderstanding is not at all surprising, however, when we view culture as originating in a mystified deferral of violence, in sacrifice, whereby human violence is rerouted via the sacred, which is a safe place for us both to abhor and adore it. This indirection is the blind spot in our relation to violence, but it is no longer as opaque or inaccessible as it used to be. Rather, it grows less inscrutable with the passage of time, whose Latinized translation is what we call secularization and which is likewise translatable as deritualization or desacralization. This is especially the case if we identify the latter with the progress of theory, the progress of representation, including progress in the representation of representation, of language itself.

All available theories of indirection are party to this progress, except where they confide in the opacity of language, in its incapacity to reflect on itself or to reveal the truth of human relations. The thematization of writing, of the gramm, is no excuse to celebrate this incapacity; it is no obstacle to progress if its thematization, in the deconstructive form of marking its exclusion by logocentrism, marks a closure to ontological delusions about representation. These delusions can be fatal, if the fate of writing in Plato or Rousseau is any evidence.

That it corresponds to the role of the sacrificial victim in culture is no accident; rather, it is essential if the role of culture is to mistake the agency of violence by investing it in the sacred (victim), which appears as the source of a violence apart from the self.

The sacred is an indirect representation of human violence. It is a false representation, but its falsity is true and verifiable (for its Popperian "falsifiability," see Livet, in Dumouchel, ed., *Violence et vérité*). The upshot is that we must cease to regard indirection as an obstacle to understanding rather than as a vehicle or a pathway to it—as a method, in a word. That is the aim of this chapter: to approach the question of violent agency indirectly, in terms of indirect victims of state violence.

These are victims not of warring states, or of the state toward those of its members whom its deems culpable and directly deserving of violent retribution, but of the state's indirect relation to violence. These are victims of covert operations, which involve the state in a relation to violence that it prefers, as the adjective clearly states, to cover up. A number of times I shall allude to the July 1985 Greenpeace episode, in which secret agents of the French government blew up a ship protesting against nuclear test bombing in the Pacific, killing a member of the crew. But Greenpeace serves here only as a pretext, a cypher for the all-too-numerous covert operations conducted by every modern industrial state. I chose the Greenpeace affair because it may be a dead issue, thus distancing the discussion from the heat of immediate journalistic policy debate. Covert operations are an eminently live issue precisely because of the dangers attending anything liable to be identified as "naked aggression," for such aggression solicits a symmetrical response whose planetary escalation is abhorred by all.

While pursuing this line of inquiry, it will be necessary to review certain themes and perspectives of deconstruction for the value they have as a critique of institutions. Though there is a world of difference between a victim and a signifier, the victim itself is a signifier of violence. It is for forensic science to decide whether the violence is natural or social—that is, human. Accordingly, the social sciences, particularly the jurisprudential, can be illumined by certain aspects of deconstruction.

Deconstruction originates as a critique of the sign and of difference that extends to the difference between the sign and the so-called thing itself. It is regularly shown that the difference between the thing and its sign may in fact be ambiguous, problematic, even undecidable. Those who resist this argument or presume to the contrary in the name of commonsense realism are charged by deconstruction with logocentrism, metaphysics, and mythology. This position consists in "the determination of being as *presence*," of which signs are the degraded replica, the fallible or fallen and therefore culpable image—the choice between Platonism or its double, naive empiricism. Confidence in such Being falls prey to the charge of ontotheology. Indivisible, indissoluble, irreducible (above all, to representation), such Being is formally identical to the Being of God, the God of philosophers, *ens realissimus, ens causa sui*, the "unmoved mover," which Derrida styles as "the face of pure intelligibility," "absolute logos," and "infinite creative subjectivity" (*OG* 13). This is the case whether we identify this Being as God, man, nature, history, truth, or anything else (*WD* 411).

This cryptotheology is not easily set aside, for it is irresistible: "Nothing is thinkable without these notions. . . . It is first of all a question of demonstrating the systematic and historical solidarity of concepts and gestures of thought which we often believe can be innocently separated. The sign and the divinity have the same place and the same time of birth. The age of the sign is essentially theological. It will perhaps never *end*. Its historical closure *is nonetheless outlined*" (*OG* 13-14). We are, by language, culture, and tradition, implicated with divinity, accomplice to sacralization, predestined to ontotheology. It is the task of deconstruction to reveal that complicity and to demonstrate, contrary to ontotheological assumptions and by way of marking their closure, that the thing we take to be irreducibly itself, originally and insignificantly itself, "*sol de non-signification*," is always already a sign. As Derrida states in his analysis of Peirce's semiology, "*The thing itself is a sign*" (*OG* 49).

I have no wish to argue too strenuously with this view, for by the logic of identity that it engages (and subverts) it allows for the symmetrically correlate proposition that accounts for so much literature, where the sign itself is a thing, or is treated as a thing. This reversibility extends to this book's central theme of the difference between a sign and a corpse, which, however mute and inert, may (by its marking, for instance) be a sign of criminal violence. Whenever there is any dispute about the difference between a corpse and a sign, or the meaning of the signs on the corpse—about the meaning, that is, of the corpse as a sign—the law intervenes, and it intervenes decisively with its restraint or its retribution. It is for the law as the supreme, unique arbiter of violence to arbitrate such differences as between a thing and a sign. This is in part the implication of Derrida's remark in *The Post Card* that, concerning any debate on the scene of representation, "the police are always in the wings" (91).

The thrust of Derrida's reading of Plato is to show that the scene of representation is the scene of a crime. On the scene of a crime, the conventional wisdom of detective literature intones *"cherchez la femme,"* which is but another way of saying: find the object of desire and you will find violently mimetic rivals, one of whom must be the criminal, the other being the victim, or a surrogate, or some other obstacle to the object of desire. In Derrida's reading of Plato, for instance, writing is the victim whose other, whose rival model, is the father-logos. The mutual object of rivalry is nothing else than each other's primacy or origin-ality.

Although it is customary to regard deconstruction as a denial of reference, it has a referent: violence, the sacred, the victim, whose complexity is what deprives deconstruction of a *"nom unique"* for what it calls differance. I have shown the homology between the encrypted destiny of the letter and the victim in chapter 2, where I sited that referent in the victim. Derrida beckons this conclusion when he defends deconstruction against "a suspension of reference."

> The critique of logocentrism is above all the search for the "other" and the "other" of language. . . . Certainly deconstruction tries to show that the question of reference is much more complex and problematic than traditional theories supposed. It even asks whether our term "reference" is entirely adequate for designating the "other." The other, which is beyond language and which summons language, is perhaps not a "referent" in the normal sense which linguists have attached to this term. But to distance oneself thus from the habitual structure of reference, to challenge or complicate our common assumptions about it, does not amount to saying that there is *nothing* beyond language. ("Deconstruction and the Other" 123–24)

According to the habitual structure of reference, there are things and signs of things; without this difference, language could not function. There are objects and there are words to designate them. But deconstruction argues that language operates out of oblivion or forgetfulness of the materiality of the signifier, incarnate in the latter as the sign of a substitution, the sign of a sign encrypted in speech. According to Girard's hypothesis, the other that summons language and that language symmetrically distances is the victim, whose designation causes a seemingly miraculous end to mimetic violence. It is not a referent in the normal sense, however: from the perspective of the violent community, it is the sacred; from the perspective of the victim, it is violence itself. Violence, the sacred, and the victim constitute the complex to which deconstruction refers. The aim here will be to view this structure on the plane of the historical referent.

Covert Action

At issue in the Greenpeace affair are state security and the unlawful means undertaken to serve that end. At issue is the finality of the law, its supra-referentiality, versus its undecidability, its internal relation to a violence it proscribes for the benefit of its members. No one is above the law or below it: "nul," as the French say, "n'est censé ignorer la loi." Privilege, private law outside or above the law, has been eradicated in modern democratic republics. But in this case the transcendence of the *law*, in the objective sense of the genitive, is compromised by the *transcendence* of the law, in the subjective sense of the genitive. A law higher than positive law, which stipulates "thou shalt not kill," is exceeded, transcended by efforts to ensure its imperium, its hegemony. It is transcended by the law of violence, which has absolute sway, for the state has violated the law it exists to uphold; it has violated the principle on which it is founded.

In modern democratic nations, it is the rule of law, not of individuals, that is said to prevail. The sovereignty of the community's collective will has replaced the violent, arbitrary tyranny of princes. Monarchical privilege, which identifies the prince as the origin, the archè, of law and therefore as beyond it, as absolutely privileged, has not so much been abolished or eradicated as displaced and disguised; the privilege now resides in the law of violence from which the law is intended to protect us. Subjects are subjected to one law, which is not the princely will but the law of violence. Monarchy, then, has been eradicated in the sense of being uprooted; for all that, it has not been abolished or eliminated, but rather evaporated, dematerialized, abstracted, ominously universalized. There is little naked violence, to be sure, for there are myriad institutions that function to clothe violence and to variously mediate, detour, restrain, divert, and accordingly soften its impact. But it is still there. Polyarchy only disguises the arcane rule of violence.

In some cases, the law is frustrated by the complexity of the institutions. In other cases, extreme cases such as I examine here, the law is undone by the simplicity of its dedication to violence. That is the case with covert operations generally. Placing itself outside the law, placing its own security, for which it exists, above, beyond, or prior to the exercise of the law, the state undoes itself in pursuit of its own purpose and destiny, its archè and telos, its essence, which is to maintain itself for the protection of its members against violence. For reasons of state, which are the *raison d'être* of the law, the state has engaged in illegal practices. It feels itself obliged to, as if in obedience to a double bind that opposes the law to itself. Whether to construe the state in such instances as lawless or excessively lawfull is undecidable. It is a condition that Girard assigns to Kafka's insight "that the absence of law is in fact identical with the law run wild and that this identity constitutes the chief burden of mankind" (*VS* 189).

Evidence of this violation in the Greenpeace episode is manifest and decisive in the form of the violent destruction of a victim. The extraterritoriality of the action and the victim only better exemplifies (or as the French say, accuses) the contradiction of the state, its outlawry. The ship was blown up in a foreign harbor, and it was done in the presumed interest of state security. Presumed? Who is to decide that if not the state, in pursuit of the (presumed) interest of its members? If, in a modern liberal state, its members are to decide those interests, they nonetheless invest such decisions in the state, in its elected representatives. We not only invest decision in the state; we invest the state with decisions, we defer to the state for decisions that we do not make, that we prefer not to make, such as whether to commit manslaughter in the interests of state security. Clandestinity, or secret agency, is essential here; it goes to the contradictory essence, the skewed ontology of all states. Secret agency is all to the purpose of the state and its members in their relation to violence, to the secretly violent destiny of the state. There are secrets that the state hides from its members for their mutual good. They reflect the secret that the state and its members hide from themselves, so that the agency of violence can remain a secret to all. That is the interest of the victimary hypothesis, according to which violent agency is always a secret, victimization being the secret and in every way occulted origin of culture.

Because there was a man on board the ship when it was blown up, the Greenpeace affair unravels all that. No one knew he was on board, or wished him aboard, or willed him dead, but there he is—or rather, is no more—a human victim of state security forces. This is essential: no one willed him dead, not directly or deliberately; decisions were almost certainly made to avoid just that. "No victims" was the ministerial mandate for the action (Derogy and Ponant, *Enquête sur trois secrets de l'état*). He is a victim not of a will to power or a will to violence but of a renunciation of will, realized as an abdication of direct and public policy in favor of clandestine state agency. There was a displacement, a deferral to the covert, indirect action by which the state and its members veil their relation to violence. This is the state secret *par excellence*, of which all other secrets are the secret, and which the Greenpeace affair unveils because it unveils the secret that the state withholds from itself: its indirect but nonetheless decisive relation to violence.

The hideous crimes of terrorist groups, such as those perpetrated under the telling banner of *Action Directe*, do not unveil this secret but rather ensure the necessity of agencies, tribunals, and methods destined to cover it up, to legitimize it. (I will return to the capital issue of terrorism.)

The state's relation to violence is not clear or decisive with regard to the state, which prefers in every instance to look away, to delegate violence, to secrete it, clandestinate it, but it is decisive with regard to the victim, who, according to my hypothesis, is the matrix of decision in every instance, in every issue.

Lest this analysis appear paranoid, let me note that it does not deny the state's goal to be the welfare of its members, consisting chiefly in internal and external security, in peace among its members and peace with other states. Rather, it affirms the relation of the state to violence that the state chooses to ignore, that for reasons of state it must ignore to maintain its semblance of legitimacy. But *chooses* is too strong a word; it suggests an ill will that could be corrected by or exchanged against a good will. My contention here is rather that ill will is to be diagnosed as an illness of the will, a debility whose name is desire and to whose mechanisms anything like a sovereign, autonomous will is lacking. Because desire originates not in a self but in another desire, it is prey to mimetic behavior in which the sovereign will has no role. If this is not a benign view of culture, neither is it a malignant one. It argues that free will is a human possibility rarely essayed, especially at the level of nation states.

The argument is structural. Freeman Dyson offers a properly homely illustration that accounts incisively for the unhomely, uncanny dynamic of violence:

> When I was seven years old, I was once reprimanded by my mother for an act of collective brutality in which I had been involved at school. A group of seven-year-olds had been teasing and tormenting a six-year-old. "It is always so," my mother said. "You do things together which not one of you would think of doing alone." That is a piece of my education which I have never forgotten. Wherever one looks in the world of human organization, collective responsibility brings a lowering of moral standards. The military establishment is an extreme case, an organization which seems to have been expressly designed to make it possible for people to do things together which nobody in his right mind would do alone. (*Weapons and Hope* 7)

From the behavior of children through that of armed hosts and the bureaucracies propelling them, Dyson's "education" betokens an economy and clarity having the force of anthropological law, whose name is mimesis.

With the Greenpeace affair, an action of the state issues in a victim. The victimage is clear, the agency is not. It is an accident rather than an action from the point of view of the state; it is a crime from the point of view of its members, one of whom is a victim who could have been any one of its members. If it is crime, violence, that the state outlaws, then this is a crime *par excellence*, a crime of violence that raises the question of the relation of the state to violence, of the state as an institution of violence, as violence institutionalized. This happens not because people love violence but because they hate it; they hate it violently, and so they clandestine it in the state. Institutions, beginning with sacrifice, exist to mediate violence and to mask its agency.

The failure of the state to adjudicate the action properly or satisfactorily is inevitable. It is legible in the failure of other states to prosecute the violence of their military and paramilitary organizations accused of engaging in overt terrorism against citizens. Argentina, Chile, and El Salvador come to mind, but, with the production of Marcel Ophuls's *Hotel Terminus*, so does the complicity of the United States in covering up the traces of the war criminal Klaus Barbi. And Barbi was but one of a host of Nazi officials who were more or less excused of their crimes so that they could be enlisted against a new foreign enemy, as Arno Mayer, among others, has testified (see *Why Did the Heavens Not Darken?* xii). The failure to mourn victims of the Third Reich, a forgetting of its crimes, is in part owed to the almost immediate recruitment by ideological opponents of Nazi bureaucrats against their new enemies—each other. It is a scandal neither side failed to publicize about the other. At that point, a new host of government officials (and taxpayers?) acquired a share, however unwitting, in crimes against humanity.

This cover-up, this failure to prosecute, is a radical injustice, a literal travesty, for it goes to the root of evil in unrestrained violence. It nonetheless obeys a structural necessity, for it derives from the parergonal (Derrida, *La Vérité dans la peinture* 63) or invaginated (Derrida, "Living on" 97) relation of the state to violence: it expels violence by absorbing it, rules it out by taking it in, by enfolding it within its institutional apparatus. For what is a secret agency if not a parergon or para-organ of violence? It is a "pharmaceutical" relation in terms of the vocabulary of "Plato's Pharmacy": like writing is for speech, violence is the remedy-poison (*pharmakon*) in which the state originates, which it expels in order to found itself. Virtually any of the Derridean anticoncepts or anathememes ("trace," "differance," "marque/ marge," or "marche/démarche") can be applied to these secret agencies, these agencies of violence secreted by the state, which function as a *supplement* to official and public organs of power, namely, the army and the police. The resistance and in every sense reluctance (from *reluctari*, to fight back) to assign blame rightly and directly, the failure to locate the proper author or origin of the crime, are proper to an institution that has been founded for the purpose of masking violence of people to themselves, of making them love in the state what they hate in one another and in themselves.

According to the victimary hypothesis, that is just what sacrifice does. It accomplishes this by attributing violence to the sacred, by alienating violence in the victim, which it sacralizes for bringing concord, unanimity, and community to its members. The sacrificial victim is arbitrarily selected; he or she need only lack the intimate communal ties that might generate reprisals, that might solicit vindication (from *vindex*, avenger)—whence the selection of kings as from above society, slaves as from below it, or orphans as defenselessly isolated within it (*VS* 11–14). It is a process of substitution and displacement, of metaphor and metonymy, if you will, that accounts for the substitution of animal for human victims and in turn reflects both the arbitrariness and the obliquity, or indirection, of violence. It is ever amiss, being a mystification of violent agency. Direct violence among group members is intolerable to the maintenance of public order, to communal life. Internally, it is to be mediated by the law, which, for the sake of communal peace, attempts to monopolize it. It is also regularly alienated, redirected toward a common external enemy. Accordingly, the criminal is regarded as the public enemy; the victim of state violence, of legal, adjudicated sentencing, is supposed to be rightly and justly chosen, being identified as the origin and author of the violence that the state restrains, expels, or punishes to vindicate its members.

The Greenpeace affair, in all its complexity and simplicity (regarding the agent versus the victim), reveals the state as heir to sacrifice. For who is the victim? Just anyone. Indeed, its being just anyone who happened to be on board at the time is what marks the dead man as an arbitrary victim rather than a declared enemy of the state or the people. He is an accidental but nonetheless innocent victim of state action, a sacrificial victim to state security. The demand for adjudication of the crime, for retribution on the part of society, expresses society's intolerance of sacrificial practices. If it is meritorious, it is also dangerous, for it is an effort to desacralize state violence and consequently destabilize state security.

On the other hand, the attempted cover-up betrays the state's implicit commitment to those same practices; it is a commitment for whose cover-up the state exists. It cannot be made explicit without naming the sacred, which the modern state exists to displace. Add to that the singularly momentous fact that the clandestine operation was conducted to protect the state's disposition and perfection of nuclear arms, which are universally recognized as means of definitive, absolute violence, and you have a line that, from the banks of the Seine to a harbor in New Zealand, stretches halfway around the world connecting violence to the sacred and both to the state.

Like the Old Testament divinity, the state jealously reserves its exclusive rights to violence. Violence is a signifier of the sacred (*VS* 148, 151), being a signifier of the mimetic desire to appropriate for oneself what the other, any and all others, has designated as desirable. It is the mimetic confluence, the common and mutual influence, of desire on the same object that makes the object dangerous to appropriate, that makes the object taboo or sacred (*VS* 144–48; see also Gans, *The Origin of Language* 8–67). This is what has happened to state sovereignty (Schell, *The Fate of the Earth* 129, 133, 187–88), to state security, whose sacralization is manifest in the total, definitive violence that has been enlisted to realize it—and that, consequently, none dares to implement. This is in every sense painfully obvious, so that Paul Virilio, without reference to either Girard or Derrida, can observe that "today the Holy War is the horizon of history" (*Pure War* 50); "belief in salvation, in peace by an ultimate weapon is idolatry" (53). In consequence, we are experiencing a "return of the sacred" (123) whereby "God has come back into history through the door of nuclear terror" (134).

I have already consulted Derrida's own contribution to nuclear criticism. Still other of his remarks are pertinent here for his reflections on the properly ontological questions envoked by the prospect of nuclear holocaust. "Why is there something rather than nothing?" This question posed by Heidegger in *What Is Metaphysics* (1929) is revived by the prospect of "remainderless destruction, without mourning and without symbolicity" (Derrida, "No Apocalypse . . . " 30). In the "groundlessness of a remainderless self-destruction of the self, auto-destruction of the *autos* itself" (30) is the question of state sovereignty that sovereign states do not pose to themselves. Such groundlessness, at once self-evident and fabulous, suggests that Schell is correct, accurate, and realistic rather than utopian, as some reviewers have averred, when he argues that we have to "reinvent politics, reinvent the world" (*The Fate of the Earth* 226).

In a sense, deconstruction says that this is what we are always already doing when it argues against any belief in immutable essences, in things or meanings apart from signs, and in substance (and other *stance* words, such as *state* or *constitution*) apart from forms; when it argues against origins and foundation that we have not confabulated out of an ontological delusion inhering in language; and, above all, when it argues that we cannot trace the world, or politics, or culture, or

institutions to a stable essence or principle or to any values that do not
bear traces of a mystification, a cryptotheologic hypostasis (see Burke
on "The Paradox of Substance" in *A Grammar of Motives*, where virtually all the gestures of deconstruction are executed). For instance,
"A foundational event cannot be simply understood within the logic of
what it founds. The foundation of a right is not a juridical event. The
origin of the principle of reason . . . is not rational" (Derrida, "Mochlos, ou le conflict des facultés" 50). This is not to deny all foundations, but only self-legitimizing, rational ones, for the topic of
Derrida's essay on Kant is the foundation of the university, which Kant
locates in a tension between theology and philosophy, in what is in
effect a mimetic rivalry between the faculties.

In the name of what do we secure the state? That is the issue raised
by the Greenpeace affair, and by all covert operations to the extent
that they work against the law on which the state is founded. It is
clearly an ethical issue. Derrida's nuclear criticism shows how it is also
both a semiological and an ontological issue, for here again his text
bears witness to a tension between the thing and the sign, the name
and its referent. Because of nuclear war's total destructiveness, Derrida observes that it can be waged only "in the name of that which is
worth more than life, that which, giving its value to life, has greater
value than life" ("No Apocalypse . . . "30). Schell and others have
made this same point about the patent absurdity of this totalizing war,
whereby all is lost in an all-out effort to win. Derrida's analysis helps
penetrate the *structure* of this non-sense, for it is not ordinary nonsense, pure contingency, "a tale told by an idiot." Far from it; meaning is lost from the excesses of the signifying process.

This war is ultimately—that is, logically, teleologically, and arche-
ologically—to be waged "in the name of something whose name by
this logic of total destruction can no longer be borne, transmitted, inherited by anything living" (30), "in the name of nothing," "in the
name of the name with only the non-name of 'name' " (31): "a name-
less war in the name of the name. That would be the End and
the Revelation of the name itself, the Apocalypse of the Name" (31).
This is the self-referential paradox of the name that names itself as
"name" and which consequently has no name, although we can give
that a name: "ça a un nom," as the French say when referring to
something pejorative. It is the sacred, which names the point where
the violence of desire becomes the desire of violence. Violence is that

which for lack of a better name we call the sacred as that which all desire and none dare appropriate.

Following on the work of Whitehead, Russell, and Gödel, Jean-Pierre Dupuy has shown that all such self-referential paradoxes and self-fulfilling prophecies exhibit the double-binding logic of the sacred. The one who falls victim by chance to the circle of violence is retrospectively interpreted as the destined savior-creator of the community:

> The cultural order and social differentiation which spring from the res-olution of the crisis may be considered as a "fixed point" of the sacred circle: produced by chance, it is experienced as a necessary order. Self-reference transforms chance into destiny. Chance and destiny have this in common that both escape, by definition, the mastery of men. But men only see the unorganized in chance, while they invoke destiny to account for what they perceive as organized. Therefore if the arbitrary can appear to them as organized, it is because they interpret it as the production of a divinity or some postulated unknown force; even if its meaning escapes them, even if they rebel against the injustice of its decrees. Such is the logic of the sacred. ("Mimésis et morphogenèse," in Deguy, ed., *René Girard et le problème du mal* 243–44)

By the sacred I do not mean what is ontologically wholly other, which culture and theology call the holy or the divinity. The Girardian sacred is other than itself, like the self-contradictory desire that engenders it. Like the neighbor whose difference I imitate and thereby deny, like the statement "this statement is false," and very like a war in the name of the name, the self-referential paradox issues in a double bind: "In every case," Dupuy pursues, "the mimetic form cannot reflect upon itself without destroying itself. Differentiation is transformed into indifferentiation when it thinks back on itself. That is precisely the self-referential paradox: the more it wishes to be other, the more it produces the same" (257).

The purely formal structure of self-referential paradoxes results in annihilating the meaning they seek to contain. When their structure informs society, the socius, what is annihilated is society. There is a *performative* (or, following Derrida's refinement on that notion: "per-verformative") dimension here that is unmistakable in our era: "Vio-lence will come to an end only after it has had the last word and that word has been accepted as divine. The meaning of this word must remain hidden, the mechanism of unanimity remain concealed. For religion protects man as long as its ultimate foundations are not revealed" (*VS* 135). It is in the name of violence, for the sake of its definitive mastery and disposition, that such a war as we have been contemplating for four decades would be waged: in the name of the sacred, which is nothing but the name we give to human violence to veil its humanity and mystify its agency. To expel it from our midst, we sacralize it. We do not recognize the name because we have veiled it as God, nature, history, law, or truth.

But now the veil is rent, the name is revealed: it is nothing, annihilation, a covert operation for *pure war:* violence is the sacred. In history this process goes by the name of the sacrificial crisis; this is the name Girard gives to Western history as an accelerating process of ever more violent indifferentiation succeeded by still more violent redifferentiation: "To think religiously is to envision the city's destiny in terms of that violence whose mastery over man increases as man believes he has gained mastery over it. To think religiously (in a primitive sense) is to see violence as something superhuman, to be kept always at a distance and ultimately renounced. When the fearful adoration of this power begins to diminish and all distinctions begin to disappear, the ritual sacrifices lose their force; their potency is no longer recognized by the entire community" (*VS* 135). There is no difficulty here in recognizing the desacralizing, de-institutionalizing progress of history. As this passage continues it becomes apparent why this progress does not result in the reduction of violence or even in a retreat of the sacred: "Each member tries to correct the situation individually, and none succeeds. The withering away of the transcendental influence means that there is no longer the slightest difference between a desire to save the city and unbridled ambition, between genuine piety and the desire to claim divine status for oneself. Everyone looks on a rival enterprise as evidence of blasphemouse designs. . . . Men set to quarreling about the gods, and their skepticism leads to a new sacrificial crisis that will appear retrospectively, in the light of a new manifestation of unanimous violence—as a new act of divine intervention and divine revenge"(*VS* 135). Substitute the word *agency* for *member,* which is what individuals and states do to veil membership in the drama (*The Bacchae,* by name), and you have the Greenpeace affair, which is but the name for covert operations, for the appropriation of violence by the law and against the law, the sacralization of violence above the law and from which the law draws its sanction. Secret agency and the sacred are synonymous as names by which the law disguises its violent foundations. Transcendence is the name humanity gives to violence at a distance; blasphemy, impiety, and evil are the names it gives to violence in proximity, that is, to our neighbor's violence.

The paradoxical observation that violence's "mastery over man increases as man believes he has gained mastery over it," that it is fueled by the means engaged to overcome it, describes the appropriately named nuclear dilemma (from *di*, two, and *lemma*, premise): the contradictorily twofold premise of victory and defeat, of victory as defeat, and defeat as victory—of violence. This is the name that names itself when it misnames itself as other. Loss of difference, of meaning, comes about as this simultaneous excess and recess or abscess of difference. This is semantically foreshadowed in the common recognition that these differences are fundamentally ideo-logical, that they proceed from abstractions, reflecting the logic or law of ideas or forms rather than of things or nature (*physis*). We find ourselves in the realm of purely formal logic, with no substance undergirding symbols. The problem is that there is no such realm, no such thing as purely formal logic. In the world of mathematics, the result is undecidability as to total verification, for there will be at least one well-defined formula whose truth-value is undecidable. In the world of people, the ultimate result is annihilation. Like pure mathematics, pure war is self-obliterating. Douglas Hofstader's fantasy, based on Gödel's first incompleteness theorem, of "a phonograph which could produce any sound whatsoever, even its own self-breaking sound, which is of course impossible" (*Gödel, Escher, Bach* 77), is realized in history, where the impossibility is history, or human culture itself.

This is not a mere semiological whirlgig. It describes the operation of a machine whose mimetic character in the form of the arms race requires no elaboration and whose internal contradictions have become transparent to opposing parties. The strategy of nuclear deterrence is purely mimetic, all anticipation and deferral, all representation. It operates by feints and fictions of reprisal, including the broadcast fiction that, lest the threat lose its credibility, we don't know what the threat catastrophically implies for all. It is an astonishing feat, as Stephen Kull describes it in *Minds at War:* we have to pretend we do not know what we know or what we do. As Girard observes of our worldwide Hamlet posture in his own contribution to nuclear criticsm, "strategic thinking, as a result, demands ever increasing subtlety; it involves less and less action, more and more calculation. In the end, it becomes difficult to distinguish strategy from procrastination. The very notion of strategy may be strategic in regard to the self-defeating nature of revenge which no one wants to face, not yet at least, so that the possibility of revenge is not entirely removed from the scene. Thanks to the notion of strategy, men can postpone revenge indefinitely without ever giving it up" ("Hamlet's Dull Revenge" 193–94). In a word, cannily poststructural as that word designates undecidable differance, "all actions and motivations are their own opposites as well as themselves" (194). The result is what Michel Foucault describes in his analysis of power as "a strategy without a strategist," though for reasons ignored by Foucault: the absence of a central, organizing agency derives from the fact that the strategy is entirely mimetic in its construction. In general, merely substituting the word *desire* for the word *power* in many of Foucault's texts gives them more positive anthropological significance (see, for instance, the chapter on method in *The History of Sexuality* 93–102).

What is crucial (indeed, cruciform) here is the mechanical, systemic, self-perpetuating structure of deterrence, the desire to allay violence by the threat of still greater violence, which Virilio rightly identifies as our religion (*Pure War* 134). It too is laden with contradictory self-reference as it means to frighten away (*de-terrere*) terror. It is remarkable above all for the way it is rigorously homologous to what we simply deplore as terrorism, which is by no means simple.

What terrorism does is replicate the contradictions of the state toward violence. The state, as Laurent Dispot points out, is principally an army and a justice system; the terrorist, *"un justicier armé"* (*La Machine à terreur* 58): "We have to take the '-ism' of terrorism seriously: it is a system" (69). This systemic, machinelike dimension is essential, for it designates an absence of will, of autonomously willing agency, the illness of a will which I identify as desire, whose illness is mimesis. I would say its essence is mimesis but for the fact that mimesis contradicts any notion of essence, of any internal self-sustaining identity. If there is a homology or structural continuity between state sovereignty and secret agency, as between deterrence and terrorism, it is because these forces are driven by the same machine, the "desiring machine." This is how Deleuze and Guattari designate human being, or being human, in *The Anti-Oedipus*, and this is just why Girard views their antipsychoanalytic and ostensibly emancipatory discourse as a "system of delirium" (*DBB* chap. 5). The manner in which Dispot defines "the contradiction of terrorism" is how I have described secret agency: "être hors la loi par un plus-de-loi [to be outside the law by an excess of the law]" (176). Terrorism exhibits the vocation of the state to violence in its relatively pure form; being, as Dispot observes, its "ascetic" form, "plus étatique que l'Etat." (58). If terrorism is "the last of religions which kill" (151), it is because, as Girard argues, the religious as such is sacrificial. It is never more lethal than when its transcendence is dethroned and democratized:

> The horror which terrorism inspires has its source, among other things, in the enduring feeling of sacrilege. Before the death of God, its representatives were protected by anointment; the people having replaced God as transcendent principle, it seems that they implicitly inherited His prerogatives and that there remains, in particular, something sacred in the idea of the immunity of the people's representatives. That is what terrorists contravene. At the same time, *they reinforce the archaism:* not only by provoking it, reawakening it, reviving it; but even more so by claiming it for themselves: they would be more representative than the existing representatives, and therefore much more sacred, much more holy. (Dispot 165–66)

Hence, violation of the sacred culminates in resacralization, but this irony is not peculiar to terrorism, or even more generally to democracy. It obeys the structural laws of ritual sacrifice, where differentiating taboos are regularly transgressed to ensure their subsequent reenforcement, where the prohibitions affecting desire enjoin their own transgression.

If there is a difference here, it is in terms of what is essential to the modern, deritualized world, namely, the absence of ritual constraints on the exercise of violence. This tradition has not altered in its structure and mechanism since the foundation of the world. What has altered is the range and intensity of world violence since the effort of the world to become its own foundation. This accords with an anthropological law of which our century is the historical confirmation: with the passing of the sacred order, of the sacred *tout court*, sacrifice becomes less and less ritual, less and less efficacious, less and less capable of uniting the community, and therefore demands more and more victims. Front-line human-wave attacks and massive internal purges serve the same logic: "that our sacrifice," as it is often said, "should not have been in vain." Otherwise stated, the decline of symbolic violence brings on an increase of real victims; their quantity mounts in inverse proportion to the ritual efficacy of sacrifice, and victimage appears more and more gratuitous, stark, indifferent, and callous. As Roberto Calasso writes, "the process of secularization does not, as it claims, succeed in exhausting or extinguishing the sacred, but only displaces it. And the power it assumes is all the more devastating and uncontrollable in that it no longer has a name, in that it cannot be recognized for what it is" (*La Ruine du Kasch* 333). With the retreat of the sacred there are no more restraints on the violent destiny of mimetic desire, the sacred being nothing but the name for the way humanity misrecognizes human desire. "It is in vain that he says 'I will,' " as Dispot writes of the man mastered by the terror machine, "he can no longer will" (103). This absence of will is especially prominent and systemic when agency is bureaucratized and disseminated in the form of state agencies.

State Agents

The case of the agent in covert operations is as complex as the case of the victim is simple (but only in the original sense of the word *simplex*, having only one fold or *pli;* the victim is necessarily a dual structure, being "good" for the evil it bears away). Any decision by the courts bearing on a single agent, a single culprit, must emerge as a frameup, a par-ergon or pseudo-work of truth-seeking justice. The attempt to trace the origin of violence to a single culprit is destined to cover up its complex origin; it is a sacrificial gesture par excellence. It is a matter of finding a scapegoat for a more generalized culpability, a more systemic participation. Such a work of detection on the part of the state must yield undecidable results, an *"hors d'oeuvre"* in Derrida's terms ("Parergon," in *La Vérité en peinture* 63), for it seeks a fulcrum, a lever of decision that does not take place, that is not punctually localizable. It seeks a malevolence, an ill will, whereas we find only the traces of mimesis, and traces of those traces.

Every decision is the mask, the mark, the margin, and the *"démarche"* of another decision. Every decision can be traced to another one, every so-called decision can be shown as bearing the traces of decisions not made, or not made in a here and now, not in so many words, not in or by a self-presencing consciousness deciding to decide (much less deciding homicide, of the same etymon). Decisions were made elsewhere, earlier, by others, and so on, in what threatens (or promises, if you are a state agent) to be a Derridean "renvoi infini sans fond d'origine."

It is worthwhile to consider at this point the *structure* of decision. From a Derridean angle, it corresponds to the dynamic of differance as it hinges actively and passively on decisions made before and after it (on the double meaning of "the hinge" [*la brisure*] as "designating difference and articulation" see *Of Grammatology* 65). We may view it as properly *disseminative* to the degree that every so-called decision is the sign and seed (engaging both meanings of the Greek *sema*) of other decisions. It conforms to the structure of the *renvoi* as "dismissal; expulsion; suspension, discharge; sending back; return; kicking back; throwing back, referral, postponement" (*Collins Robert Dictionary*) and even more to differance. This singular irresponsibility should not be viewed as cause for celebration, as it appears in some texts of deconstruction, for its measurable effects in history are devastating, as are the implications of the deconstruction of the unified subject. It can translate as the depersonalized tautology, "orders are orders," which is the administrative stuff that hecatombs are made of.

This has been scrupulously and massively documented, and I will evoke but a few of the more spectacular examples in no preferential order of gravity. Anyway, the concepts and especially the anticoncepts they engage are such as to link them inextricably.

In a prize-winning essay, "Of Accidental Judgments and Casual Slaughters," Kai Erikson places "the decision to drop" the bombs at Hiroshima and Nagasaki in quotation marks (thereby somewhat derealizing it), for it was routed through so many government channels and debates as to be nowhere traceable to a unified, conscious intention. "It became a force like gravity. It had taken life" (126) without anyone being able to trace its origin to a single creator among the, for the most part, "unusually decent and compassionate people . . . operating with reflexes that had been tempered by war" (129).

In serving its own ideological purposes by recruiting and secreting Nazi officials, the American military intelligence required legerdemain tactics of indirection. They were exceeded, perhaps, only by the camouflaged agency, individual and bureaucratic, by which the Nazi crimes themselves were licensed. Arno Mayer's book on the "Final Solution" strongly and not unwittingly favors the conclusion that

Judeocide is not traceable to any single document or recorded *diktat* of any kind. It is as if the perpetrators would not, could not, face and outright name the enormities they were accomplishing, at least not originally. On the other hand, in its final stages and worst excesses, as Raul Hilberg points out, "there were no orders . . . everybody knew what he had to do" (in Woodruff and Wilmer, eds., *Facing Evil* 111). It is plausible to argue that this indirection was necessary to the deed; not deciding it out loud or in so many words, not proclaiming it explicitly but nonetheless authorizing it by bio- and bacteriological metaphors, by administrative euphemisms, by *implication*, were the enabling conditions for the staggering atrocity, which required the complicity, the tacit assent, of every echelon of society, industrial and bureaucratic, clerical and laic, instructional and constabulary. "The built-in but fatal ambiguity which facilitated the 'Final Solution' " (Mayer 434) consisted in the simultaneously complementary and competitive collusion of ostensibly competitive goals, both exterminationist and productivist (slave labor).

At issue is what Hannah Arendt labels "the banality of evil," by which she means the "lack of imagination" and "sheer thoughtlessness" that are the necessary though not sufficient conditions for "administrative massacres." This banality is fatally linked to the "rule of Nobody" in the form of bureaucracy, which serves "to make functionaries and mere cogs in the administrative machinery out of men, and thus to dehumanize them" (*Eichmann in Jerusalem* 289). Owing to this banality Arendt observes that "with the best will in the world one cannot extract any diabolical or demonic profundity from Eichmann" (288). This is a crucial point, the search for the demonic being sacrificial rather than properly juridical.

Ever since its formulation at the Eichmann trial, Arendt's phrase has haunted journalists and social scientists for expressing an intuition they could neither unravel nor evade. It is a paradoxical phrase, conjoining what is near and known with that from which we prefer to distance ourselves, what we habitually regard as alien, as more or less monstrously other, as demonic. Ordinary and sinister, familiar and strange, the phrase conforms to the structure, the antithetical meaning, of the uncanny, and to differance as well. Banality implies superficiality, surface visibility, and proximity; it inscribes the difference of evil under erasure, it brings it home, marks it as *heimlich*. If the uncanny is to be studied in a realm called parapsychology, the proximity or alongsidedness of the prefix *para-* concerns the unconscious only as mimesis, as interdividual consciousness, as ruled by rival and model psyches unconscious of their mimesis. What is radical about radical evil is its essential rootlessness, its nomadic contagion.

In her essay "On Violence," Arendt elaborates on this disseminated rule in a way that evokes its relevance for nuclear holocaust: "If, in accord with traditional political thought, we identify tyranny as government that is not held to give account of itself, rule by Nobody is clearly the most tyrannical of all, since there is no one left who could even be asked to answer for what is being done. It is this state of affairs, making it impossible to localize responsibility and to identify the enemy, that is among the most potent causes of the current worldwide rebellious unrest, its chaotic nature, and its dangerous tendency to get out of control and to run amuck" (*Crises of the Republic* 137-38). It is just this tendency that is rightly apprehended in current strategies of deterrence, where mimesis operates undecidably as theme and structuring principle.

Though dissemination—or differance, for that matter—may characterize the structure of decision, it is not therefore the last word, the truth of this structure: seeing it thus, the seeds of responsibility would be forever and everywhere (or always already) lost—and justice, too, interdicted by this *"loi du biais."* Dissemination is not the last word on anything, despite critics who accuse Derrida of a sort of absolute relativism: "Dissemination . . . can never become an originary, central or ultimate signified, the place proper to truth. On the contrary, dissemination represents the affirmation of this nonorigin, the remarkable empty locus of a hundred blanks no meaning can be ascribed to, in which mark supplements and substitution games are multiplied *ad infinitum"* ("The Double Session" in *Dissemination* 286). Again, what has become infinite and endless from the human historical perspective is the violence of the game, there being nothing outside it to arrest the conflict of differences. As Bandera notes, deconstruction has uncovered blanks where metaphysics, since Plato, sited a king or a principle, a border or barrier whose purpose was precisely to check conflictual play. Now, it is up to humanity alone to recognize its responsibility for this play and to act on that recognition. If mimetic desire, whereby every presumed will is a stand-in, a misrecognized substitute for another's desire, is at the root of this play, then a properly free, authentically good will is necessarily defined as taking the place of the victim, as giving up one's life for another. This would be an action in which desire has no role to play, thereby lending credence to the idea, an eminently performative idea, that "the truth shall make you free." Identification with the victim can be perverted, diverted into a further conflictual play, as I have already acknowledged, but this only authenticates the undisputed privilege of the victim as the site from which truth is determined in our era.

Dissemination is the name for the indirection of truth, for its infinite substitutability, which begins with the victim. From the vantage of the sacrificial scenario, Derrida's statement that "dissemination affirms the always already divided generation of meaning" (*Dissemination* 310) takes on a baleful coloring in the light of the violent generation of meaning in the twofold meaning of the victim, of the *pharmakos*, as of the sacred itself. Derrida astutely invokes the uncanny in this context, citing Freud's attention "to undecidable ambivalence, to the play of the double, to the endless exchange between the fantastic and the real, the 'symbolized' and the 'symbolizer,' to the process of interminable substitutions." (301). I have shown this substitution as the *pharmakon* of writing, the remedy-poison to speech, its paradoxical origin and usurper, its monstrous double. I have shown that this substitution begins and ends with the victim, yet it is interminable in that the victim may be anyone; according to the nuclear scenario, it may in fact be everyone. The uncanny is a modality of the sacred in just this respect, in its unnatural duality and its potential for the proliferation of doubles and monsters (*VS* 97, 111). With writers like Poe and Kafka, it constitutes a resurgence of the sacred in a desacralized world. Its thematization in criticism is not fortuitous, being evidence of our sacrificial crisis, in which our neighbor, our double, emerges as a fantastical and fantasized reflection of our "own" desire, of a violence we cannot consciously own up to (for more on the nexus "uncanny-superstition-persecution," see Siebers, *The Romantic Fantastic*).

If responsibility is disseminative, it would seem to take on Dostoyevskian (*The Brothers Karamazov* part 2, book 6, chaps. 2-3) or Johannine proportions, engaging the whole of culture and history, including all victims and all indirect, institutional agencies that produce them. All are responsible, but none is directly responsible in view of one or another form of mediation, which the social sciences have translated as one or anther form of social or psychological determinism. As

Arendt observes, such relativism renders the administration of justice impossible: "True, we have become very much accustomed by modern psychology and sociology, not to speak of modern bureaucracy, to explaining away the responsibility of the doer for his deed in terms of this or that kind of determinism. Whether such seemingly deeper explanations of human actions are right or wrong is debatable. But what is not debatable is that no judicial procedure would be possible on the basis of them, and that the administration of justice, measured by such theories, is an extremely unmodern, not to say outmoded, institution" (*Eichmann* 290-91). Unmodern or merely modern, for this is just where a postmodern critique of justice intervenes—though without any conclusive results. It decenters the criminal/judge structure, but not so as to get past Hannah Arendt's lapidary notation on the topic: "For conscience to work: either very strong religious belief—extremely rare. Or: pride, even arrogance. If you say to yourself in such matters: who am I to judge—you are already lost" (in Young-Bruehl, *Hannah Arendt* 339). The legal profession is awash in this crisis of difference, as is evident in the countless law review debates where deconstruction and allied critiques (Stanley Fish's notion of boundless and normless contextuality) have enjoyed a hearing—to the eminent dissatisfaction of some jurists (for a sample, see Fish, "Critical Legal Studies," and Posner, *Law and Literature: A Misunderstood Relation*). That considerable clarity might be brought to these debates by understanding the law as heir to sacrifice is the tenor of these remarks.

Precisely because communities secrete victims and rely on largely unconsciously sacrificial practices to form their identity, community consensus (as advertised by Stanley Fish in *Is There a Text in This Class?*) can never be an adequate criterion for judgment. No one can confide in community consensus without consenting—*vox populi oblige*—to his or her own lynching. According to Girard, that is just what Job's interlocutors urge him to do and what he resists in his appeals to "the God of victims" (*Job* chap. 21). This is what is at stake when, according to Christopher Norris's reading of Fish, we "collapse the distinction between valid and what *counts* as valid argument within any given community of interests" (in Dasenbrock 201). It is equally at stake in Eric Santner's more sweeping view of critical controversy: "The new discourses of cultural criticism which I am calling postmodern situate themselves at the points of tension in these notions of identity"—namely: "premodern and modern notions of personal, sexual and cultural identity" (*Stranded Objects* 164, n.12). If the error of these notions is their essentialism or mythologocentrism as "an effect of various signifying practices" (ibid.), there is much to be learned from the theory that accounts for their systemic misdirection by mimetic contagion and self-delusion as it leads to victimage.

Responsibility, then, appears to be like language itself, which is never itself; it must somehow be written under erasure: "le signe ~~est~~ cette ~~chose~~ mal nommée" (*OG* 31). It is not on that account undecidable. On the contrary, it is total—or rather, it is total because it is undecidable. This is the *"double bind"* that Derrida explores in "Mochlos, ou le conflit des facultés," where he articulates a properly oceanic sense of responsibility on the part of "la communauté scientifique et de l'université":

> For example, but we could vary the examples *ad infinitum* [presumably, then, to all forms of professional responsibility], the interpretation of a theorem, of a poem, of a philosopheme, of a theologeme is only produced by simultaneously proposing an institutional mode, of consolidating the one which exists and which makes interpretation possible or of constituting a new one which agrees with the aforesaid interpretation. Whether such a proposal is declared or clandestine, it summons [*elle appelle*] the politics and policies [*la politique*] of a community of interpreters gathered around this text, and at the same time [*du même coup*] of a global society, of a civil society with or without Statehood, of a veritable regime which makes the inscription of that community possible. I will go farther . . . (40)

But that is far enough for my purposes. The contract "with the institution, between the institution and the dominant forces of society," (41) is always already signed. In this scheme of things, there is no last judgment because it is infinitely deferred. It is not, however, deferred beyond but within decisions taking place at every moment, and in the form of decisions that do not properly take place as well, decisions that are not consciously made but that issue from the structural, systemic relations between individuals and institutions and among institutions themselves. In his aim of "making as clear and as thematic as possible such a political implication, its system or its aporia," in his pursuit of clarifying this "minimal responsibility" (41), Derrida moves far enough here to point to *Things Hidden since the Foundation of the World*, where we learn that what first takes place is indecision regarding the victim.

What first takes place is the victim, the product of unanimous (minus one) violence, and what takes its place is the sacred. The sacred issues from indecision on the part of all about taking the victim for oneself, which would be tantamount to taking the place of the victim and succumbing to the unanimous violence that produced it. As I have already argued, this mimetic gesture of deferred appropriation is the first linguistic sign, the origin of all cultural deferrals to come, the origin of culture as differance. It is the first human under-taking, the first cultural *entre-prise*, representing the victim as desirable to all and therefore as taboo to all. It is all this because the unanimous, mimetic bid for the victim suffices to make it forbidden to any, making it sacred in the primary, that is, antithetical or uncanny (Freud) or disseminative (Derrida), sense of the word. This irreducible paradox, this double bind or double bid issuing from doubles, accounts for the non-instinctual attention in which Girard postulates hominization. Humanity emerges from attention to the victim in the form of abstention from the victim, if only to bide its time, bid up the stakes, pounce anew (Old English *biddan* expresses both a demand and a stay, a *prise* and a freeze, uncannily).

We are still biding our time, though with nuclear stakes, with the world at stake, we know it may be up; "No Apocalypse, not now (full speed ahead, seven missiles, seven missives)" is the title of Derrida's contribution to nuclear criticism. Its resonance with Girard's originary hypothesis about the simultaneous origin of the sacred and of the human, of their origin in deferred violence, has been discussed. This resonance might appear simply uncanny, or perhaps I should say doubly uncanny, given the way Derrida himself characterizes the first war as a rivalry of doubles, divine and human, and the first peace (and all of history and culture in consequence) as the mystified suspension of that rivalry: "You will say: but all wars are waged in the name of the name, beginning with the war between God and the sons of Shem, who wanted to 'make a name for themselves' and transmit it by constructing the tower of Babel. This is so, but 'deterrence' came into play among God and the Shem, the warring adversaries, and the conflict was temporarily interrupted: tradition, translation, transference have had a long respite" ("No Apocalypse . . . " 31).

That long respite is history, culture, and representation. Derrida does not explain how deterrence came into play. He does not have to, for God and humankind are already in their place in the myth, and

Derrida is only commenting on it. Like the Creation and the Flood, it is doubtless a foundation myth, and Derrida is committed to skepticism about such stories. But I can fill in this blank with the victimary hypothesis, which explains how a god came into play out of the interplay of rival, mimetic desires, how a god came into Being as the mystified object of an original deferral of violence, of a deferral to the desires of others, of desire as deferral. Only Girard offers an explanation for the passage from destruction to deterrence, as from chaos to creation, which Derrida fancies as follows: "God and the sons of Shem having understood that a name wasn't worth it—and this would be absolute knowledge—they preferred to spend a little more time together, the time of a long colloquy with warriors in love with life, busy writing in all languages in order to make the conversation last, even if they didn't understand each other too well" (31). This is a properly mythical representation, the passage from war to peace being assigned to an understanding, a preference, for which there is no motivation except the worthlessness of the name. But no such understanding is possible. Between rival doubles, between humanity and the god whom humanity represents as its violence, any understanding is logically impossible. An understanding about the nothingness of the name, of the object of their rivalry, of their common desire, is rationally inconceivable, for their rivalry is that misunderstanding. The object of rivalry—of the desire common to God and the sons of Shem— is a name, and that name is divinity. It is not a name that names an object except as the object of the other's desire. The object is not an object at all, but rather the name or sign of the other's desire. It is in this sense, originally and finally, that "*la chose même est signe.*" The name does not name an object truly, but another's desire falsely and indirectly. That is how the god got its name, as the name for violence, for the object of mimetic desire as it leads to violence; the name for whatever desire sacralizes, the name for whatever people kill for. God is the name for this misunderstanding, being the name for violence when violence is the object of desire. With this god no understanding can be reached, for its name is humanity. "One and one make one," as Sartre's posthumous character exclaimed, "what a misunderstanding!"

This does not mean that understanding between individuals is impossible, far from it, but that it is impossible as long as people demonize or divinize violence, desire, the adversary, the origin. Indeed, for

Marcel Gauchet it is only in the disenchantment of the world, where "it is no longer with the gods that we are at grips, but with ourselves" (*Le Désenchantement du monde* 237), that "the bond among men is conceivable and practicable" (290). If this is the occasion to celebrate the triumph of a uniquely Western reason, it is also the occasion to fathom the unique role played by Judeo-Christianity, which Gauchet persuasively appraises as "la religion de la sortie de la religion" (133ff): "The obstacle, the separation, the opacity is still there, but within the individual himself, and in the relations among individuals, and at the heart of their collective being—and without any extrinsic guarantee to prop them up and absolve them from open enquiry" (237). For Girard, this is what is essential to the context of Revelation: "The really important apocalyptic writings say nothing except that man is responsible for his history. You wish for your dwelling to be given up to you; *well then, it is given up to you*" (*THFW* 195).

This misunderstanding, then, is at its term. The "long respite" Derrida mentions, or what he later calls "the long compromise," is almost over. Sacrificial compromise with human violence has had its day. Between two wars—the first, which gave birth simultaneously to the human and the sacred, and the last, which decides the fate of humanity in its misguided (read: guided missile) quest for divinity, which deicides the human race—we have been moving toward absolute knowledge. Just in time. We require nothing less than knowledge of the absolute, of the wholly other, of the sacred as the mystification of human violence—nothing less will suffice to make the conversation last into the next century, to make the conversation between God and the sons of Shem the last one, to "outline," at the very least, "its historical closure."

So I return to some of the deconstructive premises with which I began, to clarify their cultural reference.

"The sign and the divinity have the same place and the same time of birth" because both are born of mimetic desire, which in turn is born of the sign. The sign is a mark, an effect of desire that is an effect of the sign, whence the "always already divided generation of meaning." "The age of the sign is essentially theological" because the essence of the theological is a misunderstanding of the sign, of desire. Derrida construes all of history as the history of conversation, colloquy, and writing rather than of rulers and battles, but what I have shown about *polemos* demonstrates that it is the same history. He does that not only here but also as early as *Of Grammatology,* which is the archeology, history, and closure of that history: "It is therefore as if what we call language could have been in its origin and its end only a moment, an essential but determined mode, a phenomenon, an aspect, a species of writing. And as if it had succeeded in making us forget this and in *willfully misleading* us, only in the course of an adventure: as that adventure itself. All in all a short enough adventure. It merges with the history that has associated technics and logocentric metaphysics for nearly three millennia. And now it seems to be approaching what is really its own *exhaustion* [ce qui est proprement son *essoufflement*]" (8). It is, then, as if writing were the genre or genus (as both genesis and genius) of culture and language were but a species, a subsystem, a by-product; but this "as if" only translates our misunderstanding of origins. History is the history of representation, and above all (always already according to Derrida) of misrepresentation (of violent origins according to Girard): God and the sons of Shem "didn't understand each other too well." They mislead us, they mislead each other, much like the misleading translation of *"donner le change":* "allay suspicion," "put off the track" (*Collins Robert*); but the proper sense of the metaphor suggests a qui pro quo, a substitution of doubles. History is the history of rival doubles, of *polemos* between phonè and grammè, between the king and his scribe, Ra and Theuth, God and the sons of Shem, the sons of Shem among themselves, like the sons of Adam, Isaac, Jacob, David—not to mention, as already suggested concerning Rousseau, the sons of the Revolution. "A European war may issue in revolution," Jean Juarès prophesied in 1905, "but the European war may also produce, and for a considerable time, crises of counter-revolution, of reactionary fury, of exasperated nationalism, of suffocating dictatorship, of monstrous militarism—a long succession of retrograde violence and low hatreds, of reprisals and enslavements" (in Gallo, *Le Grand Juarès* 292–93). History is the history of rival doubles, of alter nations and their throwing us off the track in the name of god, humanity, or the name itself. This observation leads back to the track of things hidden since the foundation of the earth, of absolute knowledge. This is not knowledge of God, who is *de facto* and *de jure* unknowable, but knowledge of the sacred, of sacrifice and its victims.

It is in this sense that the Greenpeace example extends to a new mode of critique focusing on the victim, of which Juarès is again prophetic. For the all-but-nameless victim of Greenpeace should remind us of Dreyfus, of whom Juarès wrote in 1898: "If Dreyfus is innocent, he is neither an officer nor a bourgeois any longer; he is shorn by the very excess of his woes of any class identification; he is no more than humanity itself, and at the most intense degree of misery and despair we can imagine. . . . Dreyfus is an exemplar of human suffering at its most poignant. He is the living witness against military lying, political cowardice and crimes of authority" (in Gallo 163). Juarès was assassinated by one of the sons of 1870 for his uncompromising opposition to France's revanchist glee in going to war in 1914.

This focus helps solve a logical conundrum that has come to haunt virtually every theory humanity has constructed about itself. What is to prevent this theory of desire from being misled by desire itself, which is what makes us human and is where our misunderstandings originate and accumulate? As with language, how can desire be its own theory without falling prey to the aporias of self-reference, without becoming in turn a name for a name, for something that has no name, which is why we have recourse to antinames like differance, trace, and so on? The answer lies with the victim—not in any perverted desire to be the victim, but in the eminently traceable fact of victimage, in its uniqueness amidst the play of rival desires, its immunity to desire being its forthright undesirability. Desire for that uniqueness, rather than for the suffering it entails, is a central focus of existentialist literature. Camus's Meursault seeks justification in his public execution (*L'Etranger*), as does Sartre's Hugo in his own political assassination (*Les Mains sales*). Deconstruction formally rejects the romanticism of this position while effectively embracing it. It is crucial therefore to purify deconstruction of its romanticism, as exemplified by its often paralytic fascination with *"des choses doubles"*: ambiguity, ambivalence, aporia.

We have been over this ground before. It is "la route antique des hommes pervers," "the ancient trail trodden by the wicked" (Job 22:15), to which Job's interlocutors attribute his stubbornness, his refusal to accept his role as scapegoat in what Girard sees as a "totalitarian trial" conducted in the name of communal solidarity (*Job: The Victim of his People*, especially chap. 16). Over and beyond the consensus on his guilt among his "friends," Job appeals to the God of victims, whereby Girard integrates his plaint with the Hebrew Bible's denunciation of sacrificial practices and with the Christian Bible's ratification of that denunciation. I will examine this claim, not in all its textual instances but via examples of its textual logic, in the appendix, but I can conclude here with something positive about knowledge, science, and theory.

What are these but representation? Especially theory, which comes from the Greek word meaning contemplation, beholding, or speculation; the *theoros* is a spectator, as of the cosmos, or a drama, or a sacrifice of which drama was to become the representation, the representation of victims like Oedipus, Ajax, Agamemnon. We need to acknowledge drama (beginning with tragedy but eventually including comedy as well, especially if the veritable deconstructions of such as Molière or Shakespeare are to be valued) as a nascent theory of sacrifice—and therefore of culture, politics, and history—rather than as something that our theories are suppose to master.

I have reviewed the theory, born of literature, that represents language and humanity as born in the representation of desire; it is the theory of desire as born in the representation of desire, of desire born in the sign. Language originates as the representation of desire. The task of science or theory as the desire for representation should be the representation of desire in the objective rather than the subjective sense of the genitive. That would be *objective* knowledge, a representation of violence that would owe nothing to the violence of representation. Where do we look? Not to the causes of violence or of desire, which, being mimetic, are ultimately untraceable, but to their unmistakable effects, the victims. A properly human science begins and ends where the human begins and ends, with the victims, with the difference a victim makes, which these days, as the Greenpeace affair testifies in all its nuclear complexity, is all the difference in the world.

6

Conclusion: Representation and Decidability

Girard has acknowledged the importance of Derridean deconstruction for his hypothesis, including its importance for an anthropology whose possibility it questions. In a sense, the analyses and discussion undertaken here have served only as a *mise au point*, a textual specification, elaboration, and complication of the following remarks from the early pages of *Things Hidden since the Foundation of the World*:

> The discovery of the scapegoat as the mechanism of symbolicity itself justifies the discourse of deconstruction at the same times as it completes it. And this discovery explains at the same time the characteristic traits of this contemporary discourse. Because much of contemporary thought is still without an anthropological basis, it remains given to verbal acrobatics that will ultimately prove to be sterile. This is not for lack of the right words; it is only too talented where words are concerned; it is the mechanism behind the words which escapes this discourse. If you examine the pivotal terms in the finest analyses of Derrida, you will see that beyond the deconstruction of philosophical concepts, it is always a question of the paradoxes of the sacred; it is never a question of deconstructing this, which sparkles all the more on that account in the eyes of the reader. (*THFW* 63-64, trans. modified)

"Verbal acrobatics" is a telling figure, suggesting stylistic or formalist preoccupations in deconstruction that I will consider at length later on. The reproach here is directed at the self-indulgent auto-affection of deconstructive texts as they exult in the paradoxes and impasses of representation rather than concern themselves with its real institutional origin: the mechanisms of the sacred as they issue from the mystified agency of the surrogate victim: "This deconstruction is still only partial; it confuses the crisis of all cultural signs with the radical impotence of knowledge and of language. It doesn't believe in philosophy but it remains inside philosophy. It doesn't see that beyond the present crisis, there are possibilities for rational knowledge about culture which are not philosophical. It revels in the pure mirroring of the sacred which is but one, at this stage, with a purely literary effect; it risks degenerating into pure verbalism (*THFW* 64, trans. modified). My goal throughout has been to counter this tendency, to avert this risk—namely, to salvage deconstruction from the dilapidation it foments, to preserve its positive contributions from a flashy sterility it tends to favor, or at least has not discouraged.

By Girard's account, much that we admire about literature, its brilliant formal effects, emerges as the sacred's last refuge, its last vestige (from *vestigium*, footprint or trace). Radiating with the same internal contradictions, with a fairly hallowed undecidability and, above all, inconsequence in today's world, poetry and the sacred seem to share the same irretrievable marginality. They reflect the same formal characteristics, and they exhibit the same formidable barrier to finite interpretation, to determinate meaning, their only difference being criticism's symmetrical repulsion to the sacred and attraction to poetry.

Criticism refuses to acknowledge in the sacred what it cherishes in poetry: ambiguity, without deference to which no self-respecting reading of a text is permitted nowadays. When considering the origin of language in chapter 3, I demonstrated this simultaneous attraction and repulsion to be the originary structure of the sacred itself. Because the victimary hypothesis focuses on the substantial effects of our repulsion to the sacred, as it results in our incomprehension of the sacrificial mechanisms informing our institutions, it yields a debate about form and substance of the first order. The sacred is only the more pervasive for being invisible in our institutions, for being the form of institutions whose perdurability and credibility depend on denying their sacrificial heritage. As Roberto Calasso writes, "unnamed, sacrifice continues to demand its victims; it becomes nomadic and displaces everywhere the sites of its cult" (*La Ruine de Kasch* 269).

It is no accident, then, that the destiny of the sacred conforms to what Derrida writes of metaphor in our era, where its ubiquity results in its effacement, where its constant detection and restriking (*retrait*) result in its retreat (*retrait*). To underline this properly uncanny destiny of metaphor, Derrida inscribes it under the single term as "le retrait de la métaphore":

> Any statement concerning anything that happens, metaphor included, will be produced *not without* metaphor. There will not have been a meta-metaphorics consistent enough to dominate all its statements. And what gets along *without* metaphor? Nothing, therefore, and rather it should be said that metaphor gets along without anything else, here without me, at the very moment when it appears to pass through me. But if it gets by without everything that does not happen without it, maybe in a bizarre sense it does without itself, it no longer has a name, a literal or proper meaning, which could begin to render the double figure of my title readable to you: in its withdrawal (*retrait*), one should say in its withdrawals, metaphor perhaps retires, withdraws from the world scene, withdrawing from it at the moment of its most invasive extension, at the instant it overflows every limit. Its withdrawal could then have the paradoxical form of an indiscreet and overflowing insistence, of an overabundant remanence, of an intrusive repetition, always marking with a supplementary trait, with one more turn, with a re-turn and with a *withdrawal* (*retrait*) the trait that it will have left in the text itself. ("The *Retrait* of Metaphor" 8)

Substituting the word *culture* for *text*, as by a reversal of deconstructive habits ("il n'y a pas de hors texte"), yields a passage on the fate of the sacred in today's world. It has in a metaphorical sense become a "victim" of its own ubiquity; the very pervasiveness of the sacrificial has disguised its efficacy—and its dangers. Its formal, ritual manifestations have disappeared, bearing away with them the mechanisms by which culture seeks to control violence. "And it would happen," says Derrida of metaphor, and I of the sacred, "that we should get along without it, without being able to dispense with it (*il passerait ceci qu'on devrait se passer d'elle sans pouvoir s'en passer*), and this defines the structure of withdrawals which interests me here" (21).

Derrida is exercising what he calls "attention to the syntactic motif" to elude the ontological delusions of "denomination" (15). It is a way of inscribing metaphor "under erasure," which is also the way to understand the sacred in Girard's text. It is necessary to insist on this because of the massive textual evidence in critical literature indicating that when people hear the word *sacred*, they just stop thinking, when what is needed is to think the sacred back to its institutional origins. The sacred is not theological or ontological in any way; it is not an entity of any kind, except according to our misconstruction of it, which is the most common misconstruction on the part of those critics who imagine Girard to be a religious thinker, an apologist for sacrifice, a pietist, or a dogmatist.

It is no wonder, then, that Derrida has been labeled by one of his most astute commentators as an "uncanny philosopher," *"un philosophe 'unheimlich'"* (Kofman). Strange and familiar, homely and sinister, the paradoxes of the uncanny are those that Derrida discovers in metaphor (as well as more generally in writing, in the gramm) and sacrifice in the victim. In its simultaneous attraction and repulsion, the uncanny exhibits the antinomial structure of the sacred, the sacralized victim, the object of desire. The uncanny is a modality of the sacred, with this difference when related to the sacrificial scenario (that is, when conceived anthropologically): it is no longer unknowable when traced to its institutional origin; its very unknowability is knowable as the mystification informing sacrificial substitution. Deconstruction is accordingly historicized rather than invalidated once its attention to the uncanny is shown to reflect "the crisis of all cultural signs." If it is to survive, it must not mistake the symptom for the cure. What is called for here is not bedazzled attention to literary effects, be they Derrida's or those of the texts he explicates, but concerted and sustained attention to the unknowable as a structure whose unknowability is generated—indeed, constructed—by the desire of the knower rather than by any property of the object of knowledge. If the sacred is not the origin of the cultural order, except as a misconstruction of violent agency, then the sacred and the cultural order are knowable once their mystified complicity is deconstructed.

Deconstruction's answer to Girard is that it does not believe in philosophy either, except as a text—philosophy in fact defining itself by denying its textuality. As Barbara Johnson states, "philosophy is defined by its refusal to recognize itself as literature; literature is defined as the rhetorical self-transgression of philosophy" (*A World of Difference* 20). Literature is further advertised as a more or less conscious or strategic critique of representation and hence of knowledge, especially theoretical knowledge. The result is a literal pro-gram, *Of Grammatology* and allied projects, that Derrida describes as not "a system but rather a sort of strategic device, opening onto its own abyss, an un-closed, unenclosable, not wholly formalizable ensemble of rules for reading, interpretation and writing" ("The Time of a Thesis" 40). These notions of strategy, the abyss, and the formalizable provide a suitable focus on which to formulate my conclusion.

The abyss Derrida refers to is not merely or entirely its "own," as he states, for its opening is wide enough to engulf virtually the whole of the human sciences. "This type of device may have enabled me to detect not only in the history of philosophy and in the related socio-historical totality, but also in what are alleged to be sciences and in so-called post-philosophical discourses that figure among the most modern (in linguistics, in anthropology, in psychoanalysis), to detect in these an evaluation of writing, or, to tell the truth, rather a devaluation of writing whose insistent, repetitive, even obscurely compulsive, character was the sign of a whole set of long-standing constraints" (40). The name for these constraints, in the form of ob-scurely violent oppositions, is logocentrism, and its critique, as I have shown, is a critique of its continuity with mythology in its covert vi-olence. Writing is the lever by which to dethrone the "transcendental signified, which, at one time or another, would place a reassuring end to the reference from sign to sign. [Derrida has] identified logocen-trism and the metaphysics of presence as the exigent, powerful, sys-tematic and irrepressible desire for such a signified" (*OG* 49). Unless we postulate humans as naturally metaphysical beings, which is a con-tradiction *in adjecto*, we have to ask where such a desire comes from, where it originates. If its destiny, its goal, is closure, "a reassuring end to the reference from sign to sign," then its other, its alternative, its wellspring, is the endless repetition, the mimesis of desire as it can lead only to conflict. The reassurance we find, or rather invest, in transcendence is born of the unanimity experienced toward the victim of previously rival desires. Considering the alternative, Plato's desire for such a signified is a quite rational and responsible one, mystagogy being found preferable to demagogy, with its consequent civil strife and sacrificial resolution.

Girard is not mentioned by name in the preceding passage, or in-deed anywhere (but once, dismissively, in *Psyché*, 621-22) in Derrida's writing, a silence that invites speculation in view of the intertwining of their discourses. But the project for a scientific anthropology seems to be engulfed by Derrida's critique nonetheless, especially as

Girard's "fundamental anthropology" is avowedly and thematically postphilosophical as it looks "beyond the present crisis" in philosophy for "possibilities for rational knowledge about culture which are not philosophical." An anthropology rooted in the victim is a strategy of detection that does not yield but reveals the very same constraints cited by Derrida, this same compulsion to disguise the agency of violence. At the bottom of the abyss, as at the epicenter of the pyramid, where Derrida places writing, is the surrogate victim. If metaphysics is sacrificial, as Derrida's readings of the *Phaedrus* and of Descartes strongly suggest, then a critical theory of sacrifice is truly beyond metaphysics.

For his part, Derrida has not shied away from marking the properly literary character of his writings: their anamorphic and labyrinthine character and above all their antic and performative disposition resist classification as either fiction or nonfiction as much as they resist formulation as a thesis. He says of his more spectacular writings withheld from his thesis defense (*The Post Card*, *Glas*) that they cannot even be classified as autobiography: "They were inscribed in a space that one could no longer, that I myself could no longer, identify as or classify under the heading of philosophy *or* non-fiction, etc., especially at a time when what others would call the autobiographical involvement of these texts was undermining the very notion of autobiography, giving it over to what the necessity of writing, the trace, the remainder, etc., could offer of all that was most baffling, undecidable, wily or despairing" ("The Time of a Thesis" 46–47). Derrida admittedly cannot dissociate his own story from the story of writing, of which he says in "Plato's Pharmacy," "we will watch it infinitely promise itself and endlessly vanish through concealed doorways that shine like mirrors and open onto a labyrinth" (128). But the text just cited points in at least two directions, depending on whether the reader focuses on the space of this writing (the labyrinth) or on the character who invests it. What traditionally occupies this space, as within the pyramid (see "The Pit and the Pyramid" in *Margins of Philosophy*), is a corpse—or, much the same thing, a monster—that, according to the sacrificial hypothesis, is identical to the mystified double generated by violence, the form violence takes in its indifference to difference.

For Derrida, who revives this corpse (the "cryptogram"), this is the space of play, of "*le jeu des différences*," known as differance, which he says we have to think "without *nostalgia*" for origins, "a lost native country of thought. On the contrary, we must *affirm* this, in the sense in which Nietzche puts affirmation into play, in a certain laughter and a certain step of the dance" (*Margins of Philosophy* 27). The motif of laughter and dancing is insistent in Derrida's writings (see "Choreographies"); it all but *denominates* the character investing the labyrinth and weaving its walls around himself (or herself, for sexual identity is perforce in play here, too). Derrida's self-portraiture as literary performer displays the ironic double, the fool, in a word, and not less for being "baffling, undecidable, wily or despairing"—that is, double in himself. "Rien ne dissemble plus de lui que lui-même [nothing is more unlike him than he is from himself]," as Diderot's narrator says in describing the *"originalité"* of Rameau's nephew (396). Closer to home, Rousseau says this of himself: "There are times when I am so unlike myself that I might be taken for someone else of an entirely opposite character" (*Confessions* 126). Barbara Johnson cites this dysunity to evoke a deconstructive difference as "what makes all totalization of the identity of a self or the meaning of a text impossible" (*The Critical Difference* 4–5). To be sure, Rousseau is very far from representing himself as a fool, either as duper or duped; his preferred self-image is that of the victim. But not much genealogy is required to show that the fool owes his problematic identity and hapless destiny to his origins in the victim.

The fool is the very figure of writing as characterized in "Plato's Pharmacy": "The god of writing is thus at once his father, his son, and himself. He cannot be assigned a fixed spot in the play of differences. Sly, slippery, and masked, an intriguer and a card, like Hermes, he is neither king nor jack, but rather a sort of *joker,* a floating signifier, a wild card, one who puts play into play" (93). We have seen the trickster's role that Theuth plays, and Derrida after him, to Plato's King Lire (who, quite like Shakespeare's, demands a representation that his demand forecloses). Now, recalling the sacrificial vocation of the fool in culture, we must indeed think this role without nostalgia. The fool, the court jester, is the king's double, representing his fallibility, his foolishness, his madness. He is also the king's surrogate at the whipping post, for he is above all the king's sacrificial substitute, the fool's immolation being symbolized by his humiliation and degradation.

If the fool mocks with impunity, it is not because Christian Majesties of yore were possessed of a humility lacking in our modern chiefs of state. Rather, the fool incarnates a principle of transgression that is neither licit nor completely outlawed. Closest to the throne and least respected at court, this principle is necessarily located, instituted, on the margins of kingship. This simultaneous proximity to and distance from the throne is that of the sacred, for the fool represents to the community a verbal and sensual license without which sovereign, arbitrary kingship is unnecessary. Kingship is the principle of order; it solves the problem of rampant desire, and the fool must be kept around because he represents the problem as stated in Plato's *Laws:* "the problem of how someone will manage a city like this, in which young men and women are well reared and released from severe and illiberal tasks that do the most to quench wantonness; and where sacrifices, festivals, and choruses are the preoccupations of everyone throughout their whole lives" (§ 835e).

The fool's undecidably mystifying and demystifying activity derives from the mystification that gives rise to kingship and continues to surround it in a monarchial tradition whose continuity depends on misunderstanding its arbitrary, violent origins. A host of anthropological literature (see Routeau, "Au Cirque," and Serres, *Le Parasite*) testifies that the fool is to the king as writing is to the father-king-logos in Derrida's reading of Plato: a parasite, an obscure, enigmatic remainder or signifier of a violent expulsion. Thus, the victimary hypothesis provides a genealogy for Derrida's writing activity. Where fools do not lack employment altogether in a desacralized, deritualized culture, as in the theater of Samuel Beckett, they turn up as the "cultural critic," whom Adorno deftly designates as culture's "salaried and honored nuisance" (*Prisms* 20). In a culture without kings or sacrifice, without carnival except as a cultural ideal forgetful of its sacrificial origins, this role inevitably devolves to the margins of philosophy, even as it yokes the latter to the entertainment industry, which is where hapless literary critics have been dwelling uneasily.

Yet this destabilizing role can yield the positive result of denying philosophy its claim to be a master discipline in the sense that things like knowledge and truth are the philosopher's job—what *they* do, *they* know—whereas literature is mere entertainment, diversion, recreation. Literary critics have never been content with that view, but neither have they ever succeeded in overcoming the marginality of their enterprise. The interest of the victimary hypothesis is that it appraises literature for its properly scientific contribution to understanding human culture. "Only a pseudo-science runs counter to the greatest works of our literary heritage. A real science will justify their vision and confirm their superiority" (*DBB* 78). Of course, this remains to be seen, to be thoroughly tested, but the alternative is intellectual despair, even if it masquerades as *"gai savoir."*

The fool is in no danger today, for there are no kings to emulate or be immolated for. His emphatically anti-thetic role is *purely strategic*, which by Derrida's own admission is a contradiction in terms.

> Strategy is a word that I have perhaps abused in the past, especially as it has been always only to specify *in the end*, in an apparently self-contradictory manner and at the risk of cutting the ground from under my own feet—something I almost never fail to do—that this strategy is a strategy without any finality; for this is what I hold and what in turns holds me in its grip, the aleatory strategy of someone who admits that he does not know where he is going. This, then, is not after all an undertaking of war or a discourse of belligerence. I should like it to be also like a headlong flight straight towards the end, a joyous self-contradiction, a disarmed desire, that is to say something very old and very cunning, but which also has just been born and which delights in being without defence. ("The Time of a Thesis" 50)

These are the very last words of Derrida's thesis defense, and their evocation of a cunning naivete, a wily bafflement, clearly exhibits the fool. Further, their insistence on nonfinality equally clearly exhibits what philosophy since Kant has described as the artwork, whose aim is but the grace of its own movement. These words are not for all that without weighty theoretical implications, for what should also be clear is Derrida's position as victim. Attention to his strategically ambiguous syntax shows his position to be his defenselessness, his defenseless delight in being. It is not a position that requires or solicits defense, for to oppose it is to oppose life itself. It reflects a decision that is disarmingly simple in its inertia: to survive, to go on living, or, as he entitles his essay, "Living On." Its desire has no goal other than the game itself, the game of representation, the play of signs.

There are obvious implications here for literature as a kind of endless, aimless textuality, delightful in its own way, but frustrating, too, especially given the historical implications of its *via negativa.*

In its nonbelligerence, this position is by definition no defense against the machinery of death, which is nothing else than the unrestrained machinery of mimetic desire as it seeks scapegoats for the mystified origins of its violence. *La machine à terreur* is sacrificial in its

mechanisms, or Girard has nothing to contribute to the understanding
of history. In our century we have seen this become the machinery of
the state itself, and we so deplore its yield of victims that we tend to
resist anything theoretical or systematic, any totalizing discourse, for
its possible complicity with totalitarianism.

This resistance is not limited to deconstruction. It shows up as well
in Richard Rorty's breezy and formulaic paean to contingency, which
he holds up as an antidote to "the metaphysical urge, the urge to the-
orize" (*Contingency, Irony and Solidarity* 96) or to seek "final vocabularies" in a "de-divinized world," to any idea that truth is to be
discovered "out there" rather than made up by us down here (3-5).
Consciously reminiscent of William James, it is an archly American
gesture: let's take off from here, leave this philosophical "stuff" (a
cherished expression) behind—"En avant, et négligeons nos morts"
as Baudelaire heard us saying ("Edgar Allan Poe, Sa Vie et ses ou-
vrages" in *OC* 320). Rorty is nonetheless allied with the deconstructive critique of ontotheology in arguing that all such confidence in
essence and quests for foundations represent but "an awkward attempt to secularize the idea of becoming one with God" (*Contingency*
198)—to whom, by definition, all is permitted, even cruelty, in service to eschatology. To this Rorty opposes "the idea that we all have
an overriding obligation to diminish cruelty, to make human beings
equal in respect to their liability to suffering" (88; see also 91–93, 95),
though he insistently links "a loathing for cruelty . . . with a sense of
the contingency of selfhood and of history" (190).

I have no desire to disagree with this claim about loathing for cruelty and suffering, but even a postphilosopher may be permitted to
inquire into the grounds of this unexamined assumption and to ask in
turn on what it is founded. Why *not* cruelty? In a world without uni-
versals (44), without a "criterion of wrongness" (75), where, as Rorty
likes to say, we have to "get rid of" or "give up" "notions like 'rational,'
'criteria,' 'argument' and 'foundation' and 'absolute' " (49)—in such a
world, "*hier ist kein warum*" is as good an answer as any other. This is
the interest of the victimary hypothesis, of a sustained, coherent, and
historical theory of victimage as it operates in culture and on our moral
sensibilities. In sum, the vocation of a postphilosophical culture is a
scientific anthropology rooted in the victim. A theory founded on the
rigorous and systematic contradictions of mimetic desire, as it solicits
and opposes its violent doubles, is one in which, contrary to Rorty,

"the rational-irrational distinction" is eminently more rather than "less useful than it once appeared" (48). Such a theory locates true rationality, and the equation between truth and rationality, in the claims of the victim against oppressive mystifications, however rational in appearance.

Since Rorty's notorious "Philosophy as a Kind of Writing: An Essay on Derrida" (in *Consequences of Pragmatism*), there has been an uneasy and nonreciprocated compact, a one-way discussion, between a revived pragmatism and deconstruction. The convergence is foregrounded by Rorty's *Philosophy and the Mirror of Nature*, which argues against the necessity or even the possibility of an epistemology. This convergence is not a mere coincidence, a happenstance of academic journalism; rather, it reflects widespread antiphilosophical tendencies within the discourse of philosophy that are symptomatic of the present "crisis of cultural signs." But here again it is important not to mistake the symptom for the cure and abandon rationality in the name of values without foundation. It is only that philosophy cannot provide foundations; it never has, not since its inception "from out of the death of Socrates." Rorty's desire to give up on philosophy is appropriate, but only because, as Eric Gans remarks, philosophy yields its best insights to anthropology.

Derrida's more rigorous critique of what amounts to a sacrificial rationality in Plato, Descartes, Rousseau, Saussure, Husserl, and others is more to the purpose, though as I observed at the outset of this chapter, its allergy to an anthropological hypothesis as foundational discourse frustrates its keenest insights.

This can be shown with reference to the recent resurgence of debate around deconstruction generated by the revelation of the wartime journalistic writings of Paul de Man. They include expressions of antisemitism that Derrida himself does not hesitate to qualify as being of an "*unpardonable* violence and confusion," as going "in the sense and the direction of the worst" ("Like the Sound of the Sea . . . " 623). I approach this debate gingerly, reluctantly, with no intention whatsoever of judging the youthful de Man; that is for only those exempt from the mimesis and resulting conformism of the human condition, who would consequently be immune to collaboration or accommodation with the variegated mendacities, blandishments, and brutalities of an alien occupying force. But the themes of the debate are of a kind that no sustained discussion of deconstruction can ignore, and least of all this discussion, concerned as it is with the historical, institutional, and ethical implications of deconstruction, with deconstruction and the public realm, including the vagaries of its journalistic representations.

De Man's brief wartime journalism has been the occasion for adversaries of deconstruction to associate it with fascism and its cognate discourses, an association that Derrida, along with a host of others, has roundly refuted. With a ringing *tu quoque*, he shows, for instance (I cannot reproduce the entirety of his vigorous and nuanced argumentation), that such "confusionist practices—amalgam, continuism, analogism, teleologism, hasty totalization, reduction, and derivation"—are endemic to the "totalitarian logic" being denounced (640–41). Deconstruction is nothing if not a vigilant attention to stereotyping (see 647, where this vigilance is fairly thematized as a value opposed to the dream of "expeditious trials"); it is above all a resistance to "totalizing violence" (645), though most often in unsuspected, intellectual forms: "What I have practiced under that name has always seemed to me favorable, indeed destined (it is no doubt my principle motivation), to the analysis of the conditions of totalitarianism in all its forms, which cannot always be reduced to names of regimes" (648). That indeed has been its interest for a correlation with the victimary hypothesis undertaken throughout this book.

Thus Derrida finds himself obliged to defend deconstruction, a term from which he had but lately attempted to dissociate himself precisely because of its journalistic misrepresentations: "deconstructions have always represented, as I see it, the at least necessary condition for identifying and combating the totalitarian risk in all the forms already mentioned" (647). The list of these forms is worth citing; they are but various forms of a single persecutory structure, but variants of the sacrificial process: "purification, purge, totalization, reappropriation, homogenization, rapid objectification, good conscience, stereotyping and nonreading, *immediate* politicization or depoliticization (it is always the same thing), immediate historicization or dehistoricization (it is always the same thing), immediate ideologizing moralization (immorality itself) of all the texts and all the problems, expedited trial, condemnations, or acquittals, summary executions or sublimations. This is what must be deconstructed . . ." (646). This is what Girard's institutional critique undertakes, especially in *The Scapegoat* (see chap. 2, "The Stereotypes of Persecution") and in *Job: the Victim of his People* (see chaps. 16, "A Totalitarian Trial," and 17, "Retribution").

Sacrifice is the only word missing from this list, though it summarizes it all. The notion all but surfaces thematically in Derrida's animadversion "to the expeditious violence of lapidary judgments, even to a symbolic lapidation" (634). Lapidation is an exemplarily sacrificial practice, a traditional way of instituting a distance between one's violence and its victim so as to delude oneself about one's distance and difference from violent origins and to deceive oneself about one's immunity to violence, or innocence of it. It is a mechanism intended to avoid contamination by a violence that the destruction of the victim is meant to resolve. Of course, it is commonplace to denounce lapidary judgments, as much as it is to denounce scapegoating. Girard's argument is that this commonplace is rooted in the scriptural deconstruction of sacrificial practices (see *VO* 74–78), whereby we have all been co-opted, so to speak, by the likes of Job, Jeremiah, Isaiah, and Jesus. This too remains to be thoroughly tested (see, for starters, Schwager, *Scapegoats*, and McKenna, ed., *Semeia 33*); at the very least, it is a more humanly interesting alternative to most current appreciations of "the Bible as literature," where literature means indeterminacy in a way that is not far from meaning nothing at all.

It has been one of the principle aims of this book to show that there is an analytic and critique of sacrifice imbedded in the discourse of deconstruction and to bring it to the surface by a correlation with Girard's reading of culture. I have yet to explain why, beyond a certain textual self-involvement that calls for its own explanation, it does not surface on its own. This can be done in terms of the baleful circumstances under consideration and without indulging in the "petty and mediocre game" (642) of putting de Man on trial. That is the Pharisaical game of "good conscience," precisely as denounced in Scripture: the game of swearing that we would not have murdered the prophets, or condemned Baudelaire, or ignored van Gogh, and so on (see Matt. 23:29–32 and *THFW* 160, 175).

The game is structural in its blindness to mimesis, a fact that Derrida intuits rather than thematizes when he urges against "reproducing the logic one claims to condemn" ("Like the Sound of the Sea . . . " 647), when he shows "it was easy to recognize axioms and forms of behavior that confirm the logic one claims to have rid oneself of" (646), and again when, in his summation, he likens de Man's accusers to the "gesture" of which the former is accused: "To judge, to condemn the work or the man on the basis of what was a brief episode, to call for closing, that is to say, at least figuratively, for censuring or burning his books is to reproduce the exterminating gesture which one accuses de Man of not having armed himself against sooner with the necessary vigilance" (651). The issue is totalization in all its forms, including "historical totalization" (641). That is what deconstruction has resisted throughout—indeed, has resisted with a thoroughness so devastating (I do not hesitate to say so total) as to cripple its chance to oppose it or to formulate a position from which to combat it: "Since we are talking at this moment about discourse that is totalitarian, fascist, Nazi, racist, antisemitic, and so forth, about all the gestures, either discursive or not, that could be suspected of complicity with it, I would like to do, and naturally I invite others to do, whatever possible to avoid reproducing, if only virtually, the *logic* of the discourse thus incriminated" (645). Derrida is issuing more of a challenge than an invitation, as the following paragraph plainly reveals. It deserves to be quoted in its entirety, not in spite of its length, but just because of it, because of the total demands it makes on our powers of interpretation and formulation.

> Do we have access to a complete formalization of this logic and an absolute exteriority with regard to its ensemble? Is there a systematic set of themes, concepts, philosophemes, forms of utterance, axioms, evaluations, hierarchies which, forming a closed and identifiable coherence of what we call totalitarianism, fascism, nazism, racism, antisemitism, never appear outside these formations and especially never on the opposite side? And is there a systematic coherence proper to each of them, since one must not confuse them too quickly with each other? Is there some property so closed and so pure that one may not find any element of these systems in discourse that are commonly opposed to them? To say that I do not believe that there is, not absolutely, means at least two things: (1) Such a formalizing, saturating totalization seems to me to be precisely the essential character of this logic whose project, at least, and whose ethico-political consequence can be terrifying. One of my rules is never to accept this project and consequence, whatever that may cost. (2) For this very reason, one must analyze as far as possible this process of formalization and its program so as to uncover the statements, the philosophical, ideological, or political behaviors that derive from it and wherever they may be found. The task seems to me to be both urgent and interminable. It has occurred to me on occasion to call this deconstruction. (645–46).

What follows is the list of confusionist practices cited earlier and the unqualified opposition of deconstruction to them, which I have already examined. It is clear by these sentences, however, that deconstruction has defined an impossible task, for whose discourse should escape whipping under such transcendental conditions, qualified as they are by the following stringent terms: complete, absolute (twice), systematic (twice), closed and identifiable, never (twice), so closed and so pure, saturating, essential, terrifying, whatever, as far as possible, and wherever? This is a case of Richard Shusterman's objection that deconstruction remains "fundamentally committed and inextricably wedded to . . . the principle of organic unity which it claims everywhere to contest" (in Dasenbrock 94): "the idea that everything is a product of its interrelations and differences from other things, that there are no independent terms with positive or intrinsic essences, rests at bottom on the idea that all these interrelated and differential terms are indeed inexorably and ineluctably interconnected" (107–8).

Special attention to the syntactic motif is warranted here: Derrida's second question requires several readings to determine whether he is referring to the discourse of totalitarianism or to its other, to what is exterior to it. The confusion here is not accidental or idiosyncratic; it is inherent, systemic with the outlandish goals that deconstruction has set for itself and its readers. It is a rhetorical question, because like the others, it is generated by a concern for integrity, for a completeness that renders formulation virtually impossible, or impossibly virtuous.

The task of deconstruction is interminable because it has set impossible demands for representation, the very demands of totalization it opposes. Consequently, totalitarianism and its cognates are unrepresentable, unformalizable, unknowable: *ignotum per ignotius.* Though Derrida has resisted the appellation, the conditions stipulated here perform a negative theology, though in reverse; this theology bears not on the being of God but on the Adversary, in the form of a discourse that nonetheless corresponds to the ontological conditions of the Scholastics' God, whose center is everywhere and whose circumference is nowhere. Like metaphor.

As long as deconstruction holds out against an ideal of a fully self-reflexive discourse, as against Hegel, it will always be right, just as Rorty will be right as long as he identifies epistemology with the idea of language as a "transparent medium" of representation (*Contingency* 75; *Philosophy* passim). But this is no more than to hold out against a theological absolute, incompletely secularized as a Laplacean dream of total explanation, and to prop it up as an improbable standard against which to measure one's intellectual good faith. In Sartrean terms (see *Baudelaire* 62), it is a rebellious rather than a revolutionary stance, for it depends on the oppressive imperium of its adversary to justify its oppositional role. It is a properly mythical activity, the role of myth ever being to stabilize antinomies, to petrify identities by means of imaginary dualisms.

Because deconstruction has sensitized us to symbolic forms of violence, we have to ask about the symbolic violence of this all-or-nothing alternative between terror and textualism. What Paisley Livingston says against the "rigorous purity" demanded by Derridean skepticism (the term in quotes being Derrida's about the unknowability, the untraceability, of "signature effects"; see "Signature, Event, Context" in *Margins of Philosophy*) applies to the conditions laid down here. Concerning the demand "to consider a belief to be knowledge only when we know with absolute certainty that it is true, " Livingston remarks that "it is possible that many of our beliefs could truly correspond to what is the case without our having this kind of absolute evidence or justification for them. Yet our skeptic prefers an absolute theory of justification that leads us to sacrifice all of these beliefs to the possibility of doubt; fear of error and a desire for absolute reliability are given first priority" (*Literary Knowledge* 52).

Something very like a literal sacrifice takes place with such transcendental skepticism: the demand for absolute certainty functions like unanimity; the result is that truth is, *more sacrifico*, the victim of a ubiquitous, unanimous host of doubts, as personified by conditions that are complete, absolute, and saturating, whatever and wherever. This effect is not willed but structural, being the inevitable by-product of a demand for purity, of a veritable purge. The fact that what is purged is the divinity, in the form of a transcendent truth, betrays the essence of sacrifice, whose role is to dehumanize and expel a violence whose sway among humans is intolerable. Deconstructions's veritable terror of error condemns formulation to silence, or to bad conscience, which is what deconstruction is. It is the bad conscience of philosophy, its consciousness of being a text, or its unconscious *tout court;* it is the bad conscience of language generally, generically, and above all genetically: for lack of an origin, language suffers from a lack of foundation, of a "ground of nonsignification" to which it might reliably refer.

Derrida repeatedly warns against oversimplifying (602, 607, 615, 647), but the symmetrical danger of overcomplexifying is not considered. Here as elsewhere, deconstruction is in danger of nuancing itself out of a job, at least an academic one—unless its role is to disfranchise everyone else, absolutely everyone who lays claim to knowledge, whatever and wherever the claim. However, unless we subscribe to risk-free conditions that render formulation impossible, an answer to his questions must be attempted. It is no good having clean hands if the process renders them incapable of grasping anything. In any event, deconstruction, whose ethical impulse as evoked by Derrida is worthy of adherence if any is, is supposed to be a risky business, and here where it counts most, where a body count is concerned, desire for a risk-free discourse is tantamount to nihilism. For despite Derrida's resistance to that appellation, what Tobin Siebers states of de Man's literary criticism in its resistance to "the initial violence of position" (de Man, *The Rhetoric of Romanticism* 118) applies *avant la lettre* (having been published prior to the revelation of the wartime journalism) to Derrida's "rules": "Nihilism in the modern world may be defined as the preference for nothingness over the risk of committing an act of violence" (*The Ethics of Criticism* 105).

If all forms of utterance, all axioms and evaluations, pale before the absolute, the absolute before which they pale and by which they are judged is the victim. The victim is not a property, still less an element, but a position from which to judge all inquisitions, determinations, and doubts, all formulation and "the philosophical and political behaviors that derive from it." The victim is not a system but that by which all systems are to be tested, by which their false coherence is belied. The victim is not a property of the system, not in a de-divinized and ostensibly postsacrificial world, but the impropriety that the system seeks to ignore in order to function. It is the system's inside turned out. It is not a transcendental criterion for all that; I have called it transdescendental, for it surges from beneath rather than from above the violent agency of institutions, hierarchies, principalities, and powers.

In this sense, neither Derridean deconstruction nor Girard's sacrificial theory qualifies as a system, at least not in the philosophical sense. What is common to both, where they coincide at a structural level, constitutes a rigorous and coherent critique of "systematicity," be it philosophical or more broadly cultural: both detect sacrificial, exclusionary mechanisms that are blind to their own violence, which is ever imputed to the element they expel. What their parallel decon-structions achieve is not just another construct, another misrepresen-tation, for the latter is a theme rather than a structuring principle in their texts. Examining historical events of indubitable magnitude shows the *real* import of their writings. The real is the victim, vio-lence, death by more or less administrative measure, and a key to un-derstanding it on firm ground is mimetic desire, conflictual mimesis, an understanding of which explains the misunderstanding of violence and of systems that secrete it. This in turn explains my continual attention to the writings of Hannah Arendt, for whom power is a historical fact, not a signifier, a motif, or a trope—though she has until lately endured fairly ritual avoidance by "serious" academic philosophers.

Derrida's plea for a reading "as open and as differentiated as pos-sible" ("Like the Sound of the Sea . . ." 648) is warranted precisely by the need to preserve this one irreducible difference between victim and persecutor. The claim of the victim has not changed since the foundation of the world, since, that is, "the voice of your brother's blood crying to me from the ground" (Gen. 4:10), where "me" is to be understood as the God of victims (see Girard, *Job* chap. 21). What has changed is the status of that claim, which has become universal. All lay claim to it in their recourse to judgment and violence. What the victim represents (human violence) is not ambiguous; what is ambig-uous is what or who represents the victim, who simulates rather than who incarnates, who realizes in her or his own flesh the experience of the victim, the ordeal of human violence. That is the task of a herme-neutic of suspicion that need not remain suspicious of its own vicious circularity once its attention is averted to the inside-out relation of the victim to the *belle totalité* that secretes it.

Responsibility implies undecidability ("Like the Sound of the Sea . . ." 639) precisely insofar as no one is at liberty—because of all the complexity described by Derrida—to decide his or her relation to the victim, short of choosing to trade places, that undesirable choice being the only one in which free decision is properly exercised, in which desire has no role. In sum, the victim is a means of anchoring interpretation to something outside it, to its ethical roots, precisely as they spring from outside the system, the totality, the community. Af-ter all, what is "terrifying," as Derrida observes, about the "desire for roots and common roots" (648) is the fact that the homogeneity (and the origineity and unanimity) of a "people" is realized only by violent expulsion of what it arbitrarily deems as its other. Yet Derrida is rightly suspicious of even this choice if it serves only as a self-exonerating exclusion:

One does not free oneself of [totalitarianism] effectively at a single blow by easy adherence to the dominant consensus, or by proclamations of the sort I could, after all, give into without any great risk, since it is what is called the objective truth: "As for me, you know, no one can suspect me of anything; I am Jewish, I was persecuted as a child during the war, I have always been known for my leftist opinions, I fight as best I can, for example against racism (for instance, in France or in the United States where they are still rampant, would anyone like to forget that?), against *apartheid* or for the recognition of the rights of Palestinians. I have gotten myself arrested, interrogated, and imprisoned by totalitarian police, not long ago, so I know how they ask and resolve questions and so forth." No, such declarations are insufficient. There can still be, and in spite them, residual adherences to the discourse one is claiming to combat. (648)

Derrida appears to be aware that every persecutor takes him or herself for a victim, striking here for having been struck there, or imagining oneself to have been struck. Residual adherences, or traces, are the specialty of deconstruction, as he goes on to say: "And deconstruction is, in particular, the tireless analysis (both theoretical and practical) of these adherences" (648). I have traced the interest of the trace, its theoretical and practical value-orienting significance, to the victim. According to Derrida's readings, the signifier, or the gramm, as well as a certain (uncertain) literature or poetic indeterminacy, is the victim of philosophy's violent will to truth, of logocentrism as it succumbs or conforms to a sacrificial mechanism.

In other words, philosophy's truth-seeking impulse obeys a compulsion to repeat—sacrifice. It obeys a ritual imperative detectable from Plato through Husserl, not to mention Heidegger, whose notorious flirtation with Nazism is not clarified by Derrida's qualification of his works as "at once terribly dangerous and madly *drôle*" (*De L'esprit*). If Derrida's readings are accurate, if, by way of minimal formulation, they state "what is the case," then sacrifice is the truth of philosophy. It is a truth that survives in the form of the victim, even if the victim takes the form of writing; indeed, especially if, as Derrida states in (non)defense of his anti-thetical (non)position, "postphilosophical discourses" consist in "an evaluation of writing, or, to tell the truth, rather a devaluation of writing whose insistent, repetitive, even obscurely compulsive, character was the sign of a whole set of long-standing constraints" ("The Time of a Thesis" 40).

In sum, Derrida unwittingly states a case for an epistemology rooted in the victim, in which all differentiations begin and by which they are to be appraised. From this perspective, his rhetorical questioning amounts to something disarmingly simple; by a virtual indictment of all discourse, it conforms to the dictum that any without sin may cast a stone at the accused. And his rule not to accept the project and consequence of totalization "whatever the cost" is justified by identifying the cost with the victim. It is not justified, however, when the cost is identified with any postulation of truth. Nor is it necessary, if truth is identified with the victim, which by Derrida's account of it is what deconstruction implicitly does, especially when it assails a transcendental notion of truth wrought by covert mechanisms of exclusion.

This is all to the good, but it is insufficient, both practically and theoretically, if it results only in exulting in linguistic bad conscience. If good conscience is bad for entertaining delusions about exemption from violence, there is a symmetrical risk of entertaining delusions about a good bad conscience, which can result in a kind of *delectio morosa* with regard to enunciation. This is the danger of a purely antithetical position, a strategy of strategy, however much it "delights in being without defense" and just because of that delight as well. If a certain idea or ideal of literature is the last veil of the sacred, then the sacralization of the veil ensures yet another vast detour around the victim. It is a question not of judging Derrida or deconstruction on this score but of completing them with reference to a mechanism that they themselves uncover at almost any turn of phrase, but that, out of modesty as well as a crippling fear of error, they fail to name.

Denomination is forsaken for the syntactic motif, a systematic dysposition that becomes a position (under erasure) of its own, however much it is inscribed under erasure by a "certain pas de la danse." Its purely negative capability is difficult to distinguish from that of the romantic writers from Keats through Sartre, whose Roquentin viscerally but ineffectually resists denomination by the Autodidacte: "I don't want to be integrated, I don't want my good red blood to go and fatten this lymphatic beast: I will not be fool enough to call myself 'anti-humanist.' I *am not* a humanist, that's all there is to it" (*La Nausée* 168). Sartre never gets the attention he deserves from deconstruction, perhaps because he already thematized the contradictions in which the latter seeks its claims to originality, beginning, as in *La Nausée*, with the monumentalizing pathology of books.

Equating totalization with totalitarianism, deconstruction prefers to do violence to itself rather than participate in the violence of logocentrism. Adopting irony as its master trope, its antisystematic openness, its emphatic irresolution, is testimony to its generosity, its *titres de noblesse*. That phrase comes to mind when considering how this strategy of self-effacement finds its formal equivalent, if not its vocational fulfillment, in what Baudelaire analyzes as dandyism, whose adherents are "at once priests and victims" of an "étrange spiritualisme" whose only sacrament is suicide. This is doubtless not a welcome denomination, but neither it is a fortuitous one in view of the timelessness of this "institution vague, très ancienne and très générale" marked above all by a "caractère d'opposition et de révolte," which can "survive everything that we call illusion" (*Oeuvres complètes* 560). At the very least it represents a permanent temptation of a poststructural, postmodern "caste provocante" whose "lois rigoureuses" place it "en dehors des lois" and that is "above all in love with *distinction*," not in its toilette in this instance but, as by a further refinement, in its textuality: "How to interpret—but here interpretation can no longer be a theory or a discursive practice of philosophy—the strange and unique property of a discourse that organizes the *economy* of its representation, the law of its proper weave, such that *its* outside is never its *outside*, never surprises it, such that the logic of its heteronomy still reasons [*raisonne*, but also *résonne*, resonates] from within the vault of its autism" (Derrida, *Margins of Philosophy* xvi). This text resonates in turn with Baudelaire's observation about the dandy's "culte de soi même" as it seeks "the pleasure of astonishing and the proud satisfaction of never being astonished" (*Oeuvres complètes* 560).

I do not wish to reduce deconstruction to dandyism, for it oscillates in every sense brilliantly between dandyism and philosophical seriousness: "Simultaneously, by means of rigorous, philosophically *intransigent* analysis, *and* by means of the inscription of marks which no longer belong to philosophical space, not even to the neighborhood of its other, one would have to displace philosophy's alignment of its own types. To write otherwise" (Derrida, *Margins of Philosophy* xxiv). A certain pathos of discipleship, with philosophy as the rival-model this writing seeks to displace and replace, is transparent here in the motif of the type. To write otherwise than philosophy, while striving for and against claims to originality, is a trademark of literary postmodernity, where ironic self-effacement cannot resist its own inscription:

> What I have not yet accepted must indeed be called divulging. The part of divulging in the slightest, most reserved, most neutral publications I still find inadmissible, unjustifiable—and above all r-i-d-i-c-u-l-o-u-s, comical a priori. Not condemnable but a priori deriving from the comic genre. There is someone in me who kills with a burst of laughter whoever appears to find it necessary, opportune, important to say what he thinks, feels, lives, or anything you like. Of course I do not escape the slaughter. In the name of what, in the name of whom publish, divulge—and first of all write, since it amounts to the same? I have published a lot, but there is someone in me, I still quite can't identify him, who still hopes never to have done it. And he believes that in everything that I have let pass, depart, a very effective mechanism comes to annihilate the exposition. I write while concealing every possible divulging of the very thing which appears to be published. For tell me what is the imperative, in the end? With sights set on whom, for whom accept to divulge? (Derrida, *The Post Card* 80).

I have no wish to deny Derrida his primal doubts, which are those of any modern writer: as Baudelaire says in correspondence, "A quoi bon ceci? à quoi bon cela?"—"what's the use," as we say—something that Flaubert and Kafka say in scarcely different terms in their letters. Self-(de)negation *positions* the writer at least since Montaigne: "Thus, reader, I am myself the matter of my book: it is not reasonable that you employ your leisure on a subject so frivolous and vain" are the penultimate words introducing the *Essais* to the reader (for the pathology of self-representation, see Beaujour, *Miroirs d'encre*). But I do not wish to grant such ironic self-deprecation any metaphysical (or rather, meta-historical) status either, for it expresses a well-founded ambivalence toward the stereotype *par excellence* of Western modernity, which Baudelaire called "cette petite propriété, le moi."

Derrida's systematic indisposition is not peculiar to his thesis defense or to his most recent defense of de Man. It is permanent and structural. This pro-gram appears early on in his writings, at the conclusion of "Structure, Sign and Play in the Human Sciences" (*WD*), where he opposes Lévi-Strauss to Nietzsche in way that inaugurates what has since become known as poststructuralism:

Turned towards the lost or impossible presence of the absent origin, this structuralist thematic of broken immediacy is therefore the saddened, *negative*, nostalgic, guilty, Rousseauistic side of the thinking of play whose other side would be the Nietzschean *affirmation*, that is the joyous affirmation of the play of the world and the innocence of becoming, the affirmation of a world of signs without fault, without truth, and without origin which is offered to an active interpretation. *This affirmation then determines the noncenter otherwise than as loss of center.* And it plays without security. For there is a *sure* play, that which is limited to the *substitution* of *given* and *existing, present* pieces. In absolute chance, affirmation also surrenders itself to *genetic* indetermination, to the *seminal* adventure of the trace" (*WD* 292).

Stated in these value-laden terms, where negative and positive are all but labeled guilty and innocent, there appears to be no choice but to surrender ourselves to the "*seminal* adventure of the trace." But Derrida knows better than *simply* to oppose these alternatives, which he describes as participating in "an obscure economy," a notion that needs closer examination.

With the invocation of Rousseau and Lévi-Strauss, it appears we are back in the Platonic dream world. Indeed, of these two interpretations of interpretation Derrida goes on to say that "the one seeks to decipher, dreams of deciphering a truth or an origin which escapes play and the order of the sign, and which lives the necessity of interpretation as an exile. The other, which is no longer turned toward the origin, affirms play and tries to pass beyond man and humanism, the name of man being the name of that being who, throughout the history of metaphysics or of ontotheology—in other words, throughout his entire history—has dreamed of full presence, the reassuring foundation, the origin and the end of play" (292). But it is important to observe that, according to Girard's hypothesis, the sacred victim is *not* a truth or an origin that escapes the play and the order of the sign, except in the mystified belief of the newborn community. As transcendental signifier, the sacred victim, who is a sign of contradiction (good and bad, desirable and taboo, mana of the structure, etc.), generates the play of differences. The sacred victim is a sign without truth, without origin—except chance—offered to active *and* passive interpretation, in which the community is born. This hypothesis is as critical of Platonism as is Derrida, for it shows that the dream of philosophy is born of oblivion, of obliterating the nightmare of victimage. What does Derrida offer with "the joyous affirmation of the play of the world and the innocence of becoming, the affirmation of a world of signs without fault, without truth, and without origin which is offered to an active interpretation"? Nothing less, nor more, than the dream of literature as rigorously antithetical to the dream of philosophy: whereas Plato dreamed of "truth as distinct from its sign, being as distinct from types, . . . memory with no sign" (PP 109), we are to envision signs as distinct from truth, types as distinct from being, signs with no memory, movement without position. The goal of the game is to keep the ball in perpetual motion while scoring an occasional victory against a Husserl or a John Searle (see "Limited Inc.," which we are to think as ending, with a bow to Joycean "inkinstinct," only with the ribbon on the typewriter), but only because they seek to arrest its play. It is the *pas de la danse* and not of negation, resonating with *Le Pas au-delà* of Maurice Blanchot, a step (*pas*) beyond or a not (*pas*) beyond, moving toward his *L'Entretien infini* and his *Le Livre* that is always *à venir.* The signs are without memory—except of other signs, other signifiers, whose model, whose literal and letterly stereotype, appears in and as Derrida's writings, where signifieds are ever detoured from their (im)possible referents by a *retour* to their homonyms, playing among what Paul Valéry called "les similitudes amies qui brillent parmi les mots." Derrida's strategy is structurally destined to self-reflection and self-imitation, where language mirrors not reality but itself, its unself, its lack of essence. It cannot fail to fetishize literature: emulating the attraction-repulsion of signifiers, it stands in relation to language as the desiring subject to the sacred victim, to whom the subject defers by virtue of the same ambivalent force that attracts his desire to it.

Of course, as I have said, Derrida knows better than simply to oppose these two interpretations, a move that would further the dialectical oppositions he seeks to evade. He underlines that we cannot simply *choose* between these alternatives, though he says they "are absolutely irreconcilable even if we live them simultaneously and reconcile them in an obscure economy," for they "share the field which we call, in such a problematic fashion, the social [human] sciences" (WD 293). There is no alternative to the obscure economy of their "common ground," "the differance of their irreducible difference." But this constrains a choice in his direction, for his indirection, his bias, differance being the "term" under erasure that generates and presides over these two interpretations and sanctions their undecidability as a consequence. The conditions he enunciates conform to the structure of the double bind: simultaneous and contradictory imperatives compelling a choice that will always have been wrong, erroneous, lopsided, and arbitrary.

In one sense, he is right: there is obviously no choice between structure and process, between guilty past and innocent becoming, for those are the defining conditions of human existence, of human freedom. We cannot deny past and present complicity with (sacrificial) institutions, nor can we resign ourselves fatalistically on that account to paralysis, to what in every sense amounts to statism. To claim or disclaim responsibility appears to result in one and the same determinism, the same logical impasse, whose rationality is undecidable. We need no longer remain in awesome, stymied contemplation of this impasse, however, now that we have an anthropological theory for it. For what Derrida's double bind propels us toward is a theory rooted in the contradictions of desire, which he has concisely described as "la cohérence dans la contradiction." His argument here unfolds precisely according to the movement of the sacrificial scenario, where a double bind affecting the victim issues in the generation of a divinity, an *ignotum x*, whose baffled contemplation protects and absolves the community from examining or confronting the contradictions of its violent foundation.

This scenario is just where Derrida leads when he summons what this differance generates, what awaits the work generated by this "*différence irréductible*": "Here there is a kind of question, let us call it historical, whose *conception, formation, gestation* and *labor* we are only catching a glimpse of today. I employ these words, I admit, with a glance toward the operations of childbearing—but also with a glance toward whose who, in a society from which I do not exclude myself, turn their eyes away when faced by the as yet unnameable which is proclaiming itself and which can do so, as is necessary whenever a birth is in the offing, only under the species of the nonspecies, in the formless, mute, infant, and terrifying form of monstrosity" (*WD* 293). These are the very last words of his essay. They give a dandy *frisson* to the work of deconstruction and to those venturing forth armed with its untruth, "the truthless truth on truth," as he says *à propos* Blanchot. They represent a properly mythical solution that we must deconstruct.

I do not think Derrida believes in monsters, which are but a figure of speech for the unknown, including (especially so) what speech cannot make known, what it is structurally destined to ignore, especially about itself. On the other hand, he concludes with this properly mythical solution as if he wanted his readers to believe in them. Yet no one can believe in monsters, at least no one who has read works like *Don Quixote, A Midsummer Night's Dream,* and Dostoyevsky's novels, which artfully and knowingly dispel such creatures. We cannot believe in monsters, for we know what they are. They are sacred, and like the sacred, they are not. When they threaten us, they are nothing but the form violence takes in its indifference to difference, the form our own violence takes when we disown it. When vanquished, they are surrogates for the victim, the form violence takes when we sacralize it, the form the victim takes when its destruction reconciles the community. The sacred and the monster are proof of a false reconciliation among violent rivals, and it is wrong to believe in them. They are indestructible as long as we cling to our illusions about desire, which is not ours to arm or disarm in pursuit of its representations, its signifiers.

To make a long story short, it has been twenty years or so since Derrida summoned a monster from the lair of Western rationality, the lure of binary logic, and in that time a theory has emerged that neutralizes the monster's terrors and its consequent attraction-repulsion for the self-delusions of desire. On this account, a rational choice is possible and necessary as long as it is poised between a discourse that generates labyrinths inhabited by the cryptogram, the phantom monster of writing itself (not itself), and a discourse that identifies the monster as the self, as what the self refuses to know in and as the self: the other's desire, the other's violence. If we know anything, we know we do not want to be party to a violence born of (self) ignorance of which we stand as much a chance as any of being the arbitrary victim.

That ought to be the last word of this book, being as well, though in mystified form, the first word of human culture, its *Überworte.* But it is highly misleading, for it gives the impression that, because deconstruction favors logical impasses and undecidability, it must favor indifference to the victim. That is untrue.

Rather, because it opposes oppression (however formally disguised) and favors the victim (however formally represented), it favors unde-cidability in the formal representation of (merely) rational alternatives. Its impasses lead to the conclusion that there is no formal solution to the problems it poses. We cannot, it argues, assume too quickly what is outside language, but language is not a solution. Yet the conformity of its logical impasses to those affecting the victim, the sacred, shows that pragmatic solutions have or obey a rationale once that rationale is located in the victim.

This rationale is manifest in Derrida's brief essay against apartheid, "Racism's Last Word," which he contributed to a catalog of essays ac-companying an itinerant art exhibit. He largely forgoes the labor of deconstructing "an evil that cannot be summed up in the principle and abstract iniquity of a system. It is also daily suffering, oppression, poverty, violence, torture . . . " (293). The thematics of deconstruc-tion are in evidence, linking "a European 'discourse' on the concept of race . . . to a whole system of 'phantasms,' to a certain representation of nature, life, history, religion and law, . . . a contradiction internal to the West and to the assertion of its rights" (294), but only in service to the "just silence" of artworks as it "calls out unconditionally." (299). These works perform a crisis of representation: "Here is an exhibi-tion—as one continues to say in the old language of the West, 'works of art,' signed 'creations,' in the present case 'pictures,' or 'paintings,' 'sculptures.' In this collective and international exhibition (and there's nothing new about that either), pictural, sculptural idioms will be crossing, but they will be attempting to speak the other's language without renouncing their own. And in order to effect this translation, their common reference henceforth makes an appeal to a language that cannot be found, a language at once very old, older than Europe, but for that very reason to be invented once more" (294). I do not pre-sume to know what language Derrida means to allude to, or even that he knows. He is soliciting some alternative to Western logos, some otherness to the "the juridico-political or theologic-political dis-course" of Europe, to its internal contradictions in its otherness to it-self. It is legible again when he "appeal[s] unconditionally to the future of another law and another force lying beyond the totality of this present" (298). But in view of a thematic and relentless em-phasis on suffering (294, 297, 299), I am reminded ineluctably of a voice, a language, an appeal that the victimary hypothesis locates in

Scripture and to which it credits the force of anthropological law. Because I have reported here and there the contention that Scripture is the origin of this appeal and the deployment of its rationale, I owe it to the reader to make at least some essay of that hypothesis, which I append to this volume.

It is appended without reference to Derrida, whose (a)structural correlation with Girard's reading of culture is independent of scriptural testimony.

Biblical Theory: Testing The Victimary Hypothesis

Hermeneutic or Hieratic?

"Instead of interpreting the great masterpieces in the light of modern theories, we must criticize modern theories in the light of these masterpieces, once their theoretical voice has become explicit." Thus René Girard offers his summary estimate on the relations between great literature and theory in the introductory chapter to a volume of his essays (*DBB* x). Substituting the word *Scripture* for *great masterpieces* gives voice to his conception of the Bible in its relation to theory.

The novelty of this claim is ambiguous. It accords to literature, and in this case Scripture, an active rather than a passive role in interpretation, such that literary theories are to be viewed no longer as instruments but as objects of a critical gaze emanating from these texts. We do not read them; they read us, and our task in attempting to understand these texts is to understand ourselves as well as they do, for what they offer is "real knowledge . . . of human relations" (*DBB* xi). As Girard states in *Things Hidden since the Foundation of the World*, "We can no longer believe that it is we who are reading the Gospels in the light of ethnological, modern revelation which would really be the first thing of its kind. We have to reverse this order. It is still the great Judaeo-Christian spirit that is doing the reading" (177).

I describe the novelty of this claim as ambiguous because, although on the one hand it scandalizes our theoretical intelligence, our scientific ambitions, on the other it appears to continue the most traditional notion of the Bible as the unique and apodictic deposit of truth.

Beyond that it communicates with a fundamental dimension of biblical self-understanding in the Jewish faith: "Before any sort of literary work, every reading formulates an appreciation, the fruit of its sovereign taste. Before the Bible, the judgment is reversed; it is the book which judges the Jew. The Torah exists, he says, but I, do I exist?" (Claude Riveline, "Présentation" 18).

Perhaps there is nothing less novel than to argue for the uniqueness and supremacy of the good book, which understands itself, rightly or wrongly, as the God book. But here too a difference obtains in Girard's claim; unlike the traditional conception, Girard's reading privileges Scripture for not its theological but its theoretic import, not its hieratic but its hermeneutic value. And this novelty emerges above all when he says that the theoretical voice in Scripture is not primarily the word of God in the traditional sense, the voice of divine inspiration or of the all-powerful divinity that speaks to Job from out of the whirlwind. Girard never writes about inspiration, only of revelation. Moreover, what is revealed does not come from on high, but from down below—indeed, from underfoot. The theoretical voice of Scripture is that of the victim, and it is thematically marked as such "since the foundation of the world": "Then the Lord said to Cain, 'Where is Abel your brother?' He said, 'I do not know; am I my brother's keeper?' and the Lord said, 'What have you done? The voice of your brother's blood is crying to me from the ground. And now you are cursed from the ground, which has opened its mouth to receive your brother's blood from your hand.' " (Gen. 4:9–10 [Revised Standard Version]).

Girard offers not a theology of revelation, which could be of interest only to believers—and intellectual curiosity seekers—but an anthropology of revelation, which is something else again. The Bible's authority is autochthonous, self-contained. Its universal interest is scientific, not soteriological. According to the orthodox conception, the opposite of revelation from on high is ordinary human representation, or imitation of reality, whereby texts are distinguished as sacred and profane. Girard creates a new paradigm, where the opposite of revelation is reflection as they both concern the structuring principles of human relations, namely, mimetic desire as it leads to violence: "If one individual," as he writes in the first paragraph of *To Double Business Bound*, "imitates another when the latter appropriates some object, the result cannot fail to be rivalry or conflict." The resolution of this conflict is destined to sacrifice, which takes place when rival desires are polarized around a single object. Its unanimous destruction or explusion generates a harmony, a com-unity for which in retrospect it is held responsible, first as the source of dissension and then, by its expulsion, as the source of reconciliation. To sacralize the victim is to sacralize violence. The object of rivalry, which is perceived as bad, as good to destroy, will be perceived by all as good in the aftermath of its reconciling destruction. It is on this misunderstanding, on the mystified agency of the victim and the violence that produced it, that culture is founded.

What Scripture reveals in a manner unprecedented and unsurpassed is the foundational role of violence and the mystified role of the victim as the structuring principle of the sacrificial resolution to human violence. Once this structuring principle is revealed and thematized it can no longer function effectively. People are face to face with their own violence, which they can no longer mistakenly interpret as divine. They are faced no longer with the difference between human and divine, profane and sacred, but with the difference between persecutor and victim, which is irreducible.

It is Girard himself who underlines in turn his lack of originality:

> The revelation of the surrogate victim as the founding agent in all religion and culture is something that neither our world as a whole nor any one particularly "gifted" individual can claim to have discovered. *Everything is already revealed.* This is certainly the claim of the Gospels at the moment of the Passion. To understand that the victimage mechanism constitutes an essential dimension of that revelation, we will not need to take up the comparative analysis and constant cross-references that were necessary in the examples of religions of violence; we need only give our fullest attention to the letter of the text. It speaks incessantly of everything we have said ourselves; it has no other function than to unearth victims of collective violence and to reveal their innocence. This is nothing hidden. There is no secret dimension that the interpreter must painstakingly seek to discover. Everything is perfectly transparent. Nothing is less problematic or easy than the reading we will offer. The true mystery, therefore, as far as this reading is concerned, is its absence among us. (*THFW* 138)

In what follows, I will not deal primarily with the workings of the victimage mechanism. Rather, I will examine the self-evidentiary claims concerning the victim in their hermeneutic and epistemological dimensions.

Everything is revealed, then; nothing is mysterious except our misunderstanding. But elsewhere Girard adumbrates an explanation of this mystery in terms of the biblical thematics of those who have eyes not to see and ears not to hear (*THFW* 177). Indeed, this theme, with its variants of obduracy, or the "hard heartedness" of a "stiff-necked people," is so insistent from Exodus through Apocalypse as to constitute a second-order revelation, a correlate hermeneutic principle that explains the nonreception of the first. Our incomprehension, our resistance to this theory, is comprehensible if we are the creatures that Girard's anthropology, after Aristotle's, declares us to be; if we are, that is, what the tale of our expulsion from the Garden represents us as being, and what the last commandment of the decalogue forewarns us as being—namely, creatures whose structuring principle is envy, mimesis, or mimetic desire. (For this reading of Gen. 2–3, see Schwager, *Must There Be Scapegoats?* 68–71; Gans, *The End of Culture* 189–202; and Oughourlian, *Un Mime nommé désir* 37–44. Martin Buber, in *Moses: The Revelation and the Covenant* 133–34, highlights the role of envy in the decalogue.)

Our relation to the world is mediated by other subjects, not by their ideas but by desire, which is neither their desire nor ours to do as we or they would with it; rather, it does with us exactly as we would not, for will and desire are antinomial, antithetical. In Paul's epistle to the Romans, this is the relation between law and sin: the law thematizes the structuring principle of our actions; law is to sin as theme is to structuring principle: "Yet, if it had not been for the law, I should not have known sin. I should not have known what it is to covet if the law had not said, 'You shall not covet' " (Rom. 7:7). Shortly thereafter, Paul proceeds to explicate the dialectics of law and sin as they affect the autonomy of the desiring or willing subject, that is, of the subject of desire. A fuller exegesis of Paul's discourse (Rom. 7:15–20) on doing not "the good I want, but the evil I do not want" would show that it provides a critique of autonomous agency as radical as anything we find in a Derridean deconstruction or a Lacanian decentering of the subject. This has been adumbrated by Antoine Vergote ("Apport des données psychanalytiques à l'exégèse: Vie, loi et clivage du Moi dans l'épitre aux Romains 7" in *Exégèse et herméneutique*). It needs to be completed with Vincent Descombes's philosophical critique of subjectivity in *L'Inconscient malgré lui*.

The same structural misunderstanding prevails in conflict as in desire. We never fail to perceive violent conflict, though we never perceive it as originating in ourselves, which in a sense it does not: it is not we or our opponent who wills the conflict but the identity of our desire (i.e., mimetic desire) that ensures it—whence the Bible's habit of thematizing our opponent as our brother or our neighbor: our double. Conflict comes from desire, from mimesis, which we never see; it is a structure, it is not a visible thing to be seen like my neighbor's wife, or for that matter, my neighbor's fist. Desire is the structuring principle of conflict; it cannot become a theme, a motif of dispute, without the conflict disappearing. But it rarely becomes a conscious theme because it is the structural origin of the unconscious (see *The Scapegoat* 110–11, 117–24).

Mimesis generates the purely formal rather than substantial difference of rivals. Mimesis is the indifference, the indifferent identity of opponents, their mechanical repetition, as clearly suggested by this passage from Jeremiah:

> For they are adulterers,
> a company of treacherous men.
> They bend their tongue like a bow;
> falsehood and not truth has grown strong in the land;
> for they proceed from evil to evil
> and they do not know me says the Lord.
> Let every one beware of his neighbor,
> and put no trust in any brother;
> for every brother is a supplanter [a Jacob]
> and every neighbor goes about as a slanderer.
> Every one deceives his neighbor
> and no one speaks the truth;
> they have taught their tongue to speak lies;
> they commit iniquity and are too weary to repent.
> Heaping oppression upon oppression, and deceit upon deceit,
> they refuse to know me, says the Lord. (9:2–6)

Even after making every due allowance for the parallelism characteristic of biblical style, there is obvious in this formal arrangement of rhythmically repeated signifiers the mechanism of repetition, imitation, or simulation by which dissimulation and its consequent violence hold sovereign sway. "They bend their tongue like a bow" conflates the two. Deception begins in self-deception—"they have taught their tongues to speak lies"—and ends in violence. It is not merely that evil, as oppression or deception, is a social phenomenon; it is represented here as self-perpetuating, as governed by a reciprocity that is supra-individual and that Girard calls "interdividual" (*THFW*, book

3). This reciprocity, which is as invisible to its participants as its evil effects are visible, structures the blindness of participants.

It is this structural blindness that is thematized in Matthew's gospel: " 'Judge not, that you be not judged. For with the judgement you pronounce you will be judged, and the measure you give will be the measure you get. Why do you see the speck that is in your brother's eye, but do not notice the log that is in your own eye? Or how can you say to your brother, "Let me take the speck out of your eye," when there is a log in your own eye? You hypocrite, first take the log out of your own eye, and then you will see clearly to take the speck out of your brother's eye' " (Matt. 7:1–5). Jesus, like Jeremiah, speaks of brothers as enemies, thematizing the opposition of like to like. Brothers and neighbors clearly denote the proximity or identity of opponents, which very identity generates their opposition and their blindness to it. Indeed, the core of Jesus' teaching in this chapter is directed toward a good reciprocity that forestalls violent mimesis by taking the initiative, by proposing that one act as a positive model: " 'So whatever you wish that men would do to you, do so to them; for this is the law and the prophets' " (12). The antithesis of this is mimetic behavior, as symbolized by the "wide gate" (13–14) through which the many enter.

Solomonic Structuralism

Wisdom, like prophecy, is the perception or the consciousness of mimesis as it leads to victimage. This is borne out in the judgment of Solomon (1 Kings 3:16–28) as commented by Girard (*THFW* 237–45). I wish to review the formal, structural characteristics of this episode to show the hermeneutic and epistemological rigor of its theoretical voice.

Of the notorious evidence in the case, I will cite only the plaintiff's insistence on there being no witnesses to the substitution of dead infant for live. " 'Then on the third day after I was delivered, this woman also gave birth; and we were alone; there was no one else with us in the house, only we two were in the house' " (18). The absence of witnesses is essential if what is to manifest itself is not ordinary jurisprudence but wisdom, evoked by Solomon as " 'an understanding mind to govern thy people, that I may discern between good and evil' " (9)—that is, as understanding of good and evil. But this wisdom is not all that extraordinary, for it is not incompatible with rational deduction based on inductive testing. The truth cannot be known unless the false reveals itself, condemns itself out of its own mouth. The true and the false cannot be revealed; they must reveal themselves. This must be true in all cases, as a general principle, if the quest for true and false is to escape the aporetic whirligigs about interpretation affecting debate today. I am referring to the idea of interpretation as groundless and undecidable perspectivism, as will to power and so on—the idea, in sum, of the hermeneutic circle as a vicious one, which emerges from the ritual concelebration of Nietzsche by philosophers, literary critics, and avant-garde Scripture scholars.

As Girard points out, and as anyone can perceive who has ears to hear, the language of the claimants is identical, the language of the one being the symmetrical reversal of the other's, the specular repetition of the other's: "But the other woman said, 'No, the living child is mine and the dead child is yours.' The first said, 'No, the dead child is yours, and the living child is mine.' " It is just this rigorous symmetry that motivates the tag line, the narrative supplement: "Thus they spoke to the King," which serves only to thematize language. What the King cannot know is who is the rightful claimant; what he cannot fail to know, to recognize (cognition = recognition) is repetition, mimesis, and because of the second he cannot know the first. "Then the King said, 'The one says, "This is my son that is alive, and your son is dead" and the other says, "No; but your son is dead, and my son is the living one." ' " (23). By repeating their words, the King repeats their repetition, thus thematizing it, so that the word, precisely as repetition or bi-petition, as doubling, as a relation of doubles, is promoted to the forefront of consciousness.

This presents, I think, another dimension of the traditional notion of the Bible as its own interpreter, as a self-glossing text (see Gerald Bruns, "Midrash and Allegory," in *The Literary Guide to the Bible*, especially 626–27). In this case, it is a dimension whereby one text refers not to another, but to itself, for attention is drawn to the symmetry-repetition here in a gesture performed by the text itself, not by any outside interpretation. The text attends handily to its own signifiers, without recourse to any other agency or authority, hermeneutic or hieratic. The text is engaging in, or simply is, an exercise in structural analysis. Its authority is methodological, not metaphysical. When the king orders the division of the prize, he is materializing this symmetry, incarnating it or carnally inscribing it, fairly spelling it out word by word: " 'Divide the living child in two, and give half to the one, and half to the other' " (25). The text identifies the true mother of the living child as the one whose "heart yearned for her son" rather than as the one driven by mimesis. When she says " 'Oh, my lord, give her the living child and by no means slay it' " (26), the mimetic symmetry is broken, the balance is upset. "But the other said, 'It shall be neither mine nor yours; divide it' ": these words bear witness not to maternal love but to mimetic desire, to a fascination with the rival that loses sight of the prize, a fascination wherein the prize is demoted to a token, a symbol, a cipher, a dead letter, a signifier. The structure of mimetic rivalry is reflected in the second woman's desire to divide the prize, whereby the false symmetry is revealed between a mother attached to her child and another attached to that attachment, the second being imitative of the first, a copy or a representation of the first. At the level of representation, it is impossible to decide between reality and copy, original and representation, because both are subject to representation. Between living and dead, life and death, it is impossible not to decide, because that is the origin of decision as *de-cidere:* to cut off or kill. Accordingly, I have argued (chap. 4) that all discussions of the undecidability of differences, as origin and copy, as theory and practice, and so on, reach their term with the victim.

The symmetry of claimants breaks down on the difference between life and death to which mimetic rivalry leads. It is perhaps a matter of indifference whether the king knows this or has just learned it. "Then the King answered and said 'Give the living child to the first woman and by no means slay it, she is its mother' " (27), whereby the text has him repeat the mother's words, returning, in archly Lacanian fashion, the message to the sender in reverse form. The relevance of Lacanian theory here is not fortuitous, for it issues from Lacan's famous "Séminaire sur 'La Lettre volée' " (in *Ecrits*), which is concerned with the mimetic rivalry of Queen, minister, and detective over the possession of a letter, a signifier, in Poe's "Purloined Letter." I submit that our fascination with the exegesis of this tale (as witnessed by *The Purloined Poe*, Mueller and Richardson's edition of commentary on it) reflects our fascination with mimetic desire, and our contagion by it as well, as each interpreter rivals with Dupin's genius in displacing the king (and Lacan, and Derrida, whose "Purveyor of Truth" in *The Post Card* would displace Lacan as arbiter of the tale's significance).

The king repeats the true mother's words; his judgment is a repetition of her claim, indeed, an imitation of it. The meaning of this text depends decisively on these repetitions and reversals, suggesting, as the scriptural saying goes, that we are saved or condemned out of our own mouths. The justice of the judgment, which Israel attributes to the wisdom of God ("And all Israel heard of the judgment which the king had rendered; and they stood in awe of the king, because they perceived that the wisdom of God was in him, to render justice" [28]), is a structural affair. Truth is a relation, but being a relation between living and dead, between symmetrical absolutes, it is by no means relative in the end.

What informs this wisdom? How shall we say it came about? Initially, the king is in a sense only imitating the claimants, repeating their repetition in the form of a child divided in two, of replacing a living child with a dead one, thus perfecting the symmetry and annulling the difference between living and dead child. By offering to divide the child, the king is in a sense imitating the false mother; it is a structured response that brings the properly sacrificial dimension of the dispute into focus.

There is no need to suppose that this is his aim or purpose; nothing is said of the conscience of the king. This is a good example of what Martin Buber is talking about when he writes that "the Bible does not concern itself with character, nor with individuality, and one cannot draw from it any description of characters or individualities. The Bible depicts something else, namely, persons in situations. The Bible is not concerned with the difference between these persons; but the difference between the situations in which the person, the creaturely person, the appointed person, stands his test or fails, is all important to it" ("Biblical Leadership," *Israel and the World* 119). Structure, not psyche, is the key.

The king cannot fail to see that the women's struggle over the child means its death, which would indeed be sacrificial, putting an end to the rivalry of mimetic doubles. It is when the sacrificial mimesis reveals itself that the true mother of the living child can be identified, that the difference between origin and copy can be decided. When she renounces the claim to the child, she risks perjuring herself, a decision incurring genuine self-sacrifice: "The good harlot agrees to substitute herself for the sacrificial victim, not because she feels a morbid attraction to the role but because she has an answer to the tragic alternative: kill or be killed. The answer is: be killed, not as a result of masochism or the 'death instinct,' but *so that the child will live*" (Girard, *THFW* 242). I elide the Christological-figural interpretation that follows in Girard's explication because what I am after is a hermeneutic principle that will ground this judgment in something other than the wisdom of God—or better still, ground the wisdom of God in something we can see and hear, namely, the language of the participants in this tragicomic drama. For self-evidence has been the theme of the Law since its promulgation: " 'For this commandment which I command you this day is not too hard for you, neither is it far off. It is not in heaven, that you should say, "Who will go up for us to heaven, and bring it to us, that we may hear it and do it?" Neither is it beyond the sea, that you should say, "Who will go over the sea for us, and bring it to us, that we may hear it and do it?" But the word is very near you; it is in your mouth and in your heart, so that you can do it' " (Deut 30: 11–14). Moreover, I could just as well relate this episode to the great Deuteronomic alternative, " 'See, I have set before you this day life and good, death and evil. . . . I call heaven and earth to witness against you this day, that I have set before you life and death, blessing and curse; therefore choose life, that you and your descendants may live' " (Deut 20:15, 19). Hebrew Scripture expresses a confidence in difference from which all our sciences, not least what we call the human sciences, have yet much to learn. If Jesus is the fulfillment, not the abrogation, of the law, its theoretical voice already informs this episode.

In the beginning of the story, a dead child is substituted for a living one. At the end, a mother substitutes herself for the child, her death for its death, risking her life for the child's. The mother identifies with the victim of the impending sacrifice, thereby rendering it ineffective. The untrue mother identifies with the persecutor-executor, with the king who would divide the child and so put an end to the sacrificial-mimetic crisis. The king's judgment is regarded as sound to the extent and as a result of renouncing identification with the persecutor, which is tantamount to renouncing sacrifice. It is the mother's identification with the victim that renders the king's judgment sound, that informs it. The king imitates the mother. The King's decision repeats the words of the mother because his decision follows on her own and imitates it: identification with the victim is renunciation of identification with the persecutor. The difference between life and death, between true and false, corresponds to the difference between victim and persecutor. The King is enlightened by a structural necessity; his wisdom is secondary to the structural revelation of the victim. Although our intellectual-scientific conscience obliges us to question its existence, the wisdom of God, such as it is, is identified here with the victim, or more precisely, it is identified as identification with the victim.

It is important to add that the victim need not speak, as in the Psalms, Job, or Isaiah; he or she need only be present for the work of interpretation to be decisive and true. Where the victim has no voice, as here and in a subsequent example to follow, it is for Scripture to represent him or her—if, as Girard argues it to be, the theoretical voice of Scripture is that of the victim.

The Law before the Good Samaritan

To explore this epistemology further, I am going to talk about a text Girard has never discussed, probably because its meaning is too obvious. That is just why I will discuss it—because my theme is the obvious. It is the text of the Good Samaritan (Luke 10:25–37), which everyone knows and understands and to whose understanding I have perhaps nothing to add. I say this not by way of apologizing, but by way of reiterating Girard's point that everything has been revealed. What has been hidden since the foundation of the world is being revealed, but it has been hidden because of the obduracy of subjects, not because of any opacity between subject and object. I am trying to get at this notion of revelation by purely linguistic and rational means, by formal analysis, to test Girard's hypothesis that Scripture as it logically culminates in the Passion provides "something tangible that can be understood rationally" (*Job* 160).

The text appears to have three parts: questions about eternal life and the law; the story proper; and a question and answer about the story. Appearances here are deceiving though, for the third part is so much part of the second that their union-separation is undecidable. As often as not, exegetes discuss the text as having two parts. This undecidability is undoubtedly strategic, for the text's narrative strategy is to generate a crisis of difference that extends to the difference between question and answer. It is tempting to get into a deconstructive bind about the impossible unity, or the "unreadability," of a text consisting undecidably of two and three parts. My aim is to show that the text successfully resists any such equivocations, that it controls its own understanding with exemplary clarity. My reading is assisted by the traditional ones of Bultmann, Jeremias, and Drury, as well as by the more "experimental" ones of Patte, Crossan, Crespy, and Funk, which appear in a volume of *Semeia* devoted to structuralist analyses of the parable. They are helpful, sometimes provocative glosses; at the same time, they provide nothing by way of arcane knowledge, that is, nothing that biblical self-glossing does not provide.

"And behold, a lawyer stood up to put him to the test, saying, 'Teacher, what shall I do to inherit eternal life?' " (25). The lawyer is a man charged with knowledge of the law, which for Jesus' hearers is knowledge as such, all that is worth knowing, all that passes for knowledge. One need not be an archeologist or biblical ethnographer to know that; one need only recall what the Law is from the time of its revelation through Moses, to recall the Law as the foundation of Israel and therefore as representing to the Hebrews, to Jesus' hearers "the only ethnological encyclopedia available or even conceivable" (Girard, *THFW* 160). But this point is important from a methodological and epistemological perspective. This is, after all, the perspective of we professors, of we men and women of knowledge—namely, we lawyers—for whom Scripture is a problem, not a solution. I think I can say without over-allegorizing that we are in a position analogous to the lawyer's toward Jesus and Scripture, whose word we are ever testing. If we are not interested in eternal life—an idea that the churches, or at least their professors, seem to have outgrown, if Thomas Sheehan's report on recent demurrers on this topic is reliable (see *The First Coming)*—we are still interested in testing such transcendent claims as it represents, for we seek to know whether Scripture is knowledge, whether it speaks with authority or instead represents an ignorance of which we have the knowledge.

I do not say that the parable intends that analogy; I suspect it does but it need not; the analogy is there, it is structural. Knowers testing the knowledge and authority of one said to speak with authority constitutes the objective situation of the text, and the text situates us accordingly. Knowledge is what the text is about, and as such it is about us when we read Scripture. It reads us reading.

The idea that the lawyer is testing (or in some translation, *tempting*) Jesus clearly suggests that his questioning is not innocent, direct, or straightforward, but strategic; he wishes not so much to know how to inherit eternal life as to know whether or what Jesus knows. His question bears not on objective knowledge or the object of knowledge but on the subject of knowledge. His question to Jesus about eternal life is the mask of a question about Jesus. This testing that is a trapping (according to the Good News translation) is a constant, insistent motif in the Gospel dialogues; it is a normal and necessary occurrence regarding one about whom such fantastical claims were emerging. It still goes on today. Nonetheless, the testing suggests the bad faith of Jesus' interlocutors, who either already know the answers to the questions they pose to him or do not know them but do not care to know them either. It is just a question of knowing whether Jesus knows them.

We are always testing one another's knowledge, and it is not always apparent or demonstrable that we do so out of dedication to the truth—be it eternal life or definitive death. Rather, there appears a properly polemical desire to trip each other up, a desire not to know the truth but to show that others do not know it. This gives us a kind of negative security, perhaps the only kind available today: we are relieved of responsibility for and anxiety about knowledge as long as we are at least sure that our neighbor is not better off, that he or she does not possess a truth of which we are deprived. There is something mimetic about this, where truth, like the Solomonic infant, is a token of rivalry and therefore ever liable to dismemberment. We imitate each other's skepticism, lest positive knowledge be a stumbling block to our self-esteem. Skepticism is the great equalizer appropriate to our democratic age. Truth is a signifier whose signified is power and prestige, notwithstanding the prestige of skeptics, from Nietzsche through deconstructionists, who reveal our self-deception.

It is doubtless because Jesus sees that he is being tested and not frankly questioned that he answers with a question. He does not answer the question but asks another question, repeating the gesture of the lawyer-interlocutor, imitating the lawyer. It is the same thing for Jesus to question the lawyer about the law as for the lawyer to question Jesus about eternal life. Mimesis is a method before it is an issue; the

test becomes a contest: "He said to him, 'What is written in the law?
How do you read?' " (26). Here I pause only to remark the repetition
of the question, its marked insistence and thoroughness as to what is
at issue. What is a lawyer's answer? What is known? What does it
mean? Understanding, interpretation, and knowledge itself constitute
the theme of Jesus' question.

"And he answered, 'You shall love the Lord your God with all your
heart, and with all your soul, and with all your strength, and with all
your mind; and your neighbor as yourself.' And he said to him 'You
have answered right [*orthos*]; do [*poiei*] this, and you will live' " (27–
28). Jesus' answer confirms the lawyer in his knowledge of the law (as
stated in Lev. 19:18 and Deut. 6:5). This is how the gospels of Matthew and Mark leave the matter, where the question bears on "the
great commandment," "the first commandment"; at issue is knowledge as such of the law as such. The difference, decisive to Luke's
narrative strategy, is that the lawyer-scribe, not Jesus, is made to answer his own question. If this is so, it is because testing itself is being
thematized and indeed tested to the fullest. In this regard, the passage is a very modern, or even postmodern, text, with its framing narrative, its *mise en abîme*, and structural reversals, which I will examine
in some detail. "But he, desiring to justify himself, said to Jesus, 'And
who is my neighbor?' " (29). For lexicological reasons, the Revised
Standard Version refers the reader to the parable of the Pharisee and
the Publican for a contextualized explanation of the word *justify*. Justification as lawfulness, righteousness, or acceptability to God bears
on the limits, the boundaries, the confines of the law—literally on the
definition of the law. What is the content of the law, what is its referent; what is the relation of words to things?

So the questioning, the testing, the contest goes on, and Jesus replies, or rather rejoins or retorts (*hypolabon*) with a story. It is important to observe the obvious: for the second time Jesus does not answer
the question put to him. There are questions and there are answers,
and it is more than implied by this textual strategy that the answer to
these questions is not in an answer, not in a word but in a deed, not in
a *res* but in a *res gesta*—a story. There is also the implication that the
answers inhabit the question and the questioner if only he or she has
eyes and ears to see and hear with—which just happens to be the cognitive theme immediately preceding this episode: "Then turning to
the disciples he said privately, 'Blessed are the eyes which see what

you see! For I tell you that many prophets and kings desired to see what you see, and did not see it, and to hear what you hear, and did not hear it' " (23–24).

The structural unity of question, counterquestion, answer, and counteranswer thematizes interpretation as a matter of questions and answers while rendering the difference between question and answer problematic. Jesus answers a question about the law, about its reference, with a story that ends with a question. He tells a story that is a question—or rather, an answer in the form of a question whose answer is self-evident, inevitable, and unequivocal. His story is the premise of a properly rhetorical question.

Now to the story nested within the story of the law and what it means; it has, predictably, two parts: "Jesus replied, 'A man was going down from Jerusalem to Jericho and he fell among robbers who stripped him and beat him and departed, leaving him half dead. Now by chance a priest was going down that road; and when he saw him he passed by on the other side. So likewise a Levite, when he came to the place and saw him, passed by on the other side' " (30–32). The man traveling from Jerusalem to Jericho is going down, as the commentators tell us, a dangerous road, one known to be infested by robbers. That is, Jesus is taking his hearers into dangerous but familiar territory, and he is taking them with a familiar companion, for such a man going from such a place as Jerusalem to such another as Jericho is one of them, a Jew. The man traveling is one of them—that is, one of us, one of our own as we listen to the story. He is also one of us as we interrogate the law in its relation to life. This performative dimension of Scripture is essential.

If the priest and the Levite help the man, their fellow countryman, that is to be expected by Jesus' hearers if neighbor-love means anything whatsoever; that is to be expected above all because it is Jesus' hearers who are placed *with* the man, *as* the man half-dead beside the road. As Robert Funk observes, the parable invites the auditor to be the victim in the ditch ("The Good Samaritan as Metaphor," *Semeia 2* 74). This is an altogether uninviting, unenviable prospect, and the narrative rather compels this identification precisely for the reason advanced by Funk: "Every narrative is constituted in such a way as to cause the reader to view events from a certain perspective" (76); the initial perspective here is unmistakably that of the victim. This point is so obvious that it is never discussed (or at least never adequately thematized in the many discussions of the parable I have consulted), though there can be no doubt that this is, as Girard says of Job's outcry, the "anchor," "the rock of interpretation" (*Job* 163, 164). It is as if most commentary emulates priest and Levite, drawing away from the centrality of the victim.

If the temple functionaries do not help the man, that is only slightly less to be expected, the expectation being of an anticlerical story with which the law and the lore of Jesus' hearers, including contemporary readers, are amply familiar. This anticlerical expectation has been widely remarked by commentators and is the occasion to note a spectacular fact about all of Scripture as inspired by the perspective informing Hebrew Scripture, as constituting its tutelary genius: it is written against the culture in which it is nested and grows and that grows out of it. This is a point richly demonstrated in Herbert Schneidau's *Sacred Discontent: The Bible and Western Tradition* (see especially 2, 10, 12, 38); because Schneidau lacks Girard's victimary perspective, however, he can offer no basis for this opposition or any positive dimension to his critique. It is the difference between a generic and a genetic theory, whereby only the latter (Girard's) solicits properly scientific inquiry.

Martin Buber is closer to Girard's perspective when he observes of biblical leadership that it goes as much against nature as against history. It comprises a history not of a successful people but of the weak and the humble and of their failures, defeats, and disappointments:

It is "against nature" that in one way or another the leaders are mostly the weak and the humble. The way in which they carry out their leadership is "contrary to history." It is the moment of success which determines the selection of events which seem important to history. "World history" is the history of successes; the heroes who have not succeeded, but who cannot be excluded from it on account of their very conspicuous heroism, serve only as a foil, as it were. . . . The Bible knows nothing of this intrinsic value of success. On the contrary, when it announces a successful deed, it is duty-bound to announce in complete detail the failure involved in the success. When we consider the history of Moses, we see how much failure is mingled in the one great successful action, so much so that when we set the individual events which make up his history side by side, we see that his life consists of one failure after another, through which runs the thread of his success. True, Moses brought the people out of Egypt; but each state of this leadership is a failure. Whenever he comes to deal with this people, he is defeated by them, let God ever so often interfere and punish them. And the real history of this leadereship is not the history of the exodus, but the history of the wandering in the desert. The personal history of Moses' own life, too, does not point back to his youth and to what grew out of it; it points beyond, to death, to the death of the unsuccessful man, whose work, it is true, survives him, but only in new defeats, new disappointments, and continual new failures—and yet his work survives also in a hope which is beyond all these failures. . . . And, finally, this glorification of failure culminates in the long line of prophets whose existence is failure, through and through. They live in failure; it is for them to fight and not to conquer. (*Israel and the World* 124–26).

Those who hunger and thirst for "oppositional practices" in texts need to recall that the prestige of the countercultural or adversarial stance is massively tributary to Scripture.

What is not expected in Jesus' story is the Samaritan who comes along, performing a double reversal of expectations. The Samaritan is not just other than the Jew, like a Roman or a Greek, but the Jew's other self, the rival brother in the worship of Yahweh. He is a social and religious outcast, not just the enemy but, on the margin of Israel, its brother enemy, its rival double. "Jews have no dealings with Samaritans" (John 4:9), a fact that need not be pointed out of any other race or people. Samaritans are regarded as a "mongrel" race (RSV). They worship God and read the Pentateuch; they are indifferent to the difference that Jews make between themselves and all others, all non-Jews. They are not merely other than Jews, but other than themselves; they are abject. They are the stuff that scapegoats are made of (see *VS* 271–72, 275). The Samaritan was the mortal enemy of the Jew because he was his half-brother according to the cultural code in which the story is told, a code informed by the Hebrew Bible.

My gloss here is the fruit of biblical self-glossing. John Drury elaborates on the model to be found for this story in 2 Chronicles 28:8–15, where Samaritans succor the defeated victims of a three-cornered struggle between Syria, Judah, and Israel (*The Parables in the Gospels* 175–76; *Tradition and Design in Luke's Gospels* 77–78). I append Robert Funk's gloss for emphasis: "A Jew proud of his bloodline and chauvinist about traditions would not allow a Samaritan to touch him, much less minister to him. In going from Galilee to Judea, he would cross and then recross the Jordan to avoid going through Samaria. To the question who among you will permit himself to be served by a

Samaritan, the answer is only those who have nothing to lose by so doing can afford to do so" (*Semeia 2* 79). Only those perfectly unenviable; only the victim in his uniqueness.

The story places the reader in a limit situation, a critical situation in the original sense of the Greek word, where it designated the point between life and death, a point to which we need always to return in questions of criticism or interpretation. Questions of meaning are questions of difference. The approach of the Samaritan, his neighborly drawing near or nigh as it symmetrically opposes the crossing over by priest and Levite, presents a crisis of value. It is one constituted by a crisis of difference that is the matrix of value, and the matrix of difference is the victim. Only Michel Crespy has adequately thematized this "centrality," as he calls it, of the victim: the movement of priest and Levite away from the wounded man and of Samaritan toward him "make[s] the wounded man the center of the narrative. It is the different relationships to him which are going to be a basis for the value judgements at the end of the discourse" ("The Parable of the Good Samaritan," *Semeia 2* 47). The victim, in a word, serves to deconstruct the differences informing the culture of Jesus' hearers. This is consistent with what Robert Jewett shows to be Scripture's structural resistance to the violence of cultural stereotypes (see *The Captain America Complex* 133–141).

The man is half-dead—not so dead as to be dead, but not so alive as to be able to help himself or even call out for help: an object, whom priest and Levite treat as abject, crossing over to the other side. The man can see and hear nothing or almost nothing; the reader must do that for him. And the text, the story in its telling, gives no choice about that in this second part: " 'But a Samaritan, as he journeyed, came to where he was; and when he saw him, he had compassion, and went to him and bound up his wounds, pouring on oil and wine; then he set him on his own beast and brought him to an inn, and took care of him. And the next day he took out two denarii and gave them to the innkeeper, saying, "Take care of him and whatever more you spend, I will repay you when I come back" ' " (33–35). There are various structural symmetries to be observed, all serving to centralize the victim: two saw and passed by, one saw and drew near; to the triply nefarious actions of the robbers—strip, beat, leave for dead—responds the triple beneficence of the Samaritan—bind up wounds, pour oil and wine, set on his beast and bring to an inn. These formally symmetrical elements are stratgegically significant, for they govern our understanding of the story, but none of them so much as the radical asymmetry affecting the actions of the Samaritan. I am referring to the fact that fully half of the narrative, sixty-six words by one count (Crossan, *In Parables* 63), is devoted to describing his care of the victim.

The reason, the strategy, is obvious: to focus on something the cultural code forbids, to make the hearer see, feel, and hear the goodness of the Samaritan. This must be spelled out in detail for it runs contrary to expectations. This pathos, this emphasis—indeed, this *realism*—is absolutely necessary. It transforms and translates the law (knowing and interpeting it) as a question not of questions and answers but of seeing and hearing. The good Samaritan, who for contemporary auditors is a cipher for concerned care, mercy, and charity, is an oxymoron to Jesus' hearers, who are nonetheless placed by this story in the ditch awaiting succor. That is the governing strategy of the story, to put the hearer in the place of the victim, to interpret the law from the place of the victim, to interpret the law as the perspective of the victim. It is little enough to say that the victim is a theme or motif of the tale; the victim constitutes the perspective from which the tale is told, or rather, from which it is to be heard and from which accordingly the law takes on meaning and reference. " 'Which of these three, do you think, proved neighbor to the man who fell among the robbers?' " (36). Jesus' question closes the narrative, consistent with the strategy of answering a question with another question. The "do you think" (*dokei*) rethematizes the issue of interpretation, thus echoing the beginning of this contest. When Jesus asks which of the three proved to be a neighbor, "do you think," "in your opinion," he is reversing the role by which he is first addressed as a teacher (*didaskalei*); the verb also communicates lexicologically with the notion of testing, proving, and examining. We do not test the law; it tests us.

The lawyer-questioner becomes again the questioned, but the question is no longer the same one. The lawyer's question—perhaps a typical lawyer's question—was theoretical; it concerned the object of neighbor love. The answer—in the form of a question—is posed from a practical point of view and bears on the subject of love: "He said, 'The one who showed [*poieisas*] mercy on him.' And Jesus said to him, 'go and do [*poiei*] likewise' " (37). The reversal of roles of questioning subject and questioned object corresponds to the reversal of the object and subject of love and the passage from theory to practice. These changes pivot on the victim.

Joachim Jeremias suggests that this formula (the one who showed/ did mercy) is used so that the lawyer will not have to repeat the hateful name (*The Parables of Jesus* 205). That may indeed be so, with the effect of testifying to the obduracy of the lawyer, but the net effect of the periphrasis is also to forestall any legalistic equation, any theoretical closure to the question of the neighbor. The neighbor is not a Samaritan but anyone, including one least expected, especially one least expected. The narrative all but says "If you want to know who your neighbor is, go jump in the lake and see, hear, feel . . . "

This story is a parable, about which—I mean parables in general— there has been much debate of a lawyerly kind in the last quarter-century, engaging many a legalistic distinction about its relation to allegory and metaphor. Recent debate has focused chiefly around the question of whether parables provide an example story to follow or something else, something more problematic and ethereal, something to wonder at rather than imitate, something regarding interpretation rather than action. (Excepting Crespy, that seems to be the consensus of the contributors of the volume of *Semeia* devoted to this parable.) There is no denying the pertinence of this debate, for that is just what the narrative is about, from initial question to final answer: the relation of theory to practice. I do not wish to enter into the exegetical and rhetorical details of the debate, except to remark the amount of intellectual energy and technico-structural expertise devoted to proving that the story does not provide its hearers or readers with a didactic example, a practical model. What is truly remarkable concerning a story so emphatically framed by the verb "do" (what must we do to inherit; do this and you shall live; the one who did mercy; do likewise, or the same [*homios*]) is the lawyerly-scholarly apprehension lest anyone should be admonished or inspired to do anything about the law. This examplifies the retrograde character of much avant-garde theorizing (semiological, structural, poststructural, etc.) about Scripture, at least as it concerns a test whose entire strategic-rhetorical valence is governed by the verb *poiein*. There has been a lot of discussion recently about a (reprehensible) "resistance to theory," but we have to ask at this point, at the point where the parable leaves us, how much of this discussion reflects a resistance to practice. At any rate, this much is clear: in the systematic and therefore doubtless strategic reversal of reference—in a context, a contest, in which reference is at issue—resistance to practice, as testimony to the power of obduracy, is just what the text is about.

To recapitulate briefly, the questioner is made the questioned, and the subject is made the object of a question that his—our—experience puts to him; from being the one who puts Jesus to the test, he becomes the one who is tested by Jesus, and we in turn by implication. The reverse is true of Jesus: from being the one who is tested, he becomes the one who puts the lawyer and us to the test in this masterpiece of trial literature whose irony continues to reverberate among us. It communicates accordingly with the trial literature that is the Passion of Jesus, where he is tested, and with the Last Judgment, as represented in Matthew 25, where he is the test, where the test, as Crespy observes (*Semeia 2* 45), is identification with the wounded, the disparaged, the suffering—the victim, in a word, who is explicitly identified with Jesus.

In sum, the questioner is made to answer his own question, made to see and hear the law as what one grasps with eyes and ears that see and hear, not with a mind bent on questions. The parable can have but one meaning for the hearer-victim. The law can have but one meaning for the victim, and that one meaning is the victim, from whose perspective we interpret the law and whose perspective we interpret as the law. The strategy of the parable is to identify the law with the victim, with the victim's perspective, to identify the law as interpretation from the perspective of the victim. This is the furthest thing from "active interpretation" in the Nietzschean sense, if that is taken to mean the aggressive imposition of meaning; it is the victim's passivity, or passion, that is evidentiary. This text is acutely aware of the contemporary "hermeneutics of suspicion" and perspectivism, which, it is fair to say, constitutes its topic, its theme. It asks only that we listen to what we say, that we take that word (*sub-specere*) literally, telling us that to interpret the law, to know the truth, we have to look around, but especially look from under, as from underfoot, from where the downtrodden are.

Bibliography

Adorno, Theodor. *Negative Dialectics.* Trans. E. B. Ashton. New York: Seabury, 1973.

————. *Prisms.* Trans. Samuel and Sherry Weber. Cambridge: MIT P, 1981.

Aglietta, Michel, and André Orléan. *La Violence de la monnaie.* Paris: PUF, 1982.

Arendt, Hannah. *Crises of the Republic.* New York: Harcourt, 1972.

————. *Eichmann in Jerusalem: A Report on the Banality of Evil.* New York: Viking, 1965.

Aronson, Ronald. *The Dialectics of Disaster.* London: Verso, 1983.

Bandera, Cesareo. "Literature and Desire: Poetic Frenzy and the Love Potion." *Mosaic* 7 (1975): 33–52.

————. "Notes on Derrida, Tombstones and the Representation Game." *Stanford French Review* 6.2/3 (1982): 311–25.

Barnet, Richard J. "Defining the Moment." *New Yorker* 16 July 1990, 46–60.

Barthes, Roland. *Roland Barthes.* Trans. Richard Howard. New York; Hill and Wang, 1977.

Baudelaire, Charles. *Oeuvres complètes.* Ed. Marcel Ruff. Paris: Seuil, 1968.

Beaujour, Michel. *Miroirs d'encre: Rhétorique de l'autoportrait.* Paris: Seuil, 1980.

Beneveniste, Emile. *Indo-European Language and Society.* Trans. Elizabeth Palmer. London: Faber, 1973.

Blanchot, Maurice. *Après Coup.* Paris: Minuit, 1982.

————. *La Folie du jour/The Madness of the Day.* Trans. Lydia Davis. New York: Station Hill, 1981.

Bloom, Harold. *Agon: A Theory of Revisionism.* New York: Oxford UP, 1982.

————. *The Anxiety of Influence.* New York: Oxford UP, 1973.

Borch-Jacobsen, Mikkel. *Lacan: Le Maître absolu.* Paris: Flammarion, 1990.

———. *Le Sujet freudien.* Paris: Flammarion, 1982.

Bruns, Gerald. "Midrash and Allegory." *The Literary Guide to the Bible.* Ed. Robert Alter and Frank Kermode. Cambridge: Harvard UP, 1988.

Buber, Martin. *Israel and the World.* New York: Schocken, 1963.

———. *Moses: The Revelation and the Covenant.* Atlantic Highlands, NJ: Humanities, 1988.

Bultmann, Rudolph. *The History of the Synoptic Tradition.* Rev. ed. New York: Harper, 1968.

Burke, Kenneth. *A Grammar of Motives.* Berkeley: U of California P, 1969.

———. *The Rhetoric of Religion: Studies in Logology.* Boston: Beacon, 1963.

Burkert, Walter. *Greek Religion.* Trans. John Raffan. Cambridge: Harvard UP, 1985.

———. *Homo Necans: The Anthropology of Ancient Greek Sacrificial Ritual and Myth.* Trans. Peter Bing. Berkeley: U of California P, 1983.

Calasso, Roberto. *La Ruine de Kasch.* Trans. Jean-Paul Manganaro. Paris: Gallimard, 1983.

Caputo, John D. "Heidegger's Scandal: Thinking and the Essence of the Victim." *The Heidegger Case: Philosophy and Politics.* Ed. Joseph Margolis and Tom Rockmore. Philadephia: Temple UP, 1991.

Cavell, Stanley. *Disowning Knowledge in Six Plays of Shakespeare.* Cambridge: Cambridge UP, 1987.

Chenu, M. D. *Nature, Man and Society in the Twelfth Century.* Trans. J. Taylor and L. Little. Chicago: U of Chicago P, 1968.

Clifford, James, and George E. Marcus, eds. *Writing Culture: The Poetics and Politics of Ethnography.* Los Angeles: U of California Press, 1986.

Crossan, John Dominic. *The Dark Interval: Towards a Theology of Story.* Niles, IL: Argus, 1975.

———. *In Parables: The Challenge of the Historical Jesus.* New York: Harper, 1973.

Dasenbrock, Reed Way, ed. *Redrawing the Lines: Analytic Philosophy, Deconstruction, and Literary Theory.* Minneapolis: U of Minnesota P, 1989.

Deguy, Michel, ed. *René Girard et le problème du mal.* Paris: Grasset, 1982.

Deleuze, Gilles, and Félix Guattari. *Anti-Oedipus: Capitalism and Schizophrenia.* Trans. Robert Hurley, Mark Seem, and Helen Lane. Minneapolis: U of Minnesota P, 1977.

de Man, Paul. *Allegories of Reading: Figural Language in Rousseau, Nietzsche, Rilke and Proust.* New Haven: Yale UP, 1979.

———. *Blindness and Insight: Essays in the Rhetoric of Contemporary Criticism.* New York: Oxford UP, 1971.

———. *The Rhetoric of Romanticism.* New York: Columbia UP, 1984.

———. *Wartime Journalism: 1940–1943.* Ed. Werner Hamacher, Neil Hertz, and Thomas Keenan. Lincoln: U of Nebraska P, 1988.

Denvir, John. "William Shakespeare and the Jurisprudence of Comedy." *Stanford Law Review*. 39.4 (1987): 825–49.

Derogy, Jacques, and Jean-Marie Ponant. *Enquête sur trois secrets d'état*. Paris: Laffont, 1986.

Derrida, Jacques. "Of an Apocalyptic Tone Recently Adopted in Philosophy." Trans. J. Leavey. *Semeia 23* (1982): 62–97.

―――. "Choreographies." Trans. Christie McDonald. *Diacritics*. 12.2 (1982): 66–76.

―――. "Deconstruction and the Other." *Dialogues with Continental Thinkers: The Phenomenological Heritage*. Ed. Richard Kearny. Manchester: Manchester UP, 1984.

―――.. *La Dissémination*. Paris: Seuil, 1972.

―――. *Dissemination*. Trans. Barbara Johnson. Chicago: U of Chicago P, 1982.

―――. *L'Ecriture et la différence*. Paris: Seuil, 1967.

―――. "Entretien avec Jacques Derrida." *Digraphe* 42 (1987): 14–27.

―――. *De L'esprit*. Paris: Galilée, 1988.

―――. *Glas*. Paris: Galilée, 1974.

―――. *De la grammatologie*. Paris: Minuit, 1967.

―――. *Of Grammatology*. Trans. G. Spivak. Baltimore: Johns Hopkins UP, 1976.

―――. "Like the Sound of the Sea Deep within a Shell: Paul de Man's War." Trans. Peggy Kamuf. *Critical Inquiry* 14 (1988): 590–652.

―――. "Limited Inc." *Glyph 2* (supplement). Baltimore: Johns Hopkins UP, 1977.

―――. "Living On." *Deconstruction and Criticism*. Ed. H. Bloom. New York: Seabury, 1979.

―――. *Margins of Philosophy*. Trans. Alan Bass. Chicago: U of Chicago P, 1982.

―――. "Mochlos, ou le conflit des facultés." *Philosophie 2* (1984): 21–53.

―――. "No Apocalypse, not now (full speed ahead, seven missiles, seven missives)." Trans. Catherine Porter and Philip Lewis. *Diacritics* 14.2 (1984): 20–31.

―――. *L'Oreille de l'autre: Otobiographies, Transferts, Traductions*. Montreal: VLB, 1982.

―――. *Positions*. Trans. Alan Bass. Chicago: U of Chicago P, 1981.

―――. *The Post Card: From Socrates to Freud and Beyond*. Trans. Alan Bass. Chicago: U of Chicago P, 1987.

―――. *Psyché*. Paris: Galilée, 1987.

―――. "Racism's Last Word." Trans. Peggy Kamuf. *Critical Inquiry* 12.1 (1985): 291–99.

―――. "The *Retrait* of Metaphor." Trans. and ed. *Enclitic* 2.2 (1978): 5–33.

———. "The Time of a Thesis: Punctuations." Trans. Kathleen McLaughlin. *Philosophy of France Today.* Ed. Alan Montefiore. Cambridge: Cambridge UP, 1983.

———. "D'un Ton apocalyptique adopté naguère en philosophie." *Les Fins de l'homme: à partir du travail de Jacques Derrida.* Paris: Galilée, 1981.

———. *La Vérité en peinture.* Paris: Flammarion, 1978.

———. *La Voix et le phénomène: Introduction au problème du signe dans la phénoménologie de Husserl.* Paris: PUF, 1967.

———. *Writing and Difference.* Trans. Alan Bass. Chicago: U of Chicago P, 1978.

Descombes, Vincent. *L'Inconscient malgré lui.* Paris: Minuit, 1977.

Diderot, Denis. *Oeuvres.* Ed. André Bailly. Paris: Gallimard, 1951.

Dispot, Laurent. *La Machine à terreur: De la Révolution française au terrorisme.* Paris: Grasset, 1978.

Drury, John. *The Parables in the Gospels: History and Allegory.* New York: Crossroads, 1985.

———. *Tradition and Design in Luke's Gospels: A Study in Early Christian Historiography.* Atlanta: John Knox, 1977.

Dumouchel, Paul, ed. *Violence et vérité: Autour de René Girard.* Paris: Grasset, 1985.

Dumouchel, Paul, and Jean-Pierre Dupuy. *L'Enfer des choses: René Girard et la logique de l'économie.* Paris: Seuil, 1979.

Dupuy, Jean-Pierre. *Ordres et desordres: Enquête sur un nouveau paradigme.* Paris: Seuil, 1982.

Duras, Marguerite. *The War.* Trans. Barbara Bray. New York: Pantheon, 1986.

Dyson, Freeman. *Weapons and Hope.* New York: Harper, 1985.

Elias, Robert. *The Politics of Victimization: Victims, Victimology and Human Rights.* New York: Oxford UP, 1986.

Erikson, Kai. "Of Accidental Judgments and Casual Slaughters." *The Best American Essays 1986.* Ed. Elizabeth Hardwick. New York: Ticknor & Fields, 1986.

Fischer, Michael. *Does Deconstruction Make any Difference? Post-structuralism and the Defense of Poetry in Modern Criticism.* Bloomington: Indiana UP, 1985.

Fish, Stanley. "Critical Legal Studies." *Raritan.* 7.2–3 (1988): 1–20, 1–24.

———. *Is There a Text in This Class: The Authority of Interpretive Communities.* Cambridge: Harvard UP, 1980.

Foley, Richard. *The Theory of Epistemic Rationality.* Cambridge: Harvard UP, 1987.

Foucault, Michel. *Histoire de la folie à l'âge classique.* Paris: Gallimard, 1972.

———. *The History of Sexuality, Volume I: An Introduction.* Trans. Robert Hurley. New York: Random House, 1978.

Freud, Sigmund. *The Standard Edition of the Complete Psychological Works of Sigmund Freud*. Ed. James Strachey *et al*. London: Hogarth, 1953–74.

Friedländer, Saul. *Reflections of Nazism: An Essay on Kitsch and Death*. Trans. Thomas Weyr. New York: Avon, 1984.

Fusell, Paul. *Thank God for the Atom Bomb and Other Essays*. New York: Random House, 1988.

Gallo, Max. *Le Grand Juarès*. Paris: Laffont, 1984.

Gans, Eric. *The End of Culture: Toward a Generative Anthropology*. Berkeley: U of California P, 1985.

———. *The Origin of Language: A Formal Theory of Representation*. Berkeley: U of California P, 1981.

———. "The Victim as Subject: The Esthetico-Ethical System of Rousseau's *Rêveries*." *Studies in Romanticism* 21 (1983): 3-31.

Gauchet, Marcel. *Le Désenchantement du monde: Une Histoire politique de la religion*. Paris: Gallimard, 1985.

Girard, René. *Deceit, Desire and the Novel: Self and Other in Literary Structure*. Trans. Yvonne Freccero. Baltimore: Johns Hopkins UP, 1965.

———. *"To Double Business Bound": Essays on Literature, Myth, Mimesis and Anthropology*. Baltimore: Johns Hopkins UP, 1978.

———. "De la folie." *L'Esprit moderne dans la littérature française*. Ed. Reinhard Kuhn. New York: Oxford UP, 1972.

———. "Hamlet's Dull Revenge." *Stanford Literature Review* 1.2 (1984): 159-200.

———. *Job: The Victim of his People*. Trans. Yvonne Freccero. Stanford: Stanford UP, 1987.

———. "The Logic of the Undecidable: Interview with René Girard." *Paroles Gelées* 5 (1987): 1-24.

———. "Myth and Ritual in Shakespeare: *A Midsummer Night's Dream*." *Textual Strategies: Perspectives in Post-structuralist Criticism*. Ed. Josué V. Harari. Ithaca: Cornell, 1979.

———. *The Scapegoat*. Trans. Yvonne Freccero. Baltimore: Johns Hopkins UP, 1986.

———. *Things Hidden since the Foundation of the World*. Trans. Stephen Bann and Michael Metteer. Stanford: Stanford UP, 1987.

———. *Violence and the Sacred*. Trans. Patrick Gregory. Baltimore: Johns Hopkins UP, 1978.

Hamacher, Werner, Neil Hertz, and Thomas Keenan, eds. *Responses: On Paul de Man's Wartime Journalism*. Lincoln: U of Nebraska P, 1989.

Hamerton-Kelly, Robert., ed. *Violent Origins: Walter Burkert, René Girard and Jonathan Z. Smith on Ritual Killing and Cultural Formation*. Stanford: Stanford UP, 1987.

Harris, Marvin, *Cultural Materialism: The Struggle for a Science of Culture*. New York: Vintage, 1980.

Heidegger, Martin, *Basic Writings*. Trans. David Farrell Krell. New York: Harper, 1977.

Hofstader, Douglas A. *Gödel, Escher, Bach: An Eternal Golden Braid*. New York: Vintage, 1979.

Horwich, Paul. *Truth*. London: Basil Blackwell, 1990.

Hume, David. *A Treatise of Human Nature*. 2nd ed. Ed. L. A. Selby-Bigge. Oxford: Oxford UP, 1978.

Jeremais, Joachim. *The Parables of Jesus*. New York: Scribners, 1963.

Jewett, Robert. *The Captain America Complex: The Dilemma of Zealous Nationalism*. Sante Fe: Bear, 1984.

Johnson, Barbara. *The Critical Difference: Essays in the Contemporary Rhetoric of Reading*. Baltimore: Johns Hopkins UP, 1980.

———. *A World of Difference*. Baltimore: Johns Hopkins UP, 1989.

Kavanagh, Thomas. *Writing the Truth: Authority and Desire in Rousseau*. Berkeley: U of California P, 1987.

Kerenyi, Carl. *The Religion of the Greeks and the Romans*. Trans. Christopher Holmes. New York: Dutton, 1962.

Kermode, Frank. *The Sense of an Ending: Studies in the Theory of Fiction*. New York: Oxford UP, 1966.

Kofman, Sarah. "Un Philosophe 'unheimlich.' " *Ecarts: Quatre Essais à propos de Jacques Derrida*. Paris: Fayard, 1973.

Kuenzli, Rudolf. "Derridada." *Esprit Créateur* 20.2 (1980): 13–21.

Kull, Stephen. *Minds at War: Nuclear Reality and the Inner Conflicts of Defense Policy Makers*. New York: Basic, 1989.

Lacan, Jacques. *Ecrits*. Paris: Seuil, 1966.

Levi, Primo. *The Drowned and the Saved*. Trans. Raymond Rosenthal. New York: Summit, 1988.

———. *If Not Now, When?* Trans. William Weaver. New York: Summit, 1985.

———. *If This Is a Man*. Trans. Stuart Woolf. London: Penguin, 1979.

Lévi-Strauss, Claude. *Tristes Tropiques*. Paris: Plon, 1955.

———. *Tristes Tropiques*. Trans. John and Doreen Weightman. New York: Atheneum, 1973.

Lifton, Robert Jay. *Death in Life: Survivors of Hiroshima*. New York: Random House, 1969.

Livington, Paisley. *Ingmar Bergman and the Rituals of Art*. Ithaca: Cornell UP, 1982.

———. *Literary Knowledge: Humanistic Inquiry and the Philosophy of Science*. Ithaca: Cornell UP, 1988.

Lyotard, Jean-François. "Phraser après Auschwitz." *Les Fins de l'homme; à partir du travail de Jacques Derrida*. Paris: Galilée, 1981.

——. "Réponse à la question: "Qu'est-ce que le postmoderne?" *Critique* no. 419. (1982): 357–367.

MacIntyre, Alasdair. *A Short History of Ethics.* New York: Collier, 1966.

Maier, Charles S. *The Unmasterable Past: History, Holocaust and German National Identity.* Cambridge: Harvard UP, 1988.

Marx, Karl. *Capital.* Trans. Samuel Moore and Edward Aveling. New York: International, 1974.

Mayer, Arno. *Why Did the Heavens Not Darken? The "Final Solution" in History.* New York: Pantheon, 1988.

McKenna, Andrew. "Allodidacticism: Flaubert One Hundred Years After." *Yale French Studies* 63 (1982): 227–44.

——. "Biblioclasm: Derrida and his Precursors." *Visible Language* 12.3 (1978): 298–304.

——. "Biblioclasm: Joycing Jesus and Borges." *Diacritics* 8.2 (1978): 15–29.

——. "Double Talk: Two Baudelairean Revolutions." *New Orleans Review* 10:4 (1983): 99–108.

——. "Flaubert's Freudian Thing: Violence and Representation in *Salammbô.*" *Stanford French Review* 12.2-3 (1988): 305–25.

——. "*Tartuffe,* Representation and Difference." *Papers on French Seventeenth-Century Literature* 16.30 (1989): 77–93.

Mearsheimer, John J. "Why We Will Soon Miss the Cold War." *Atlantic Monthly* August 1990, 35–50.

Miller, Mark Crispin. *Boxed In: The Culture of Television.* Evanston, IL: Northwestern UP, 1988.

Molière, Jean-Baptiste Poquelin. *Oeuvres complètes.* Paris: Garnier, 1962.

Muller, John, and William Richardson, eds. *The Purloined Poe: Lacan, Derrida and Psychoanalytic Reading.* Baltimore: Johns Hopkins UP, 1988.

Nietzsche, Friedrich. *On the Genealogy of Morals.* Trans. Walter Kaufmann. New York: Vintage, 1967.

Norris, Christopher. *The Contest of Faculties: Philosophy and Theory after Deconstruction.* London: Methuen, 1985.

Nozick, Robert. *Philosophical Explanations.* Cambridge: Harvard UP, 1981.

O'Keefe, Daniel Lawrence. *Stolen Lightning: The Social Theory of Magic.* New York: Continuum, 1982.

Ong, Walter. *Ramus, Method and the Decay of Dialogue.* Cambridge: Harvard UP, 1958.

Oughourlian, Jean-Michel. *Un Mime nommé désir: Hystérie, transe, possession, adorcisme.* Paris: Grasset, 1982.

Pachet, Pierre. *Le Premier Venu: Essai sur la politique de Baudelaire.* Paris: Denoël, 1976.

Pascal. Blaise. *Pensées.* Ed. Léon Brunschvicg. Paris: Garnier, 1958.

Plato. *The Collected Dialogues*. Ed. Edith Hamilton and Huntington Cairns. New York: Pantheon, 1964.

Posner, Richard A. *Law and Literature: A Misunderstood Relation*. Cambridge: Harvard UP, 1988.

Radkowski, Georges-Hubert de. *Les Jeux du désir: De la technique à l'économie*. Paris: PUF, 1980.

Riveline, Claude. "Présentation." *La Bible au présent: Actes du XXIIe Colloque des intellectuals juifs de langue française*. Ed. Jean Halpérin and Georges Levitte. Paris: Gallimard, 1982.

Rorty, Richard. *Consequences of Pragmatism*. Minnesota: U of Minnesota P, 1982.

——. *Contingency, Irony and Solidarity*. Cambridge: Cambridge UP, 1989.

——. *Philosophy and the Mirror of Nature*. Princeton: Princeton UP, 1979.

Rose, Gillian. *Dialectic of Nihilism: Post-structuralism and Law*. New York: Basil Blackwell, 1984.

Rousseau, Jean-Jacques. *Confessions*. Trans. J. M. Cohen. New York: Penguin, 1977.

——. *Oeuvres complètes*, 3 vols. Ed. Bernard Gagnebin and Marcel Raymond. Paris: Gallimard, 1964.

Roustang, François. *Dire Mastery: Discipleship from Freud to Lacan*. Trans. Ned Lukacher. Baltimore: Johns Hopkins UP, 1982.

Routeau, Luc. "Au Cirque." *Esprit* (May 1980): 51–74.

Ryan, Michael. *Marxism and Deconstruction: A Critical Articulation*. Baltimore: Johns Hopkins UP, 1982.

Santillana, Giorgio de. *The Crime of Galileo*. Chicago: U of Chicago P, 1955.

Santner, Eric. *Stranded Objects: Mourning, Memory and Film in Postwar Germany*. Ithaca: Cornell UP, 1990.

Sartre, Jean-Paul. *Baudelaire*. Paris: Gallimard, 1947.

——. *La Nausée*. Paris: Gallimard, 1937.

——. *Les Séquestrés d'Altona*. Paris: Gallimard, 1962.

Saussure, Fernand de. *Course in General Linguistics*. Trans. Wade Baskin. New York: McGraw, 1966.

Schell, Jonathan. *The Fate of the Earth*. New York: Knopf, 1982.

Schmitt, Carl. *Political Theology: Four Chapters on the Concept of Sovereignty*. Trans. George Schwab. Cambridge: MIT P, 1985.

Schneidau, Herbert. *Sacred Discontent: The Bible and Western Tradition*. Berkeley: U of California P, 1977.

Schwager, Raymond. *Must There Be Scapegoats? Violence and Redemption in the Bible*. Trans. Maria L. Assad. New York: Harper and Row, 1987.

Semeia 2: The Parable of the Good Samaritan. Ed. John D. Crossan. Missoula, MT: Scholars Press, 1974.

Semeia 23: Jacques Derrida and Biblical Studies. Ed. Robert Detweiler. Decatur, GA: Scholars Press, 1982.

Semeia 33: René Girard and Biblical Studies. Ed. Andrew J. McKenna. Decatur, GA: Scholars Press, 1985.

Serres, Michel. *Genèse.* Paris: Grasset, 1982.

————. *Hermès III: La Traduction.* Paris: Minuit, 1974.

————. *Le Parasite.* Paris: Grasset, 1980.

————. *Rome: Le Livre des fondations.* Paris: Grasset, 1983.

Sheehan, Thomas. *The First Coming: How the Kingdom of God Became Christianity.* New York: Random House, 1986.

Siebers, Tobin. *The Ethics of Criticism.* Ithaca: Cornell UP, 1988.

————. *The Romantic Fantastic.* Ithaca: Cornell UP, 1984.

Silverman, Hugh, and Donn Welton, eds. *Postmodernism and Continental Philosophy.* Albany, NY: SUNY P, 1988.

Sollers, Philippe. "Is God Dead? 'The Purloined Letter' of the Gospel." *To Honor René Girard.* Stanford French and Italian Studies no. 34. Saratoga, CA: Anma Libri, 1986.

Starobinski, Jean. "Rousseau in the Revolution." *New York Review of Books* 12 April 1990, 47–50.

Turner, Victor. *The Ritual Process: Structure and Anti-Structure.* Chicago. Aldine, 1969.

Ulmer, Gregory. *Applied Grammatology: Post(e)-Pedagogy from Jacques Derrida to Joseph Bueys.* Baltimore: Johns Hopkins UP, 1985.

————. "The Post-Age." *Diacritics* 11.3 (1981): 39–56.

Unger, Roberto. *Passion: An Essay on Personality.* New York: Free Press, 1984.

Updike, John. "Modernist, Postmodernist, What Will They Think of Next?" *New Yorker* 10 Sept. 1984, 135–42.

Vergote, Antoine. "Apport des données psychanalytiques à l'exégèse: Vie, loi et clivage du Moi dans l'épitre aux Romains 7." *Exégèse et herméneutique.* Paris: Seuil, 1971.

Virilio, Paul. *Pure War.* Trans. Mark Polizotti. New York: Semiotext(e), 1983.

Voegelin, Eric. *Order and History III: Plato and Aristotle.* Baton Rouge: Louisiana State UP, 1957.

Williams, Bernard. *Ethics and the Limits of Philosophy.* Cambridge: Harvard UP, 1985.

Woodruff, Paul, and Harry Wilmer, eds. *Facing Evil.* Lasalle, IL: Open Court, 1988.

Young-Bruehl, Elizabeth. *Hannah Arendt: For Love of the World.* New Haven: Yale UP, 1982.

Index

A Note on the Author

ANDREW J. MCKENNA received his Ph.D. from Johns Hopkins University. He is currently professor of French at Loyola University, Chicago. His publications include articles on critical theory, Flaubert, Molière, Baudelaire, Rimbaud, Borges, and others.